PRAISE FOR *RADICAL BELONGING*

"This book is a wholly necessary contribution to our world. An expansive guide to the impacts of living in an oppressive world, this book offers an antidote to mainstream 'bootstrapping' self-help culture and illuminates real solutions for how we can thrive while pushing to create a world where social justice is present for everyone."

—**Matt McGorry, activist and actor on** *Orange Is the New Black*

"What Bacon offers in *Radical Belonging* is paramount: an opportunity for readers to reimagine healing, relationships, and connection, and to refocus our activism on community care."

—**Melissa A. Fabello, PhD, author and former managing editor of** *Everyday Feminism*

"This book is an absolute must-read for anyone interested in making the world a better place. Lindo Bacon blends thoughtful analysis, poignant storytelling, important scientific evidence, and a trauma- and social-justice-informed perspective to help people understand and cope with the all-too-common experiences of discrimination and disconnection. *Radical Belonging* offers hope that we all are capable of transforming our pain into healing and growth—not through narrowly individualistic approaches that would have us 'pull ourselves up by our bootstraps,' but through the much more effective avenues of compassion and community."

—**Christy Harrison, MPH, RD, dietitian and author of** *Anti-Diet: Reclaim Your Time, Money, Well-Being and Happiness Through Intuitive Eating*

"I read *Radical Belonging* through tears. Tears of solidarity from the vulnerable personal stories which give a voice to anyone who has ached to belong. Tears of sadness from seeing our hostile culture laid out in such painfully plain terms. Tears of happiness at feeling deeply 'seen' in a way that is rare. And tears of gratitude for being able to read a book that couldn't feel more appropriate or needed than it is right now. Thank you Lindo Bacon, for boldly gracing our world with this collection of perfect words during this imperfect time."

—**Jes Baker, activist and author of several books, including** *Things No One Will Tell Fat Girls: A Handbook for Unapologetic Living*

"Dr. Lindo Bacon has written the book I didn't know I so desperately needed. *Radical Belonging* seamlessly weaves together what we know about physical health, mental health and social health, all through the lens of a candid, vulnerable, wrenching memoir. Dr. Bacon's work shows that health isn't just a matter of 'calories in, calories out,' bloodwork, or after-visit summaries—it's also fundamentally shaped by how we are rejected or embraced by the world around us. Thank you, Dr. Bacon, for such an important and hopeful book. It is beautiful, timely and essential reading for all of us."

—**Your Fat Friend (@yrfatfriend on social media), anonymous essayist**

"Powerful, beautiful, tragic, poignant, maddening, heartbreaking, educational! If you have had any connection whatsoever with trauma in your life (spoiler alert: if you are human, you have) you simply must experience this book!"

—**Jon Robison, PhD, author of** *The Spirit and Science of Holistic Health* **and**
How to Build a Thriving Culture at Work

"Lindo Bacon's new book, *Radical Belonging*, is both informative and comforting. Remember the best things about Mr. Rogers' kid's show? He was reassuring you that you are good, just as you are. Here's the adult-sized version—and then some. It's a powerful message, and Dr. Bacon backs it up with clear, easy to follow stories and examples about how we all navigate privilege, oppression, and hierarchy, and often times, take on stress we have no business carrying. This book is an easy read in the best possible ways, and full of diverse examples tracking many marginalized identities. Readers will also find some real talk on why self-love alone won't save us and why we need to weave stronger community support for one another. That's the key here—interconnectedness. And Lindo Bacon is actually discussing how that might work—rather than just telling us it's a good idea."

—**Kimberly Dark, professor and author of several books, including**
Fat, Pretty, and Soon to Be Old: A Makeover for Self and Society

"What does it take to truly feel a sense of belonging? As a storyteller, researcher and social justice advocate, Lindo weaves together a compelling and compassionate guide that will forever change the way you see yourself and others. The world needs Lindo's roadmap to promoting connection and liberation with awareness to make this world more inviting and inclusive for every body."

—**Judith Matz, psychotherapist and author of several books, including**
The Diet Survivor's Handbook

"A book that is as brave as it is necessary, giving us the insights gained through Lindo's experiences as a brilliant academic, a powerful activist committed to leveraging privilege to create social justice for others, and a person experiencing gender-based oppression. *Radical Belonging* dismantles the victim-blaming myths that can keep us isolated and stop us from connecting with other marginalized people. Instead, we get a road map to use intersectional experience to create community in which we truly belong."

—**Ragen Chastain, fat activist, athlete, and author of**
Fat: The Owner's Manual: Navigating a Thin-Obsessed World With Your
Health, Happiness, and High Self-Esteem

"Lindo Bacon delivers an intimate portrait of their own experience of being in a body that has been rendered socially unrecognizable. They remind us that we've all been placed in the same state of dis-embodiment. The evidence of our dissociation from one another, and our own selves is damning. Bacon reminds us that in order to move toward a more just world, we must first reconnect with the very parts of ourselves that we have wanted to excise. It is a challenge that we must accept in the interest of collective healing."

—**Sabrina Strings, PhD, associate professor of sociology at the University of**
California, Irvine, and author of *Fearing the Black Body: The Racial Origins of*
Fat Phobia

"From start to finish, Lindo Bacon made me feel at peace with *Radical Belonging*. A work that successfully validates our diverse lived experiences and reveals the true problems are located within our oppressive culture, not our bodies. Let this book be a meaningful homecoming for one and all."

—**Rebecca Scritchfield, RDN, EP-C, author of** *Body Kindness: Transform Your*
Health from the Inside Out—and Never Say Diet Again

"Lindo Bacon's refreshing honesty, compassion, and vulnerability in sharing their personal story make *Radical Belonging* an accessible read for those who are on their own healing journey as well as for professionals. I am especially enthusiastic about this book's potential to radically transform the way people connect with one another, something I believe is absolutely necessary for the survival of the planet. Chapter after chapter, I could feel my hope for the fate of the human race expand. I will be recommending *Radical Belonging* to every single person I know."

—**Connie Sobczak, author of** *Embody: Learning to Love Your Unique Body*
(*and quiet that critical voice!*) **and cofounder of The Body Positive**

"*Radical Belonging* is a lifeline out of the excruciating pain of personal and societal separation. Lindo Bacon's heartfelt book identifies the necessity of belonging, the personal and cultural cost of separation, and a guide to building belonging within ourselves and our communities. I have been waiting my whole life for this book."

—**Stephanie Zone, PsyD, professor and psychologist**

ALSO BY LINDO BACON
(WRITING AS LINDA BACON)

Health at Every Size: The Surprising Truth About Your Weight

Body Respect: What Conventional Health Books Get Wrong, Leave Out, and Just Plain Fail to Understand About Weight (coauthor)

Radical Belonging

HOW TO **SURVIVE** AND **THRIVE** IN AN UNJUST WORLD (WHILE TRANSFORMING IT FOR THE BETTER)

Lindo Bacon, PhD

BenBella Books, Inc.

Dallas, TX

BenBella Books, Inc.
10440 N. Central Expressway
Suite 800
Dallas, TX 75231
www.benbellabooks.com
Send feedback to feedback@benbellabooks.com

BenBella is a federally registered trademark.

Printed in the United States of America
10 9 8 7 6 5 4 3 2 1

Library of Congress Cataloging-in-Publication Data:
Names: Bacon, Lindo, 1963- author.
Title: Radical belonging : how to survive and thrive in an unjust world (while transforming it for the better) / Lindo Bacon, PhD.
Description: Dallas, TX : BenBella Books, [2020] | Includes bibliographical references and index. | Summary: "Lindo Bacon, author of the highly regarded and consistently selling titles Body Respect and Health at Every Size, returns with another groundbreaking book that explores the deep ramifications people experienced when "othered" in society and provides a guide for creating a world where all bodies are valued and everyone belongs"—Provided by publisher.
Identifiers: LCCN 2020011328 (print) | LCCN 2020011329 (ebook) | ISBN 9781950665341 (paperback) | ISBN 9781950665495 (ebook)
Subjects: LCSH: Identity (Psychology) | Body image. | Self-acceptance. | Transgender people--Identity. | Belonging (Social psychology)
Classification: LCC BF697 .B2426 2020 (print) | LCC BF697 (ebook) | DDC 155.2—dc23
LC record available at https://lccn.loc.gov/2020011328
LC ebook record available at https://lccn.loc.gov/2020011329

Editing by Ashley Collom
Copyediting by Karen Wise
Proofreading by Amy Zarkos and Cape Cod Compositors, Inc.
Indexing by WordCo Indexing Services
Text design and composition by Aaron Edmiston and Katie Hollister
Cover design by Kim Baker
Printed by Lake Book Manufacturing

Distributed to the trade by Two Rivers Distribution, an Ingram brand
www.tworiversdistribution.com

CONTENTS

AUTHOR'S PREFACE

I write this in April 2020 in the midst of the coronavirus pandemic. At this moment, life seems apocalyptic. I'm confined to my house under "shelter at home" orders. When I leave, I arm myself with hand sanitizer, don plastic gloves when shopping, and am vigilant to stay six feet from other people. It's surreal seeing others with their expressions hidden and voices muffled behind face masks, as if we're all characters in a bad horror movie.

The effects of the coronavirus are painful and will live on long after this current stage of physical isolation. We are experiencing a collective trauma. We're watching our world make a tectonic shift.

Humans weren't meant to live in isolation, as valuable as it may be temporarily. Cutting ourselves off from one another is effectively forsaking not just our freedom, but our humanity. We are biologically wired to need connection with others. Our interconnectedness is part of the very meaning of life.

The proliferation of the virus demonstrates the truth, and the challenge, of that interconnectedness: we are not safe when those around us are not healthy and safe. Our fates are linked, and we are all as vulnerable as the most vulnerable among us. If the cheap burger I eat comes from a restaurant that denies paid sick leave to its waiters and kitchen staff, that makes me more vulnerable to illness. A market-based system that doesn't adequately provide for everyone along the supply chain fails, catastrophically.

The fallout of the virus shines a glaring light on inequities baked into our culture. The microbe itself may not discriminate, but its impact falls particularly hard on already disadvantaged and discriminated-against communities, like Black people, Indigenous people, and other People of Color, trans people, disabled people, and older people, who are more likely to lack a financial cushion and less able to work from home. They are also less able to avoid infection, more likely to get very sick, and less able to access the quality health care they may need if they do get sick.

During times of uncertainty and change, fear, anxiety, depression, rage, hopelessness, and other troubling emotions amp up. Stress-related disease runs rampant, and substance use, eating disorders, addictive behaviors, and other coping behaviors spike. It is understandable that we are reaching for life preservers during this time of profound separation and uncertainty.

Health, including mental health, is inherently political, and collective dis-ease manifests in individual lives and bodies.

As disheartening as current times are—and may, by this book's publication, still be—opportunity can come from crisis. These early days of the pandemic are revealing that what was once thought impossible is, indeed, possible. The multi-trillion-dollar US stimulus budget shows that, with enough political will, we can make money out of thin air. The dramatic decline in air pollution as countries are brought to a standstill by the virus shows that changes in habits can clean the sky. Life under lockdown is teaching us lessons in valuing the workers who sustain us, consuming less, and living simpler and more sustainable lives. I am heartened, too, as I witness beautiful acts of compassion and generosity of spirit.

It has taken the coronavirus to remind us of the interdependence of humanity—and that connection is our most valuable resource. We need to nurture it as if our lives depend on it. Because they do.

If there is a silver lining to this pandemic, it is that it has made our crisis of belonging evident—and exposed Radical Belonging as necessary, not just helpful, for survival. The way through this is together. The themes of this book are more important now than ever. Join me in the pages that follow for hope, inspiration, and a path forward.

PROLOGUE

I t's hard to be yourself and feel belonging in a culture that is hostile to your existence.

Think of someone you love. I'm willing to bet that when you think about the people you cherish, it's probably your dearest wish that they have access to every tool and opportunity possible to be themselves, be loved, and flourish in a welcoming world.

My parents wanted this for me. They wanted me to be loved and cherished. They wanted me to fit in and flourish.

That's why they chose to name me Linda. *Linda* means beautiful, the "a" signifying female—facts I learned at my bat mitzvah, a Jewish ritual that marks the day a girl becomes a woman, at age thirteen. I'll never forget my father's speech. He was so proud, he told us, as my mother beamed at his side, of how I was living up to the name they had chosen for me.

Beautiful.

It was a magnificent, tender hope for my life. My success-oriented parents intuited, correctly, that feminine beauty is currency, a success lever in our society, and perhaps even a precondition for success—one that arguably overshadows character development and earned achievements. They believed (and everything in our world and their experience confirmed) that the main tool a girl needs is beauty. My parents' hearts told them that femininity and feminine beauty would be the keys that unlocked hearts and doors for me. Like all parents with hearts full of love, they wanted that for me.

They wanted *everything* for me.

Naming me Linda was an aspiration, an invocation and a plan. Not that my parents had any ties to its origins, which are Spanish and Portuguese. Their disdain for Brown people, in fact, made this more an act of cultural appropriation than admiration. Yet, for them, the definition was powerful: I would be beautiful. I would be welcome in the world. I would belong.

There was, however, a flaw in that formula:

I was not a girl.

And femininity? Not my thing.

I had my breasts removed in 2016.

It's a surgery those of us in the transgender community call "top surgery." I was fifty-two. Post-surgery, bandages removed, standing in front of a full-length mirror in the surgeon's office, was the first time I recognized my body as my own, in every way. It looked right. *Yes, this is my body.*

I remember asking when the swelling would go down. I'll never forget hearing the doctor say: "That's not swelling. Those are your pectoral muscles." I love the symbolism of that moment, that my well-developed (gym-honed) strength, previously hidden behind my breasts, was now exposed. I recognized the reflection as my own in every way. This was my body.

I belong in this body. Finally.

After a lifetime of seeing a stranger in the mirror, this was liberation.

All bodies are perfect as they are. This idea is foundational in the mainstream body positivity movement. The message is, succinctly, "Don't change your body. Change the culture."

When I first considered top surgery, I was concerned that people who read my books, heard me speak, or looked to me as a leader in the body positivity movement would feel betrayed. What if they think I am a hypocrite? After all, I'd spent my life campaigning for self-acceptance and body acceptance.

Here I was, apparently, *not* accepting my body.

That's not entirely accurate. My personal and professional work in the body positivity movement did help me build up and achieve some measure of body acceptance. Before my surgery, I could "accept" my body as a perfectly fine and even attractive body. I appreciated how my body functioned. I reveled in having all parts of my body touched—even and especially the breasts that looked so foreign to me. Yet, despite the relative state of body positivity I had achieved, there was no mirror that reflected my true self back to me. My body-positive gaze required conceptual gymnastics. *Yes, that is indeed a fine body reflected in the mirror. It just isn't mine.*

Given my leadership position in the body positivity community, I worried that other people would find it deeply ironic and even presume me untrustworthy when they learned that I struggled to belong not just among other people, but within my own body. Yet, my struggles, first for body acceptance and later for body liberation and belonging, are actually the source of my insight.* I have had to develop deeply personal tools and strategies—and then practice them, continually—to heal my relationship with my body and our culture. My professional training, my time as a professor, and my lived experience of struggling to belong and be myself are the reasons I can offer tools and resources to help you belong in your body, too.

Body alteration has been liberating for me, letting me feel more at home in my skin. It wasn't a rejection of my body; it was an alignment of my physical self with my gender. Surgery was part of a freeing transition to body liberation. Now, I am more comfortable in my body, which means I can more often be my authentic self and am more accurately seen by others. All of this leads to greater intimacy and joy. I've dismissed the idea, which I used to promote, that we should never seek to change our bodies. I've stopped saying, "This is the body you have, embrace it." Instead, I share

* "Nothing about us without us." These empowering words have fueled the disability rights movement over the years, expressing the conviction of people with disabilities that they know what's best for themselves. Too often we look to "experts" to define the experiences of groups, ignoring and devaluing the real expertise that comes from lived experience.

a more liberating message: "All bodies deserve respect and care." Respect and care take on different meaning for each of us.

Too many of us feel alienated from our bodies. This isn't your personal failing; it means that our culture is failing you. It's not easy to experience personal body liberation in a culture where so many bodies are actively excluded and subject to stigma and discrimination; where we all face barriers in getting over our preconceptions about bodies and seeing ourselves and others for who they are; where the toxic culture gets inside us and becomes our physically embodied experience, affecting our health and longevity and instilling an unconscious bias that causes us to act against our chosen values.

Not coincidentally, this alienation and lack of belonging—within myself and in every social space I occupied—was the beginning of my eating disorder and substance abuse, fueling a range of maladaptive behaviors that challenge me to this day. Being othered, and the body shame spurred by this separation from others, is not "just" a feeling. Being erased and devalued creates structural and material realities that make it harder to regulate our emotions, and influences our relationships, our health and longevity, our finances, our ability to realize dreams, and ultimately whether or not we will be accepted, loved, or even safe.

Our pain gets internalized, wreaking havoc on our survival system and making us more vulnerable to a range of ills: learning disabilities, depression, anxiety, diabetes, high blood pressure, heart disease, cancer, stroke, chronic lung disease, compromised immune systems, digestive disorders, musculoskeletal disorders, liver disease, and early death, as well as sexually transmitted infections, financial stress, poor academic and work performance, and insomnia, to name a few.

It can also show up in an array of behaviors and disorders that help us adapt to difficult situations but don't serve us well in more favorable circumstances, including hypervigilance, heightened anxiety and suspicion, attention deficit disorder, attention deficit hyperactivity disorder, obsessive compulsive disorder, substance abuse, and eating disorders. It can also appear as dysfunctional and maladaptive behavior such as disordered thinking, difficulty concentrating, panic attacks, learned helplessness, self-hatred, hopelessness, depression, or a survival reflex that involves violence.

Oppression, by removing us from belonging, is absorbed into our bodies and is literally killing us.

That's why my body of work as a scientist, author, professor, speaker, and advocate for body liberation always comes back to the themes of belonging or not belonging.

To justice.

To being seen as an individual rather than a type.

To feeling comfortable in our own skin.

To feeling welcome in our world.

These are the issues I've been exploring across the years in my own work, in my communities, and in my books, *Health at Every Size: The Surprising Truth about Your Weight* and (coauthored with Lucy Aphramor) *Body Respect: What Conventional Health Books Get Wrong, Leave Out, or Just Plain Fail to Understand about Weight*. *Body Respect* and *Health at Every Size* are, at their core, me wrestling with belonging.

So, too, is this book.

FOREWORD

I hated going to my therapist every week. Every Wednesday morning I would wake up with a pit of dread in my stomach that would last with me through the day. At the end of my work day I would sigh and get into my car and drive to my therapist's office.

Things would not improve once I got to my appointment. I would start to explain an issue that I had encountered that week. I would talk about the sexism I faced at work. I would talk about my fears as a Black woman in a racist society. I would talk about my fears of intimacy in a world that was unsafe for women. I would try to figure out why I felt so sick all of the time, why there were some days where I was so tired that my arms and legs felt like they were made of lead. I would look over through tears at my therapist for a sign of understanding, and I would see nothing but confusion. I would blink back my tears, embarrassed. I would talk about something a little less personal. At the end of the session, the only advice offered to me was to come back again the next week. I would leave feeling like I had pulled myself apart, piece by piece, for an audience that could do little more than yawn and then leave me to pick up the pieces.

And every day I went back, for months and months. Why did I go back? I went back because something was *wrong* with me, and when something was wrong with you, you sought professional help. I went because I had been told time and time again that therapy worked. Therapy helped.

So if therapy wasn't helping, the problem must be me.

One day, I decided to take a risk and voice my shame to a friend. I confessed that I hated therapy. I hated my therapist. I wasn't getting any better and I didn't know if I ever would feel better. I felt guilty and broken and embarrassed.

My friend thought for a few seconds and then said, "It sounds like you need a new therapist."

The suggestion brought forth immediate denials from me. No, I didn't need a new therapist. My therapist had already invested so much time on me, and I owed it to him to fix whatever was wrong with me that was stopping him from being able to help me.

My friend looked at me, shocked, and said, "You deserve to have a therapist you like."

I was, mind you, a full-grown woman in her thirties at the time, and yet I couldn't quite grasp what she was telling me. Why on earth did I deserve to like my therapist?

My friend continued, "Ijeoma. You are a queer Black woman. You are a single mother. You've been going through a lot of shit. Your therapist is a white man who doesn't seem to listen to you and has no reference point for what you've experienced in life. He doesn't sound like someone you'd want to talk to on a good day, let alone when you are in crisis. I'm pretty sure you are supposed to like your therapist."

And right then I realized that the reason why I had insisted on going to this therapist over and over and over was because I did not believe that I was supposed to like my therapist, because I did not believe that therapy was ever designed for someone like me. I had devalued myself because traditional therapy had devalued me.

Western therapy and mental health counseling had not been developed for me. The majority of mental-health professionals did not look like me, had not grown up like me, and would never face many of the issues around race, sexuality, or class that I faced every day. I was a fat, queer, poor, Black woman trying to seek connection, healing, and guidance from a straight, white, upper-middle class man who had been trained to help people like him. It was never going to work. And if I was ever going to feel better, I was going to have to start with the idea that I deserved care that made me feel better.

I began the long search for the right therapist. After some trial and error, I finally found a promising candidate. She was not Black—there were no Black therapists in my area. But she was queer, and she had experience working with issues around food insecurity and financial hardship. She openly identified as a feminist. She had spent years counseling survivors of sexual abuse. And when we sat down for our first conversation, she discussed the limits of her work experience. She had worked with Black women for years, she said, but she had never been a Black woman. So while she had become well versed in issues impacting Black women in America, she would never be able to connect as directly to my lived experiences as a Black therapist would. But she would listen to me, and trust my ability to reliably convey what was happening to me, and offer the best counseling she could give. Would that be enough for me, she asked. She understood if it would not.

I immediatcly started crying with relief. In years of seeing different therapists, I had never once heard from a professional that if therapy wasn't working for me, it might not be because *I* wasn't a good fit. It might not be me that was broken.

I am a whole person. I am a fat, Black, queer woman. I'm a mother. I'm a sexual assault survivor. I'm a writer. I'm an activist. I'm a feminist. In me lies victory, trauma, humor, despair, love, and so much more. And yet, when I tried to engage with traditional practices of mental health—like medicine, therapy, or self-help books—I was never given space to bring my entire self along the journey. Often, the rejection of my whole self in the mental health and self-improvement fields mirrored the same rejection I felt from the broader world. It was constantly reinforced that I was the piece that didn't fit.

Over the years I have—first with that important therapist and then with my own work with community support networks—come to realize that not only do I need to be seen and accommodated as a whole person in society in order to be healthy, but that it is an obligation of society to make sure that we are seeing and caring for everyone. I have come to see how, in a world built to cater to people who are white, cisgender, abled, straight, and male, not only are systemic oppressions and injustices making people sick, they are also building barriers to any attempts at healing or wellness.

But we all deserve connection. We all deserve care. We all deserve compassion. *Radical Belonging* is a rare book in which I saw some reflection of myself in every chapter. It is a book that endeavors to hold space for people who have consistently been told that they don't fit in the framework of mental health and healing. This is a book that affirms that we are not the wrong shape, we are not the wrong size, and we are not broken. It is a book that I wish had been written many therapists ago, but I'm so glad it exists now. I want to reread it with my partner, with my friends, so we can, as Bacon puts it, "restore the connection that was interrupted by a culture of othering."

I deserve that connection, my community deserves that connection, and you do too.

—Ijeoma Oluo

INTRODUCTION

THE GENDERED ME

I'm walking toward a women's restroom. I'm now an adult in midlife, at a conference I'm soon to keynote. A stranger and I reach the door at the same time. She sees me and does a double take. If the two of us are heading into the same bathroom, clearly, one of us is getting it wrong. She looks for the signage, confirming that she really did see a stick figure with a skirt. Yes, she is in the right place.

Reassured, she takes a closer look at me. This time she reads me as a woman, deciding we're both in the right place. At the same time, it's clear to both of us that I've witnessed her confusion. Her thought process was displayed on her bewildered face. Now she's mortified and clearly worried that by first assuming I was not a woman, she's insulted me. She offers me an awkward, stumbling apology.

Yes, the interaction hurt. But it wasn't her double take that made me feel bad. In fact, the exact opposite is true: I liked it.

Typically, I code as "woman" to most people, and that's largely how I'm treated. But my intrinsic sense of gender is not "woman." I don't really relate to it, so when people see me and think "woman," I feel erased. I don't feel seen for who I truly am. It was in that moment when she wasn't sure whether I was a woman that I felt truly seen. Almost as if she understood, for a fleeting moment, that I was not a woman.

What hurt wasn't her confusion, it was her apology. It said to me that *not* fitting into a category of woman, as I don't, is wrong and shameful. Implicitly, her apology for not seeing me as a woman meant that something is wrong with me and my body and the signals I send out.

I'm genderqueer. *Genderqueer*, similar to the term *non-binary*, refers to a person who doesn't identify as either a man or a woman.

Being perceived as a girl, and then as a woman, has always made me feel alienated—from others and from myself—and no amount of feminist analysis or psychotherapy has helped me move beyond that. I know, of course, that there are many ways to do "woman." That haircuts and clothing—even the category "woman"—are social constructs and that some women are more comfortable in so-called men's suits than clothing designed for women. That some women play football or can change the oil in a car. A woman doesn't have to present herself as über-feminine, or feminine at all, to be a woman. For a long time, that's the argument I made to myself. Maybe I was just a different kind of woman, one that didn't adhere to femininity and the usual constructs?

You might be thinking that, too, wondering, *Why can't you just expand your definition of woman and take your place there? Understand that the culturally accepted definition is too limiting, but who you are is still "woman"?*

Believe me, I've thought about that. For decades, I took that to heart. I've studied feminist theory. I've explored gender academically and through psychotherapy, as a professional and as a client. I've questioned whether it was a difficult childhood that caused me to reject the title of woman so I wouldn't have to feel I've failed as a woman. Or whether I was just looking for access to male privilege. I have even explored the question of whether my short stature—I'm 5 feet tall—makes me excessively needy for attention! The answer I always come back to—one that rises up from within me—is that gender identity is intrinsic and deeply felt, going well beyond choice or adjustment or history or biology. I simply don't experience myself as a woman.

Nor do I understand myself as "man."

That is why I feel most comfortable as genderqueer, a category that defies definition. In this gray area, I feel less confined by false expectations, less erased and freer to be myself.

It's not uncommon for my declaration of being genderqueer to be met with eye rolls. Particularly if you are cisgender, never having experienced this kind of misalignment yourself, you may find it hard to believe I'm not a woman. (*Cisgender* refers to people whose gender identity matches the one conventionally associated with the sex they were assigned at birth.*) You may think I can and should just change my attitude. It's common for those with identities centered in dominant culture (who are straight or white,† for example) to consider their own experiences universal and be unaware of others' very different experiences.

This is an example of cisgender entitlement, in which people privilege their own perceptions and interpretations of other people's genders over the way those people understand themselves. Entitlement can cause people to scoff at identities like trans or genderqueer and to pathologize those who claim those labels. (*Trans* is shorthand for *transgender*, an umbrella term encompassing people whose gender identity differs from that assigned at birth. It includes many diverse ways in which gender identity is experienced.)

---

* The phrase "sex assigned at birth" replaces the old concept of biological sex, acknowledging that someone, often a doctor, is making a decision for someone else. That assignment may or may not align with a person's gender. It is also made with incomplete information about an individual's biological makeup.

† I capitalize Black, Brown, Indigenous, and People of Color when referring to people to highlight the need to properly recognize these groups. On the other hand, I use lowercase when referring to white people. This stylistic difference helps to bring attention to the systemic bias that typically centralizes white experiences and invisibilizes the experiences of Black, Brown, Indigenous, and other People of Color. Language is rarely easy, and this decision was made after careful review and consultation with many People of Color, both scholars and laypeople. This style choice is consistent with that used by the Brookings Institute. More detailed and nuanced explanation is articulated in their report, "Not just a typographical change: Why Brookings is capitalizing Black."

Unacknowledged entitlement runs rampant in all categories of dominant identities. Consider white people who declare they are color-blind, for example.* Only someone from the dominant culture, who's never felt the frequent, subtle prejudice of minority status, could say this. When you break down the language—color-blind = "People of Color, we don't see you"—it no longer seems so virtuous. People of Color, meanwhile, know that white people do see them differently, as "other," and have no choice but to live in a racialized reality.† They have no option to be color-blind.

No one wants to have conversations in which others suggest we don't exist, let alone matter. Yet, I find myself arguing again and again in discussions and interviews, for the very fact of my existence, the reality of my daily life, while being shot down by people who have not only not lived my experience but also lack the humility to acknowledge as much. Projecting their biases onto me, they say to "get over myself." They never consider that the problem lies in their limited worldview, not in me.

Scientific ideas change over time, and if you are caught in the old worldview that sex and gender are binary categories—or that you can know someone's sex or gender by looking at them—it's time to update your education. It is now standardly accepted among those who study these issues that neither sex nor gender are binary—and this is not just cultural, but biological. Both sex and gender are social constructs, and the relationship between an individual's sex and gender is complex. The best way to navigate the complexities of knowing others' gender identity is to lighten up on your ideas about categorizing people and recognize the authority of each individual to define their own gender.

---

* I use the word *color-blind* to critique this commonly understood phenomenon. However, I also want to draw attention to the ableism of using the term *blind* in this metaphorical sense, which can perpetuate a negative view of blindness. Words are not just words, but tools that help shape and inform our perception of the world. When we use pejorative metaphors about a group of people, it's a lot easier to see them as less deserving of respect and inclusion as people in a more favored group. Best to avoid the many negative disability metaphors that have slipped into common usage. Examples of metaphors to avoid: "The economy has been *crippled* by debt." "He was *deaf* to my protests." "That joke was so *lame!*"

† The juxtaposition of capitalizing People of Color in a sentence where white is not capitalized can be jarring. See my explanation in the footnote on page 3.

For those who have a hard time accepting genderqueer as an identity, there's an easy rule of thumb I'd like to suggest, which can be applied across the range of marginalized identities:

You don't have to understand someone's
perspective to respect that it's valid.
You don't have to be comfortable with someone's
perspective to treat them with respect.

Trust that others understand their lives better than you do. Let marginalized people teach you about their experience, rather than imposing your beliefs on them. Your "expertise" or beliefs about their identities doesn't supersede their experience.

Developing your cultural humility allows you to experience the richness that diversity brings. The world is a much more interesting place when we open ourselves to everyone's uniqueness.

Still disagree? Perhaps an analogy can help. A friend describes being raised in an impoverished small town where there was little cultural diversity, with foods limited to their specific cultural tradition, mostly rice and beans. When she first moved to San Francisco and was exposed to the diversity of food options, she was blown away. Kung pao chicken?! Sticky rice with mango?! She had no idea what she had been missing. Food suddenly became a lot more interesting, a source of delight and wonder. The prospect of congee with her morning tea gave her new reason to bounce out of bed with enthusiasm.

I promise you, right now you are missing out on so much possibility because your prejudice, conscious or unconscious, limits your ability to see the rich diversity of our world. This is not a personal indictment; we all are. As we increase our cultural humility and openness to truly seeing others, our world becomes so much more exciting. Prejudice, which is often unconscious and unintended, limits and hurts everyone, not just those on the margins.

When I returned to my childhood neighborhood recently, I was thrilled to reconnect with Lisa, the fat girl who was mercilessly teased in high school, and to learn of her current groundbreaking research in cancer treatment. It made me wonder. That fat (or queer or disabled) kid we shunned in high school, what amazing gifts does she offer the world that we were denied seeing because of our prejudice? (I use the word *fat* as a descriptor, stripped of any pejorative connotations. If you find it jarring, that's probably because you're accustomed to hearing it as an insult. Hang in there with me. My hope is that reading further in the book will help defuse the term for you.) Lisa is caring, compassionate, and smart. How did I miss out on seeing this back then? My high school experience would have been much different if I had had the friendship of a lovely person like Lisa. Instead, I missed out, too caught up in my idea about fatness, preoccupied with status, and stuck in the belief that she wasn't friend material. It pains me, too, to think about the hours and hours of time I'll never get back spent trying to fit in with the judgmental and narrow-minded popular kids. Opening to the people behind our stereotypes will go a long way to enriching our lives.

Developing your cultural humility around diverse identities—and quashing the gender binary—will help all of us. If you fit better in those gender boxes, what they're costing you may not be as obvious. Roles and expectations hurt cis people as much as they hurt trans people by placing limits on acceptable careers, ways of managing emotions, connections with others, and even possible wardrobes. It's just harder for cis people to see the toll the gender binary takes because no one is hassling them about which bathroom to use.

My hope is that we can all learn a new gender etiquette where we don't force our assumptions about gender onto other people. I'd like us to dump the outdated notion that penises and vaginas define gender. Even if you're cisgender, do you really want your gender identity to be reduced to what's between your legs? Let's also dump reliance on suits, skirts, ties, makeup, or voice to determine gender identity. They're just ways we express ourselves. They may help to communicate our gender identity, but they don't define it.

When you assume you know someone's gender, it's like saying you know someone else better than they know themselves. Want to know someone's gender? Ask!

Consider, too, that maybe it's not so important to know. After all, if your intent is to know how to treat someone, do you really need to treat people differently based on gender?

OTHERING AND BELONGING

Belonging is an urgent, fundamental, and universal human need. My parents, by naming me Linda, wanted me to have the tools they thought I needed to belong—in this case, feminine beauty. They knew, as we all do, that the quality of our lives is often defined by our relationships with others and how valued we feel. That's why it hurts so much when I get misgendered, as I was by my parents, as I was in the bathroom at the conference, and as I am in much of my life. Misgendering is a reminder that I'm not seen or accepted for who I am—and, in a world organized along a strict gender binary, a declaration that I don't belong. When we are not seen for who we truly are, we never feel that we belong. I carry this lifelong legacy. At times it can be crushing, dehumanizing, and very, very lonely.

My feeling of not belonging is not unique. Many of us experience that feeling of unbelonging—not being seen for our full humanity—whether we're not white enough, or young enough, or pretty enough, or slim enough, or are marked by an accent. My older friend experiences this when she roots through her coin purse with arthritic hands, not fast enough for the impatient people behind her in the grocery line. My Black colleague experiences this in department meetings, when she is alone in a sea of white faces. My fat friend experiences this unrelentingly, as if her sexuality and intelligence are erased with every disapproving look she is subjected to. My blind friend shares that people often raise their voices when speaking to him, though he doesn't have a hearing impairment.

I try to be aware of the ways I contribute to other people's feeling of unbelonging, like my participation in a mostly white workspace, and the fact that I'm not being more proactive about changing that work culture. There are also more explicit moments, like when I hosted a dinner party and didn't invite my friend who is disabled because my house isn't wheelchair accessible. In both cases, I knew what was happening was wrong but allowed myself to be hemmed in by the difficulty of solving the problem and my fear of uncomfortable conversations.

"Othering" is the problem of our times—and has been the central problem for much of our history. It refers to the process of designating someone as "not one of us." This makes it easier to see them as less worthy of respect and dignity. Whether that means body-based bias, different ethnic groups warring for territorial dominance, walls constructed to exclude immigrants, laws that limit the freedoms of certain groups, institutional and social constructs that afford opportunities to some while excluding others, or basic inequities like who gets food, water, housing, and employment, identity-based differences feed oppression.

Our bodies are the primary signifiers of our identities. Every time we enter a room, our body precedes us, affecting how others perceive us and treat us, and how they mete out opportunities or roadblocks. The focus in this book is the challenge of inhabiting our physical bodies in a culture that privileges some bodies over others: how we get disconnected, the damages that result, and how we can heal and do better, both as a community and as individuals.

You know the story about the emperor who had no clothes?* How people clapped and cheered for his gorgeous new ensemble even though he was actually naked?

Imagine being in that crowd. Imagine seeing everyone around you respond with enthusiasm and praise for the emperor's new robes. Imagine looking at him and thinking, *But he's naked.*

At the same time, however, you are aware that every other person can see his clothes. Their certainty and unanimity make you question yourself. You start to doubt your own perceptions and the evidence you've gathered with your own eyes. *Hundreds and thousands of people are seeing his clothes,*

---

* *The Emperor's New Clothes* is the title of a fairy tale by Hans Christian Andersen about an emperor who pays a lot of money for magical clothes that, he is told, can be seen only by wise people. The clothes do not really exist, but the emperor doesn't admit he can't see them as he doesn't want to appear unwise.

you think to yourself, *yet I cannot. This many people can't be wrong. It can't be possible that he's actually naked. Is there something wrong with my eyes? What's wrong with me?*

That's what it was like for me to have a deeply felt, interior sense of who I was (genderqueer, and definitely not a girl or a woman), but have everyone around me act as though I was someone else (a woman). I felt like an imposter in my own skin. For decades, I thought the fault was in me, that only I saw the emperor naked, so I tried to clap and cheer and play along—all while feeling deeply ashamed that I couldn't see or be what everyone else saw in me.

That's why, despite my parents' loving hopes for me—*Linda means beautiful*—femininity and feminine beauty were not tools I could use to be myself or belong.

Coming to the realization that I was genderqueer (non-binary)—and always had been—and then choosing top surgery was a relief. It was freedom. It was a decision to trust my own perceptions and bodily intelligence. It was a decision to be who I am rather than perform an acceptable self for others. It was a decision to finally belong in my own body so I could also belong in the world. It meant liberating myself to be who I am.

It also meant demanding and allowing others (and you) to see me as I am. This book is in part a coming out story, written for me, so I can authentically be seen. If you can't see me—and few people see my gender without my making the declaration—then I never have opportunities to truly connect, to feel loved and accepted for who I am.

If you're immersed in self-help circles or follow mainstream magazines, sometimes it seems as if we're being recruited into the cult of authenticity. At every turn, we're encouraged to be ourselves, to show up authentically.

Yet what doesn't get articulated is the backstory, that a call to authenticity is politically laden and the path heavily influenced by privilege and disadvantage. It's a lot easier to be your authentic self when the world tells a story that your authentic self has value.

Many of us become estranged from our authentic selves because we learn that those authentic selves aren't valued. We're forced to perform acceptable selves or hide pieces of ourselves (when possible) in order not to be punished, scorned, laughed at, rejected, bullied, or discriminated against. Inauthenticity becomes a survival tactic, a war waged on our true selves that generates shame and disconnection. We direct the pain at ourselves, sometimes taking the form of depression, anxiety, self-harm, substance abuse, even diabetes. We never truly know if the people we're interacting with actually care about us, which can be soul-assassinating. It's like gaslighting ourselves. We're then engaged in pseudo-intimacy, which is laborious rather than nourishing.

True intimacy, on the other hand, flourishes when we come together as our authentic selves. True intimacy is life-giving and energy-boosting. It's where empathy, compassion, and care blossom. There are limits to the intimacy possible, however, when you have to present your socially acceptable self rather than your authentic self, when you're on guard and managing impressions.

Have you ever felt like the people at work or school don't really know you, so it's a profound relief to get home and drop the facade? Can you even drop the facade at home?

When we cannot be ourselves, we are deprived of authentic relationships we can trust. We are deprived of belonging.

No one deserves that. Yet in an unjust culture that values some bodies over others, we're set up for it. Hiding our authentic selves can be a smart, protective survival strategy. Had I come out as a genderqueer teen in my hometown, things wouldn't have gone well. It was hard enough to stop my parents from going forward with their plans for shock therapy to cure me of perceived lesbianism. I can't imagine the consequences had they realized that what they really were observing was gender transgression. It doesn't surprise me that so many trans kids attempt suicide. In one large survey, for example, more than half of transgender male teens, 29.9 percent of transgender female teens, and 41.8 percent of non-binary teens reported that they had attempted suicide.[1]

Each of us belongs here. We deserve to belong to each other. And we certainly deserve to belong in our own bodies.

My purpose in writing this book is to heal from a toxic culture and move into belonging—and to help others do the same. We can create refuge for each other and help shift the world around us—until one day, all bodies are valued and all of us belong.

EMBODIED

None of us reading this book is doing it without a body. Belonging is fundamentally about bodies, and thus so is justice and injustice. When harm is inflicted upon someone, it is not abstract; it is material. It is inflicted on a body or a group of bodies.

Loving our bodies is how we fortify ourselves, sure, but loving each other is how we create collective body liberation.

So, let's make our body positivity movement, our lives, and our culture about *being, belonging,* and *body liberation.* Let's do the healing, but rather than reducing our movement to a quest for individualist self-love, let's name being and belonging—to ourselves and each other—as one of the main aims of a collective, inclusive, transformative body liberation.

Chapter 1

IT'S NOT YOU, IT'S OUR CULTURE

You belong in your body. You belong in this world, and we belong together.

You wouldn't know that by looking at the current state of our world. Consider the astronomical rise in inequality in the United States in income, education, housing, and health care, pushing the middle class into the lower margins, lessening the possibility that anyone other than the über-rich can better themselves financially, and contributing to growing disenfranchisement, alienation, social isolation, and divisiveness. We are increasingly disconnected from ourselves, from each other, and from the world around us.

The fallout is heart wrenching: depression, anxiety, suicide, drug addiction, and violence are all on the rise. Also on the upswing are hate crimes, intimate partner violence, sexual assault, and incarceration.

We can—and must—do better.

The truth is, we don't need to create connection with each other, or even within ourselves. It is already there. What we need to do is restore the innate connection that has been severed by a prejudicial culture.

Being and belonging are our birthright and our future. Let's reclaim them.

THE FIRST PLACE WE'RE NOT ALLOWED TO BELONG IS IN OUR BODIES

When we talk about belonging, we're usually discussing how we relate to other people. We understand loneliness, isolation, and lack of belonging as something that happens between people and in our world, broadly. Loneliness or isolation usually focus on rejection or exclusion by people or systems, being shut out of a group, not fitting in, or being discriminated against by others. All of these things are important and true, but missing from the conversation is the fact that the first place we're not allowed to be ourselves and belong is in our own bodies. Forced alienation from our physical selves is perhaps the precondition for loneliness and social isolation.

For some of us, disconnection began at a young age. We cried and no one responded by feeding or holding us. Or, we observed violence in our environment. The world—and our security—felt precarious. Not knowing otherwise, we thought the problem was us. We looked at our bodies, with their material needs, their urge for safety, for love and acknowledgement, as inadequate or too much. Our needy bodies betrayed us.

For others, the disconnect came later, when the first signs of our differ- ence started emerging, perhaps as an effeminate boy or a masculine girl, or a kid who doesn't grow out of their "baby fat." Society drills into us that our selves and our bodies are unacceptable, and we need to focus on changing. For those with some disadvantaged identities—people with dark skin, folks with disabilities, women—the cultural hostility to their very existence is immediate. It's the air that all of us breathe. It's so ubiquitous that it's nearly invisible.

"Somewhere, on the edge of consciousness," writes Audre Lorde in *Sister Outsider*, "there is what I call a mythical norm, which each one of us within our hearts knows 'that is not me.' In America, this norm is usually defined as white, thin, male, young, heterosexual, Christian, and financially secure. It is with this mythical norm that the trappings of power reside within this society."[1]

Those of us who don't fit into the "mythical norm"—which is to say, most people, since very few people hold all of those dominant identities in one embodied bundle—are tasked with the impossible, unachievable, lifelong project of hiding who we are. We are coerced and conditioned to endlessly work on our bodies and ourselves to more closely accommodate to this mythical norm. The alternative is to live with the knowledge that our appearance will always and automatically telegraph "wrongness" and limit opportunity. The less we resemble the norm, the more likely we are to suffer the consequences—socially, financially, physically, and more.

It's hard to convey the all-encompassing brutality that comes with learning over and over—at four, five, twelve, fourteen, and every day of your life—that you do not belong in your body. A lifetime of slow-burning self-immolation is ignited by the realization that your body is an enemy to be coerced, controlled, and transformed into something else—ideally, something not you. Even worse, it's your job to inflict that ceaseless punishment on yourself. Diet. Straighten your hair. Mask your feelings. Our culture's violent demands alienate us from our own bodies. We learn, again and again, that we cannot be ourselves. Convinced that our bodies are defective and deviant, we cannot settle into or be at home in our own skin. Those of us outside the mythical norm must dissociate from our bodies and regard them from a forensic distance. Our bodies, many of us get trained to tell ourselves, are not our selves. The body is an external thing, a problem to be solved.

I grappled with this growing sense of defectiveness, of alienation from my own body, across my entire childhood—and I did it without the language to explain what was wrong. A fat kid knows that they are fat and that other people don't like their fatness. There are words for it. A trans kid often doesn't even know that trans is a thing. They just think they're being rejected and punished for something so awful that it's formless and nameless. In place of words, they cultivate only a growing sense of wrongness. At the time, I didn't know there was such a thing as being trans, nonbinary, genderqueer, or two-spirited, nor did I know there had always been people like me. I wish there had been someone who did have the language and knowledge to sit me down and say, "Kid, there's nothing wrong with you. You're just trans. It's a thing. Here's what might help you navigate it . . ."

Instead, without language and with negative, forceful messaging coming at me from all angles, I grew to distrust my own body and my own perceptions. I learned not to let my guard down, relax, or be myself—because it was made abundantly clear to me that expressing my true self and my gender identity in my body was absolutely not acceptable. I got rejected and punished for it, over and over. For me, puberty, my teen years, and young adulthood were marked by danger and pain. Not being allowed to belong in your own body is like tap-dancing through landmines every day of your life while trying to make it look like you're moonwalking.

I must have done an extraordinary job of hiding my pain from those close to me. Nothing proved this better than, as an adult, receiving a text from my brother on the anniversary of our father's death. "Remembering the good times," it read, with a photo from my bat mitzvah. I was stunned. I knew he meant it as a well-intentioned, sentimental reminder that we belong to each other. In our family photo he saw a picture-perfect scene of upper-middle-class North American "normalcy" and success—a heterosexual couple and their three kids, all white, slender, seemingly able-bodied, and cisgender. I'm at the center, smiling gamely in my lacy floral dress. What my brother didn't see was that behind the practiced smile, beneath the designer dress, well-coiffed hair, and professionally applied makeup, was a genderqueer kid in drag. It was excruciating. When I look at this photo, I remember one of the most painful days I had ever experienced in my then thirteen-year life.

A bat mitzvah (and, for boys, a bar mitzvah) is a Jewish coming-of-age ritual. It marks the transition from childhood to adulthood, signifying that a girl is now a woman. For a girl who wants to become a woman, I imagine this is a wonderful, hopeful milestone. For me, however, it was terrifying. I knew things were only going to get worse.

Everything and everyone in the world told me I was a girl. I was never quite so sure. Even in the liberal 1960s, '70s, and '80s, though, and until recently, there were no other possibilities I could see for myself. This was the source of my acute and enduring anguish. As far as I knew, the world was composed of boys and girls, men and women—and, like the crowd at the emperor's naked parade, everyone seemed confident that they were one or the other. My parents, for example, thought they had a daughter, a tomboy for sure, but definitely a girl. That hybrid identity—both girlboy and neither—was closer to who I was than anything else. For a while, as a kid and a preteen with a body relatively unmarked by visible signs of gender, I could flourish in that liminal space. As I moved into puberty, however, my body started to change, and so did the way people interacted with me. My bat mitzvah, as the threshold between tomboy and woman, was the dividing line. Crossing the threshold required a survival tactic that would haunt me long after. If it's possible to mark the start of an eating disorder, that would be the day.

My body was becoming more and more of a problem. It was betraying me by sending signals to the world that I was a woman, when I knew I was not. The unrelenting messages I got about my wrongness meant that I could not exist as I was in my own body. The contrast between the excruciatingly narrow possibilities for gender (man or woman) versus what I knew of myself meant that I could not be me, in this body.

This is a kind of death.

It's so obvious that it looks ridiculous when I write this, but without a body, you don't exist. We are not separable from our bodies. We *are* our bodies, and to make someone feel that they can't be at home in their body—the source of their life—is a death wish visited upon them. To make matters worse, the way socialization works is that in pursuit of belonging, we get enlisted into committing crimes against ourselves and our own bodies.

Coercion, erasure, marginalization, othering, dehumanization, discrimination, exclusion, and alienation are targeted forms of abuse, violence, and death that are inflicted, largely with impunity, on certain bodies.

Those of us outside the mythical norm become targets. We are under unrelenting pressure to modify our perceived bodily failings. To survive, we have to objectify our own bodies and can't relax into them. We can't belong, not even to ourselves.

White supremacy and colonization, for example, make it hard for People of Color to appreciate their bodies. How can you value your body when it stands as your main barrier to opportunity and respect? (Of course, it's not your body that is the barrier; it is the oppressive culture's *ideas* about your body that are the problem, but you may not see that—and it doesn't matter to your oppressors, anyway.) How do you find value in your body when the way you adorn yourself, whether with a hijab or afro or turban, is scorned and ridiculed? Black people lose jobs for locs and braids. People have to objectify and dissociate themselves from their bodies in an attempt to manage their lives, to create safety, to get jobs, to get through the day without getting murdered—literally, spiritually or otherwise.

The signs of this crisis are everywhere, from decreasing levels of empathy and trust to soaring rates of suicide, depression, loneliness, and mass violence.

Over and over, we learn that we don't belong in our bodies.

If we have to scan our environments . . .

If we're at increased risk for rape, violence, and murder . . .

If we can't trust other people with our true selves . . .

If huge amounts of our energy, cognitive power, and money must be devoted to ameliorating our unacceptable bodies . . .

If our life spans are shortened . . .

If we don't survive pregnancies or our infants aren't surviving . . .

If police can shoot us with impunity . . .

If we can't use the restroom without fear of violence . . .

If we have to diet . . .

This continual vigilance, the constant shaming, the overbearing systemic violence isolates us, keeps us self-interested (not out of a desire to optimize but rather out of desire to survive) and keeps us from forming relationships, groups, and even movements to exert our power. All the while it contributes to a physical stress response that increases our risk for disease, addiction, other self-harm, and even early death. It erects barriers and complications that steal our creativity and drain us of energy for full participation in life.

When you are not allowed to belong in your own body, that is violence. It is oppression and a function of oppression. Body liberation is about taking our bodies back and making ourselves at home in our own skin.

THE SECOND PLACE WE'RE NOT ALLOWED TO BELONG IS EVERYWHERE

First, we're not allowed to be ourselves or belong in our bodies. Then, we're not allowed to take those bodies out into the world.

Consider for a moment a breastfeeding parent who feeds their baby every couple of hours, for as much as forty hours per week. If they're not welcome to breastfeed in public, that means they must avoid public spaces for the equivalent of a full workweek, every week. They're going to have to dart in and out, plan and carefully time essential activities, and reduce the amount of time they spend outside their home.

Or consider a person who uses a wheelchair. I'm shocked to see how frequently my friends with disabilities are unable to participate in activities I take for granted. The many restaurants, movie theaters, houses of worship, and retail stores they can't access. The extra time they need to budget for difficulties with public transportation (Elevator breakdowns! Short boarding windows! Inadequate space!). Not to mention their safety concerns; every person I know with a physical disability has faced interpersonal violence and feels vulnerable to more.

The conventionally accepted medical model of disability focuses on the limitations of the disabled body itself, rather than on the structural barriers, negative attitudes, and societal exclusions these bodies face. That my friend couldn't enter my house because we couldn't get his wheelchair up the stairs is a problem that can be solved. His body was never the problem; the structural barrier was.

Accompanying him as he uses "accommodations" like ramps and elevators heightens my sense of our crisis of belonging. As we enter an elevator for the local train, our conversation drops because we need to stop breathing in order to avoid inhaling the stench of urine. I think about the desperation of whoever used the elevator as a bathroom, what might have driven them to use the elevator. By the time we reach street level, I'm acutely aware how each of us—me, my friend who is disabled, that unseen person who peed—has been dehumanized not because of who we are, but because society won't support our basic needs. People don't urinate or defecate on city streets because they want to; they do it because they've been stripped of other options and their dignity.

Consider too, the ways fat people are excluded from full participation in the world. One example is the downsizing of plane bathrooms. Kimberly Dark, sociologist, author, and storyteller, dramatizes it brilliantly in her performance piece, "Things I Learned from Fat People on the Plane." Fortunately, she jokes, she's been doing yoga for thirty years, so she can get one leg up on the wall and pee standing up. Sadly, most people—fat or otherwise—cannot. Those bathrooms weren't accessible for Dark—and she's not alone.

Imagine if public restrooms were available only for women. Imagine how challenging—perhaps impossible—it would be for men and people of other genders to have a life and venture out in public.

That's what trans people face, daily. Now the hotly contested issue is whether trans people should have the right to use the bathroom that represents their true gender. Let's be clear about what's really going on. Anti-trans bathroom laws aren't actually about "privacy" or the risk of sexual assault—*they are about trans people's right to exist in public space*. When we can't use public bathrooms, we can't spend prolonged time in public. This means we can't work, go to school, access health care, engage socially . . . We can't exist out in the world.

Consider, too, the plausibility of the fear that has been raised: the idea that men will disguise themselves as trans women to sneak into women's bathrooms and sexually assault women. First, remember that sexual assault is illegal, even if trans people are allowed to use bathrooms that correspond to their gender identity. Trans bathroom protections do not legalize harassment, stalking, violence, or sexual assault. Moreover, there's no evidence that these crimes increase with passage of trans bathroom bills. Media Matters debunked that myth, confirming with experts and officials in twelve states and seventeen school districts that enacted protections for trans people that they had no increase in sex crimes after their policies were implemented.[2] Safety should be a primary consideration, which is precisely why these protections are necessary. Research has shown that transgender people are frequently harassed or physically assaulted while trying to use public restrooms. Providing legal protections will go a long way toward ensuring safety for all.[3]

There's historical irony in the knowledge that some of the most intense civil rights battles have been fought over the right to pee. The US civil rights movement fought for the end of prohibitions against Black people using "white" bathrooms. The disability rights movement mobilized around access to public bathrooms. And the feminist movement spoke out against employers' failure to provide enough bathrooms to accommodate women in the workforce.

Consider my struggles at my local gym. Given the binary option of either a men's or women's locker room, I feel coerced into misgendering myself and choose the women's, where I'm frequently subjected to glares, stares, and the occasional obnoxious comment. One time, when I was in that locker room complaining to a friend about the situation, another woman piped up with "But you look like a woman, I don't get why people would hassle you." I understood her intent. She was trying to comfort me, to be helpful, but she didn't see that she was adding to the hurt. I don't want to look like a woman, to "pass." I want to be seen.

If public spaces don't welcome or accommodate your body, it's because our culture has decided that your body is not supposed to exist there.

THE THIRD PLACE WE'RE NOT ALLOWED TO BELONG IS TOGETHER

First, we're not allowed to be ourselves or belong in our bodies. Then we're not allowed to take those bodies out into the world. So how are we supposed to meet each other, know each other, or be ourselves with each other?

Together, the first two barriers (not belonging in our own bodies or in the world) undermine our abilities to belong to each other—in partnerships, families, groups, and communities. I experienced this, intimately, in my own family.

I vividly remember the day my mother bought my bat mitzvah dress.

I awoke in an empty house. My parents and brother were out shopping for suits. (I have an older sister, too, but she was no longer living with us.) Expecting a few hours alone before they returned from their jaunt, I snuck into my brother's room and found the black velvet suit (this was the '70s!) he had worn at his bar mitzvah three years earlier. Hanging next to it was a white tux shirt and black bow tie, unworn since. I coveted all of it. I slipped on the shirt and then the suit. As I adjusted the tie, I imagined what it would feel like walking through the world wearing this suit.

There I was, modeling in front of his mirror, feeling oh-so-right expressing my masculinity, when my mother unexpectedly burst into the room. Busted. She stared in stunned silence for a moment, obviously horrified, and then said, "Straight to your room and take it off this moment, young lady, before your brother and father see you." She followed me into my room, making sure no one else witnessed my shame, which was clearly her shame as well.

"You're going to be a woman now," she said. "No more dressing or acting like a boy. It's time to grow up." Later that day, she bundled me into the car to go pick out the frilly dress I was to wear.

My childhood innocence was shattered. I got the message that my authentic expression of gender was inappropriate and shameful. To survive in my family, I would have to hide my masculinity. There was no sanctuary for me, and therefore no belonging, in my own home.

Even during my father's speech at my bat mitzvah about what a beautiful young woman I was becoming, I wondered: Is he saying this because he means it or is he trying to make it true by saying it? (I still don't know.) Had he picked up on something about my gender identity that didn't fall neatly into the category of girl (or boy)? My mother certainly had sussed that out, to our mutual distress. She was intervening, intensively, to try to turn me into a proper woman.

Of all the traits he could have been proud of, my dad chose "beauty," the one from which I felt most estranged. Femininity was being forced on me. Beauty was a weapon wielded against me rather than a tool I could

wield. For me, puberty, the bat mitzvah, and all the humiliating prepa-
rations leading up to it, plus the gender training that came right after
(a horrendous and traumatizing modeling school experience was next in
my mother's well-meaning attempts to feminize me) were a crushing reinforcement of my alienation.

Not coincidentally, this alienation and lack of belonging—within me
and in every social space I occupied—coincided with the beginning of my
eating disorder and substance abuse. Which is tragic when you remember
that the bat mitzvah ritual is supposed to center on becoming a thinking,
participating member of a spiritual and learned community. Instead, it gets
tangled into a cult of womanhood and manhood. In my mind, personhood
would accomplish the ultimate goal so much better.

Some synagogues are catching on to the power inherent in avoiding
this gender binary by adapting the plural term, *b'nai mitzvah*, as a way to
denote a "they" mitzvah.* In these ceremonies, *b'nai mitzvah* is used as a
gender-neutral alternative to either *bar mitzvah* or *bat mitzvah*. The traditional prayers are altered, in Hebrew and in English, so that *they* is used in
place of *he* or *she*.

BRINGING IT HOME

It would be wonderful if you could always carry with you the knowledge
that you are okay just as you are. But that's a hard thing to maintain in
this culture. Few of us feel as if we really belong, be it in our own bodies or
interacting in the world. We don't all get the love and respect we deserve.

Sometimes we join others in rejecting those parts of ourselves not valued by others. Our complicity in an alienating system may be most painful
of all. Many of us not only feel alienated, we feel alone in our alienation. We
keep silent about it, which allows it to perpetuate. Ashamed of our feeling

---

* The general intent in using the word *b'nai* is inclusivity. But linguistically speaking, it's still
gendered terminology. *B'nai* is masculine plural, which in Hebrew (as in most languages that
have grammatical gender) covers any group that isn't all female; all mixed-gender groups,
even groups of a thousand women and one man, devolve to masculine form in the plural.

of alienation, we treat it as a personal inadequacy, something to hide. Our feelings of unbelonging come to dominate our psyches.

To manage these consequences, we try to manage impressions. We intuit biases to try to defuse them. We modify ourselves. We censor ourselves, watching not just what we say but the tone or accent we say it in. We are forced to hide parts of ourselves, or to perform acceptable versions of ourselves, all in order to fit in and belong. Because when we don't belong, there is danger—to our physical persons and to our innermost selves.

The tragedy of social and systemic exclusion is that the rejection turned against our bodies manifests as maladies: depression, anxiety, addictions, eating disorders, gastrointestinal disorders, metabolic diseases, and more. Our bodies are punished when the real culprit is not us but our unjust culture.

It's not we ourselves who are to blame for feeling that we do not belong, but rather the structure under which we live that continually perpetuates violence against us.

I want all of us who feel like outsiders to know that our voices are not only necessary but desperately needed to get us out of this mess we're in right now.

No matter what cultural messaging may say, we deserve to feel that we belong in our bodies. We are human, we are whole, we are powerful— together and alone.

Chapter 2

THIS IS YOUR BRAIN ON STRESS

t's hard being human. People we love die. Relationships end. Others can be unkind. There are hundreds of ways to miscommunicate or touch on an old wound when interacting with people we care about. We don't always get what we want or deserve.

Life would be overwhelming if we didn't come well-equipped with regulatory mechanisms to manage the stress thrown our way. Fortunately, our bodies are biologically wired for survival.

The human survival response spans a wide range. If the stressor is physical—say, an oncoming car that bolts out as you're crossing the street—your body will be flooded with energy, kicking your muscles into high gear so you can scramble to the curb. If the stressor is social—say, getting picked last for the dodgeball team—it can protect you from immediate pain by dampening your emotions. To protect against future stress, it can also increase your alertness, making you vigilant and more aware of your circumstances.

While those are valuable tools on occasion, the stress response can become maladaptive and hair-trigger in damaging ways. It may be hard to find the "off" switch. Dampened reactions can devolve into chronic depression, while alertness can escalate into chronic anxiety and hypervigilance. Hundreds of other disorders and diseases can also result.

In this chapter, we'll dive into biochemistry to understand our survival system. We'll look at how this system gets hijacked by chronic stressors and hard circumstances like oppression. You will become knowledgeable about how your brain works and understand how our unjust culture gets coded inside of our bodies, leaving us vulnerable to a range of ills, from chronic depression to diabetes to drug abuse. Later in the book we'll build on this scientific foundation, putting our focus on rewiring your brain for optimal resilience, health, well-being, and connection with others. Throughout, we'll make the connections between how social systems affect brain development—and how you can change those social systems.

THE STRESS RESPONSE

Stress is like a toxin that some of us chronically bathe in. It changes the chemistry of our brains and our bodies.

If you bear the shame of feeling that something is wrong with you, or you're not good enough, it wears on you.

If you struggle financially, it wears on you.

If you've experienced abuse or neglect, it wears on you.

If you've experienced a traumatic event, it wears on you.

If you're otherwise treated poorly, it wears on you.

Scientists use the term "allostatic load" to refer to this cumulative wear and tear on the body. The growing nervous system is particularly vulnerable during childhood, which means that hard times when you were a kid—childhood abuse and neglect, parental substance abuse, and family violence, for example—permeate particularly deeply, especially in the absence of positive, supportive relationships.

The concept of allostatic load helps us understand how the stress of hard life circumstances (such as discrimination or poverty or limited work options), coupled with the feeling that you have no control over these adversities, disrupts your internal survival system. The result is decreased resilience, disrupted well-being, and increased risk for disease. It's the primary reason why, in every country, people at relative social disadvantage suffer from more disease and die earlier. It also drives higher rates of suicide and alcoholism.

The false belief that you do have control* and that your circumstances are your own fault leads us to internalize the cultural ideology, feel shame, and become our own oppressor—all of which heightens the stress response. If you're going someplace where you anticipate being treated poorly, if you're constantly scanning your environment to see if there is a wheelchair ramp or to gauge whether your fat† body will fit in a seat, or if you're feeling isolated as the only Person of Color in the room, then that hypervigilance, however necessary and useful, can also induce further stress.

When we're quick to anger or we dive into depression, it can feel like something's wrong with us. It's better conceptualized as the way we embody our world. There are smart reasons you do the things you do—it's about a self-protection system that sometimes goes awry.

So much of our response to our day-to-day lives is rooted in brain chemistry, which adapts in response to coping with stressors like trauma, inequity, and hard circumstances. Depression, anxiety, anger, reactivity, hypervigilance, distrust, and substance abuse are just normal adaptive and self-protective strategies. How we act is a response to the crap we deal with.

Although social injustice contributes to allostatic load, this does not mean that individuals with more privileged circumstances never experience a high allostatic burden and associated maladies. However, there is a clear gradient: A high allostatic burden tracks closely with social power.[1] There are undeniable protective benefits of higher social power and undeniable toxic elements of lower social power.

---

* One familiar example of this is the bootstrap myth, the idea that people, if properly motivated and willing to work hard, can pull themselves up by their "bootstraps" and become successful. This belief denies the inequity in opportunity.

† Reminder: I use the word "fat" as a neutral descriptor, stripped of pejorative connotations.

The term "marginalized people" is used to convey the idea that the needs and voices of certain groups of people get set aside while other needs and voices are centered. This book centers the experiences of marginalized people. For those with more privileged identities, I have a hunch that reading this book requires a different mindset than you're accustomed to. One privilege of having a dominant identity is not having to see that your perspective is but one of many. I've heard it said: "When you're accustomed to privilege, equality can feel like oppression." It can be challenging to change that mindset; when you are accustomed to everything being about you, sharing space can feel like being left out. For example, the trauma chapter centers on the trauma of oppression and how it affects marginalized people, in contrast to chapters on trauma in the majority of books, which place their emphasis on trauma arising from discrete individual events. This emphasis is merely that: an emphasis. It is not to suggest that trauma is reserved for oppressed people or that discrimination is unharmful to those who simultaneously benefit from it.

In one of her early books, *Feminist Theory: From Margin to Center*, author, professor, and social critic bell hooks*, who is Black, discusses the experience of living in the margins while white people are living in the center: "To be in the margin is to be part of the whole but outside the main body . . . Living as we did—on the edge—we developed a particular way of seeing reality. We looked both from the outside in and from the inside out. We focused our attention on the center as well as on the margin."[2] In other words, marginalized people have long employed the skill of seeing from both perspectives, by necessity. This book challenges those with dominant identities to learn and adopt the same skill. If you find yourself feeling left out, get curious about what that's about. Discomfort is not a bad thing. You can take advantage of it as a learning opportunity.

---

* bell hooks does not capitalize her name in an effort to place emphasis on her work rather than her name.

STRESS IN ACTION

Our emotions happen to us much more than we make emotions happen. That's why one morning, after I went to the gym and was misgendered yet again, I found myself on an emotional treadmill.

At six in the morning, I roll out of bed, still sleepy, and figure I can energize my day with exercise. I arrive at the gym and punch in my code. The front desk person I usually banter with isn't there. I've never seen this new guy before. He glances as my record comes up on his screen, and says, "Enjoy your workout, Ms. Bacon."

Ouch.

Today's a sensitive day. I was in low spirits from the get-go, and it's not so easy to let it slide. Yet another kick-in-the-gut reminder that I'm not truly seen.

You've felt this, right? That feeling of being invisibilized is common for those who don't fit the "mythical norm." Maybe you're a queer woman, for example, and you had the familiar experience where the dude at the bar muscled in on your conversation with your girlfriend, hitting on her and ignoring you. The sexual/romantic dynamics between you and your date weren't seen and respected. Not only was the intrusion on your space angering, but it also made a statement that you weren't deemed attractive enough to even be noticed.

Or maybe you felt it when a salesclerk asked the stylish white guy behind you if he needed help, obviously thinking you weren't important enough to warrant attention.

Or maybe a bystander stopped you from administering emergency medical care to a hiker, not anticipating that a Woman of Color might actually be a trained health provider.

Or maybe you were flipping through magazines in the waiting room and couldn't find anyone who looked remotely like you.

Back at the gym, I speak up.

"Hey, I'm not a woman."

He's perplexed. However I explain it, he's not getting it. I try again and there's a tiny glint of understanding.

He's a nice guy. This was just an out-of-his-realm experience. (Oh, what a luxury for cis people to not have to think about gender!) But he's rising to the occasion.

His coworker chimes in, offering me some words of support. This is good, I know, and better than I usually get. I appreciate being in the progressive bubble of Berkeley, California. But it's still not enough. I'm holding on to my hurt.

"Sorry," he says, flipping the screen to show his colleague and me that it says "female," so it wasn't entirely his fault for assuming.

Now I'm perplexed. When I signed up there were three options: "male," "female," and "not specified." I chose the last one. Of course, "not specified" doesn't acknowledge me, but at least it's better than having to choose "male" or "female."

I explain this and ask not to be categorized as female. I point out that even my driver's license doesn't say "female." Under "gender," there's an X, which signifies "non-binary." (How progressive are we in California!)

"Ah," the guy says, "that 'not specified' category is for staff only. The system must have bumped you into female."

"Can you change it?"

"No, we have only 'male' or 'female' for members."

Pedaling the stationary bike, I can't stop thinking about it. Rationally, I know this is a little thing. Can I really blame him? Of course he saw me as a woman; I embody many cultural signifiers that we're taught to assume mean "woman." The cultural attachment to the binary makes being genderqueer a constant coming out.

I try not to turn the feelings against my body for sending the wrong messages. I am just so tired of, and infuriated by, these unrelenting microaggressions.* It's the proverbial paper cut. ("Death by a thousand cuts" refers to a dramatic negative effect that occurs so incrementally

---

* Microaggressions are the daily indignities, slights, and insults, whether intentional or unintentional, that have to do with a person's membership in a group that's discriminated against or subject to stereotypes. We'll discuss these in more detail later in this chapter.

and imperceptibly that you don't give it value as significant at the time of each individual "cut."* Yet they take their toll additively.)

I go home, but the incident still weighs on me. I try to work, but my mind keeps wandering. My body responds. It responded in the moment, with a flash of pain, and now the internal sequences are in motion. I'm physically shaky. My heart races. I can't calm down.

The internal dialogue is one I've played out many times. *Just get over yourself,* I admonish. *It's going to happen in our unwoke culture. Rise above it.* But the rational understanding doesn't dissipate the felt experience.

I need to produce several thousand words for an article I promised; my professional livelihood depends on it. Instead of writing, however, I'm distracted. I channel my energy into a project not of my making, chronicling the microaggressions I've experienced as a gym member. The project escalates to two painstaking letters; three infuriating phone calls; four fruitless, in-person conversations with gym representatives; and a partridge in a pear tree. It's a battle I should never, ever have had to take on.

Advocating for myself for the most basic recognition, respect, and access—access I'm entitled to and pay for—steals resources I could be using to grow my relationships, career, writing, volunteering, and parenting. It's a huge and unnecessary drain on my time and energy. (I'd hazard a guess that oppression is one of the greatest brain drains of all time. Imagine the potential that could be released if we eradicated or diminished it.)

Transphobia steals so much from me. The self-advocacy logistics I'm enlisted into are the least of it. I feel as if I always have to fight for recognition, for my rights, always be adversarial. Advocating for our own personhood and our most basic needs can make us feel burdensome—as if we're being difficult, or as if it's our fault. I shouldn't have to advocate for being treated with respect. The time waste. The emotional energy required. Not to mention that it raises my blood pressure, keeps me irritable and on edge, and contributes to my insomnia.

---

* The term actually has gruesome roots, referring to a type of torture and execution previously practiced in China and Vietnam that involved using a knife to methodically remove portions of the body over a prolonged period of time, until death resulted.

My friends who are wheelchair users know this all too well. They need to advocate for "special accommodation" when the reality is that the world around them is specifically disregarding their needs and limiting their ability to participate.

A few months later, at the same gym, for amped-up reasons, I have a full-blown panic attack—thankfully, the only one I've ever experienced. It feels like I'm having a heart attack, as if I'm about to die. The panic attack is not solely the result of the particular incident. It's the culmination of a history of misgendering, kind of like the icing on the stress cake.

I am trained as a psychotherapist, physiologist, nutritionist, and researcher. For thirty-plus years, I have used this training professionally and personally. I have worked to heal myself of drug abuse and an eating disorder. I have a loving partner who is herself a psychotherapist. I have resources, and I use them. Even so, I am not immune. Having the tools doesn't protect me from the trigger and the response. It's biologically wired into me.

It's vital to understand that triggers, and our biological responses to them, will always exist. This is somewhat at odds with our body positivity and self-help movements, where there is a wealth of material available about practicing self-love as a panacea of life's ills. I've met many people who've read the blog posts, taken the courses, and joined the movements. They experienced the life-altering epiphany that our culture is fatphobic and that diet culture (my previous work focus) is a problem. They're actively working on revaluing themselves, and because of that, many become convinced that it's necessary to exist in a state of perpetual self-love. Often, they are fine there until something unexpectedly cruel or discriminatory gets lobbed at them. Sideswiped by astonishment—and disappointment—when something happens that plunges them into a maelstrom of anxiety, fear, and shame, they think such things shouldn't hurt or derail them anymore. "I know better," they reason, "and I've done the work. Where did I fall short?" They're ashamed of being ashamed. They interpret the pain and grief triggered by a dehumanization or microaggression as evidence that they haven't been successful at practicing self-love.

If this has ever happened to you, it's not because you failed to love yourself. No amount of self-love could have prevented the situation, or prevented your own physiological response and emotional reaction. Your reaction resulted from two things: a culture that is hostile to your body and targets you for abuse (which, of course, is going to hurt) and your natural, normal biological response to that painful stimuli. It's not you, it's the biology of oppression.

When you start experiencing emotional cascades as a result of triggers you thought you'd deactivated or "should be" immune to, this doesn't mean you've failed to do the work or to move forward. Instead, it means you're human and your brain and sympathetic nervous system are functioning well and doing their jobs. Their job is to keep you safe, and negative emotions are great for that. Scared of snakes? You'll back away and stay alive. Experiencing a "they're a predator" feeling from someone? You won't let them past the door and you'll stay alive. People who don't experience fear or physical pain—and there are some who have a rare genetic defect or brain injury that creates this outcome—have short lifespans. Their broken bones and other health issues go undetected. A painless or fearless life is not something to aspire to. Instead, it's better to build our capacity for managing and learning from our pain. Fear, shame, anxiety, depression, and hypervigilance can be our friends.

Think of a line of dominoes standing up. If you tip one, it initiates a sequence. This is how your brain and your body work, too. Some event external to you—a microaggression, insult, hostility—kicks off the line of dominos going from your brain straight through to your sympathetic nervous system.

By the way, there's an update to the gym story. My advocacy efforts did have impact. In their words, "In our future system roll-outs and upgrades, users will be able to select additional categories other than male or female . . . Our Equal Opportunity Policy Statement and Restroom and Locker Room Accessibility policies have already been updated to include references to 'them' or 'they.' . . . The requests for [gender-inclusive] signage options and lockers in our all-gender bathrooms have been escalated for consideration."

I am glad to see change happening and don't want to appear ungrateful. But this particular victory was won at great emotional and biological cost—mine. It would have been a hell of a lot easier if the impetus had come from cis folks. For them, the fight might have been less personal and vulnerable, not triggering as much of a stress response. This is a call for all of us to rise up and champion causes other than our own. To make it easier for you, in the Appendix I've provided materials you can use to educate others. Perhaps you will want to supply your favorite café with the fact sheet to help them be more inclusive and inviting with just a simple change in bathroom signage? You might then be more likely to run into me there! Seriously, think about it: These "little" gestures translate to welcoming more people into our communities, making them so much more interesting.

I also want to thank my friends who had my back. Part of my advocacy included convening an impromptu "Social Action Advocacy Coalition" and threatening a social media callout against the gym. I'm not sure the company was sufficiently motivated to do the right thing because it was right. However, they did appear to respond to the threat of negative attention.

And really, I'm settling by seeing this as a victory. I want something better: a culture of inclusion, not accommodation. These problems could be solved with gender-inclusive bathrooms and changing rooms. It seems so simple. But the arguments get hurled back: It's too late or too expensive or against their religion—and besides, why can't you be like everyone else, then we don't have to do all this extra work. I'm asked to be patient. Change takes time, they say. Your anger won't help anyone understand.

What they're really saying is I just don't matter as much. And no matter how good I am at emotional regulation, this imprints on my biological system. Injustice is embodied.

Let's map it out so you'll know inside and out that having these physical responses is not a personal failure. It's just basic human biochemistry.

THE BIOLOGY OF STRESS

I'm a science nerd. Understanding the science that supports an idea gives me a confidence that motivates me to make changes. Some early readers of the book had a different experience and felt a bit overwhelmed by this section. I invite you to consider your style. If scientific detail appeals to you, keep reading. If you want the short synopsis, skip to page 49.

In this chapter we'll focus on neuroscience (the study of the structure and function of the nervous system and brain) and endocrinology (the study of glands and hormones). We will explore the brain and how it interacts with other systems in our bodies. But don't be fooled. While we're focusing on the body, what we're really looking at is how we embody the outside world.

Your central nervous system is composed of your brain and spinal cord, and your endocrine system is composed of glands. These are the main actors in the communication and regulatory system of your body. Nerves, neurons, and neurotransmitters help conduct information in the nervous system, while hormones are the chemical messengers that conduct information through the endocrine system.

The brain structure known as the hypothalamus connects these two communication systems, playing a pivotal role in activities essential for day-to-day survival of the individual and for the continuing survival of our species. Its overall role is to collect and integrate information from the body by organizing neural and endocrine responses that help keep our internal conditions in a healthy range, known as homeostasis. For example, the hypothalamus senses when our temperature moves out of homeostasis and sends hormones to the sweat glands to slow or facilitate heat loss through evaporation. Much homeostatic regulation is, like temperature regulation, automatic and below our awareness.

The hypothalamus communicates with the rest of the body through the autonomic nervous system. The autonomic nervous system controls involuntary body functions, including breathing, blood pressure, heartbeat, and the dilation or constriction of blood vessels and airways in the lungs. It has two components, the sympathetic nervous system and the parasympathetic nervous system, which have somewhat opposite roles.

The sympathetic nervous system acts like a gas pedal, triggering the "fight or flight" response and providing the body with a burst of energy to respond to perceived dangers. The parasympathetic nervous system serves as a brake, prompting a "rest and digest" response that calms the body.

In addition to these automatic functions, our hypothalamus also triggers our conscious awareness to motivate us to help in regulation. It acts behind the scenes, so, for example, if you feel discomfort with the temperature, you may put on a sweatshirt or strip down.

Pleasure, pain, and distress are important aspects of the regulatory system as they motivate us to act in ways that support homeostasis and survival. The distress we feel may come softly, perhaps as a vague sense of unease, or loudly, in the form of anxiety, a panic attack, or depression. The point of distress is to mobilize you to take action to get out of your discomfort and back into balance.

It may be hard to recognize anxiety, panic attacks, and depression as attempts at health and mobilization, but stay with me. My hope is to help you to see these as gifts and to support you in accepting and heeding them, so that in the long run, you will ultimately become happier, healthier, and more connected. Pain and distress may not be fun to experience, but as we accept them as part of our humanity, we can value and appreciate their role not just in our survival, but in making us better and more resilient people. The usefulness of pain can be difficult to come to grips with, especially when you are going through it. Yet painful experiences can be regarded as lessons that enable us to better handle similar occurrences in the future. They can also lead to greater capacity for compassion, love, empathy, and connection with others.

We are wired for survival. That's why you feel hungry: to motivate you to eat and acquire the energy and nutrients you need. It's why food can taste good, to reward you for eating. It's why sex can be pleasurable, to motivate human connection and procreation. Of course, these systems can get messed up because of difficult personal experiences and our cultural baggage around sex, food, and weight. Yet, healthy systems are wired into us, and we have the capacity to restore and heal those connections.

The anatomy of the brain is most easily understood from the perspective of evolutionary history, using the triune brain model, which divides the brain into three regions representing the gradual acquisition of the brain structures through evolution. While this model is undoubtedly an oversimplification—in reality there is no such neat division—it provides a helpful overview of functioning.

The three regions are as follows:

- Reptilian brain: your primal or instinctual brain
- Limbic system: your emotional brain
- Cortex: your rational or thinking brain

These three sections of the brain are connected to each other and to the remainder of the body through neural pathways and hormones.

The most primitive part of the brain includes the main structures found in a reptile's brain: the brainstem and the cerebellum. This part of the brain controls the body's survival functions such as heart rate, breathing, body temperature, and digestion and is the main coordinator of the fight-or-flight survival response. The brainstem connects the brain to the rest of the body through the spinal cord. Its main job is to keep you safe.

The limbic area, which sits atop the reptilian brain, is composed of the hippocampus, amygdala, thalamus, and hypothalamus. Referred to as the "emotional brain," the limbic area plays a role in how we feel, remember things, and interact with others. Its main job is to keep you connected to others.

The cortex, the last primary structure to evolve, is often referred to as the "thinking brain." It's involved in language, rational and abstract thought, imagination, and creativity, to name just a few functions. Its main question is "What can I learn?" Of special interest is the prefrontal cortex, which connects to both the emotional and instinctual areas of your brain.

A well-developed and well-connected prefrontal cortex is critical to making good decisions and managing emotions and bodily functions. It's what allows you to pause, consider the emotional and bodily messages you are getting from the limbic system and brainstem, obtain insight into what's going on, and have empathy for others. It regulates impulsive desire, helps you do the right thing, and controls the reactive impulses that may solve a problem temporarily (saying "Shut up" when someone is driving you nuts) but create long-term consequences in the end (goodbye, friendship). It also allows you to have healthy digestion, preventing the instinctive triggering of the digestive tract that could result from unchecked anxiety.

A less developed and less connected prefrontal cortex, on the other hand, a hallmark of a high allostatic load, means that you get stuck in survival mode and your instinctual brain rules. Your ability to regulate your emotions is reduced, and you are quickly triggered and reactive, unable to make thoughtful decisions. You are also more vulnerable to being triggered by the environment, such as a food advertisement driving you to eat even if you're not hungry. Normal social anxiety can lead to drinking too much or other "reactive" behaviors, such as overexercising, gambling in a destructive way, compulsion, hoarding, anxiety, rage, violence, and overachieving in work or with other goals at great cost to relationships and well-being. You are also more prone to a range of diseases, from depression to diabetes to irritable bowel syndrome.

The prefrontal cortex is the last part of the brain to fully develop and isn't completely developed until about age twenty-five. That's one reason why kids may lack good judgment and need mature adults to guide them. Of all our brain structures, the frontal cortex is least constrained by genes and most shaped by the environment.

Studies on socioeconomic status show that by kindergarten, disadvantaged kids already display differences in their prefrontal cortex that result in difficulties in emotional regulation. This partly explains why some kids have trouble controlling their impulses ("acting out").

While challenges around emotional regulation are part of being human, your degree of reactivity tells a lot about the functioning of your prefrontal cortex. For instance:

- How good are you at emotional regulation?
- When things go wrong, are you quick to anger?
- When circumstances are beyond your control, do you become stressed and anxious?
- When you don't get what you want, do you feel sad and dejected?
- When your kid doesn't do what you want, do you become irritable and crabby?

Our brain's primitive stress response is intended to help us survive stress in our environment. Stress is a biological response to threat that triggers your sensory organs to send a message to the brain structure known as the amygdala. The amygdala, often called the "fear center," interprets the sensory information and considers stored memories (like what happened the last time we were in a similar situation), judging whether the situation is stressful.

If the situation is determined to be stressful, the amygdala quickly alerts the hypothalamus, which activates the sympathetic nervous system by communicating through your nerves to the adrenal glands. The adrenal glands then release the hormone epinephrine (also known as adrenaline) into the bloodstream.

Epinephrine has several effects: Your heart will beat faster, increasing blood flow to your muscles and other vital organs, including your heart. This will raise your pulse rate and blood pressure. You will breathe more rapidly. Airways in your lungs will open more widely so you can take in more oxygen. You become more alert as your brain receives extra oxygen. Your sight and hearing, as well as your other senses, become sharper. Epinephrine also causes sugar and fat to be released from storage sites into your bloodstream, making energy readily available throughout your body.

After the initial surge of epinephrine slows, and if your brain perceives that the threat is still present, your hypothalamus secretes corticotropin-releasing hormone (CRH), which triggers the pituitary gland to release adrenocorticotropic hormone (ACTH). ACTH then travels to the adrenal glands, prompting the release of the hormone cortisol. Cortisol keeps your body revved up and on high alert, releasing a flood of glucose (sugar) to keep you energized while tamping down insulin production to ensure that the glucose doesn't go into storage. It also narrows the arteries, while the epinephrine increases heart rate. The combined effect forces blood to pump harder and faster. Cortisol also suppresses the immune system and the gastrointestinal system so as not to "waste" energy on less essential functions.

Once the threat dissipates, the parasympathetic nervous system—the "brake"—dampens the stress response, causing cortisol and epinephrine levels to fall.

Sometimes, instead of the fight-or-flight response, a "freeze" response, wherein you dissociate or otherwise feel numb and disengaged, gets triggered. During freezing, the two counteracting components of the autonomic nervous system, the sympathetic and parasympathetic nervous systems, are activated.

Your past experiences team with your biology to dictate why certain circumstances trigger a fight-or-flight versus a freeze response. Evolutionary biologists maintain that a big driver is the degree of hope you have about your ability to activate change, such as ever getting out of debt or finding a partner, and that this is often below the level of conscious control.

Typically when we think of stress, we think primarily of the pathways leading up to and ending with the cortisol response, but there is now evidence that in certain stressful situations, a hormone called oxytocin is released along with cortisol. Oxytocin, nicknamed the "cuddle hormone," initiates what's been called a "tend-and-befriend" response to stress, elevating feelings of attachment, connection, trust, and intimacy and helping you get out of your stressful situation.

The tend-and-befriend response drives us to pay more attention to what we can do for others and encourages us to reach out for support when we feel that what we're going through is more than we can fix on our own—be it financial problems, an illness, or the loss of a loved one. It's not as well-honed in most people as the fight-or-flight response.

From an evolutionary perspective, tending or nurturing oneself and others, along with befriending others and expanding and maintaining social networks, is advantageous. We'll focus on developing the tend-and-befriend reaction in chapter 8, on Connection.

SHORT-LIVED STRESS CAN BE GOOD

Moderate, short-lived stress is valuable and energizing, often improving alertness and performance. As an example, I feel stressed before I teach. This low-level stress response makes me alert and focused, without many negative effects. Stress can also boost memory. From an evolutionary perspective, memory strengthening makes sense because remembering stressors from the past can help you respond to similar future situations.

Stress is good when it is moderate and transient, and when it happens in a relatively safe setting.

Stress is problematic when it persists for a long time or is chronically activated, adding to your allostatic load. It's also more likely to be problematic if you can't predict the onset, how bad it will be, or how long it will last.

Why does predictability result in dampening the stress response, including reduced cortisol and epinephrine secretion? It takes more energy to process something that is new. If something is predictable, the brain can use the information to minimize cost and effort and act more quickly. Also, if you have a warning, you can plan coping strategies. When I was told that I'd have a surgical drain for a week post-surgery and that I would be much more comfortable once it was removed, I planned for it by taking time off work, being prepared with binge-worthy Netflix ideas, and having my partner available to take care of me. By planning my coping strategy, I was able to manage the stress more easily. In contrast, if I thought it was never going to change, I wouldn't have taken care of myself and wouldn't have modulated the stress.

The biggest challenge to your stress system comes from the situations where you feel that you have no agency (control) in your life. The more agency you have, the better you are at mitigating the damages of a stress response. (That's largely why, contrary to popular thought, executives are less likely to have heart attacks than janitors.)

CHRONIC STRESS CAN BE BAD

Chronic, as opposed to occasional, stress imposes a very different experience.

With chronic stress, you can become hypervigilant, acting as if the world is unsafe, regardless of whether it actually is. This makes sense if experience has shown you that you can't trust your environment. Then, even if there's no monster under the bed, you're on high alert.

You may also be distrusting, constantly anticipating and scanning the world for threats. If someone turns you down for a social event, you leap to the interpretation that they don't like you, not even considering that they may have had previous plans.

You may be easily triggered, reacting in ways that seem inappropriate or out of proportion.

You may get lost in ruminations. This is your brain reviewing information to make sure you're alert and safe.

You may have difficulty sleeping, because you are thinking too much and sometimes feel a sense of dread. This is about keeping you prepared in case something terrible happens.

Chronic activation of the stress response also amps up neural connections and activity in the amygdala, which, if you remember, is considered our "fear center." High levels of stress make the amygdala larger, resulting in more fear and anxiety and heightened excitability.

As cortisol levels rise, signals in your hippocampus (the area of the brain associated with learning and memory) deteriorate.

Sustained high levels of cortisol can also cause your brain to shrink, resulting in a reduction of synaptic connections between neurons and a smaller prefrontal cortex. (In case you don't remember, the prefrontal cortex regulates "thinking" behaviors like decision-making, concentration, and judgment.) In addition, fewer new brain cells are produced in the hippocampus, meaning that chronic stress might make you struggle to learn and remember things, in addition to setting up an environment of vulnerability to disorders like depression and Alzheimer's disease.[3]

Excess cortisol also suppresses the immune and digestive systems, making energy available for more essential functions. On a long-term basis, suppressing the immune system can result in increased vulnerability to viruses like colds, increased cancer risk, susceptibility to developing food allergies, and possibly a higher risk of autoimmune disease, among other maladies. Suppressed digestive and absorptive functions also means you are more vulnerable to digestive problems like diarrhea, constipation, irritable bowel syndrome, and colitis. It could also exacerbate ulcers.

What's more, high cortisol levels can deplete you of dopamine, the "feel-good" hormone. When your brain is low in dopamine, you may feel lethargic, unmotivated, and unenthusiastic. It's as if low dopamine sucks the fun out of life. You may try to compensate with mood and energy boosters, like coffee or methamphetamine.

An increase in cortisol can also lead to a decrease in serotonin production—that's the hormone that helps give you a sense of well-being. A decrease in serotonin can make you feel anger and physical pain more readily while also contributing to depression.

People who have had repetitive activation of their stress response also experience spikes in the stress hormones epinephrine and cortisol more quickly and disproportionately to a situation and take much longer to return to baseline than those who haven't.

THE STRESS OF INJUSTICE

I want to pay particular attention to the stress of injustice, as it can take a silent toll on your body. It isn't easy dealing with ongoing poverty, misgendering, ageism, ableism, or racism, whether you're facing overt discrimination or microaggressions, which are subtler and thus harder to identify and address. You may be "dealing with it" and getting by, but not without consequence. Each emotional (or physical) blow adds to your allostatic load. While a single blatantly traumatic event bumps up your allostatic load substantially, so too does the accumulation of small, less explicit stressors over time.

Perhaps you hear "microaggressions" and dismiss them as insignificant, "just little things that hurt people's feelings." Don't be fooled; these regular, subtle cuts inflict much damage. Feeling dismissed, alienated, insulted, or invalidated has a biological impact.

Each emotional insult may not stand out, but their accumulation over a lifetime is in part what defines a marginalized experience. It can be difficult for someone who doesn't share an identity to understand the severity of a particular individual microaggression without having that historical experience. It can even be difficult for those of us who are victims of those microaggressions. I get that "kicked in the gut" feeling sometimes for little things. If someone doesn't smile at me, for instance, and I get upset, the intensity of my response (hurt) may have little to do with what's happening in the moment. That missing smile may have triggered a lifelong sense that I'm disregarded. Even so, I may blame myself for my physical response and for blowing things out of proportion.

We are all also guilty of laying microaggressions on others at times. Here are some common examples of things I've done (and learned from):

- Clutching my backpack more tightly when passing a Black man on the street (signaling that Black men are a threat)
- Asking someone who isn't white "Where are you really from?" (signaling that People of Color are not "real" Americans)
- Assuming a female physician is a nurse (signaling that women can't achieve advanced education)
- Assuming that a Latinx customer in a posh store is a salesclerk (signaling that Latinx people aren't affluent enough to shop there)*

I may not have intended to hurt people, but my actions still cause pain. Each time we experience one of these slights, our body reacts, producing a stress response. In this way, being subjected continually to microaggressions turns into trauma in our bodies.

I don't want to be that person harming others in this way. I'm learning to listen more and to be more attentive to the impact of my words and actions rather than cling to my innocent intentions. Our intentions don't really matter if we're hurting someone else.

We don't know what we don't know, which is part of why we need to listen more. What we heard may be very different from what the other person thought was said. We express ourselves within the context and history of a racialized and otherwise deeply discriminatory society. Focusing on intention diverts attention from the harm being done. Even if harm isn't intended, consequences are inevitable, and wrongs will need to be rectified. We need to reflect on these problematic interactions and

---

* *Latinx* is a gender-neutral word that refers to people of Latin American cultural or racial identity in the United States. The -x suffix replaces the standard -o/-a that is typically used in Spanish to denote male or female.

find the learning so we can take responsibility and try to do better next time.

Learning opportunities become derailed when we focus on our intent. Jay Smooth, a radio host and social commentator, articulates this well when he explains the difference between the "What They Did" conversation and the "What They Are" conversation.[4] Smooth points out that if you focus on intent, the conversation revolves around whether you are a good person. If we apply it to the above examples, it turns the conversation to whether I'm racist or sexist. By focusing instead on the person who is hurt, I call my actions into question, not my character. This provides better opportunity to learn and grow.

On the other hand, intent matters a great deal in how we choose to respond to someone who hurts us. Intent influences whether we respond in anger, shrug our shoulders and walk away, or risk a discussion that could ultimately deepen understanding. Context matters; all are valid responses!

YOUR BRAIN ON DIET CULTURE

When it comes to fat people, the cultural narrative suggests that microaggressions are somehow a service to fat people, that expressing health concerns is beneficial "tough love." Fat bodies are portrayed as diseased and wrong, capable of becoming healthy and thin if only the individual exerts enough effort. The relentless judgment of fat bodies is a good thing, the argument goes, as it can spark incentive for change.

No. No. No. We need to see these "health" admonishments as the microaggressions they are, promoting disease, not health. Stereotyped assumptions about someone's weight are oppressive. Think about what it must be like for larger people—that is, most people living in the United States—to confront daily in the media, doctors' offices, workplaces, and even their homes that their bodies are unattractive and constitute a horrifying public health crisis. That stigma shows up in the health of fat bodies. An opinion piece coauthored by psychologists, sociologists, and behavioral scientists in the journal *BMC Medicine* made a convincing argument that

bias against fat people is actually a driver of the so-called obesity* epidemic, reviewing and citing seventy studies as evidence.[5]

Our bodies are not meritocracies. Some people will never be thin, even
if they turn down that cheesecake or regularly run marathons. Furthermore,
nobody has complete control over their health, regardless of the lifestyle
that they lead. Healthism—the belief system that identifies health as the
responsibility of the individual and ranks pursuit of health above all else—is
harmful and misguided. By positioning health at the level of the individual,
it neglects the social determinants of health and obscures the reality that
some people have better access to high-quality health care and are more able
to engage in health-promoting behaviors, such as getting regular exercise.
The result is that people who are sick, disabled, or "unhealthy" feel that the
absence of health is the result of their individual failure, wearing away at
feelings of self-worth and giving others license to stigmatize them. It also
requires people to continually strive for better health to be deemed worthy,
and serves as the foundation for many moralizing and restrictive ideas about
life choices. Eating nutritious foods is portrayed as being good, while chocolate is sinful. The idea that everyone is morally obligated to engage in this
quest for "health" hurts more people than it helps.

To return to our discussion of hypothalamic control, let's delve deeper
by examining the hypothalamus's role in managing our weight—or, more
precisely, our body fat. What follows is an example of how diet culture has
put us at odds with our own hypothalamic control.

You've heard the common "wisdom" that weight management is "a
simple matter" of calorie control, right? What doesn't get mentioned is
that what's in control is your hypothalamus, not your conscious mind. The
system is not so simple after all.

This is why: Diets. Don't. Work.

There's irony when we consider that dieting has probably contributed to why we're fatter these days than ever before. Dieting is actually a
well-established predictor of weight gain, as shown repeatedly in research.[6]

---

* I use the language "so-called obesity epidemic" to draw attention to my discomfort with the
  word *obesity*. As you will read later in the text, I consider *obesity* to be a stigmatizing term.
  Hereafter, the word *obesity* will occur in quotation marks, signifying that I am using the term
  to refer to others' usage.

When we examine the body's regulatory mechanisms, it shouldn't be surprising that few people sustain weight loss from calorie reduction diets or exercise routines. Scientists have found that our bodies will trigger numerous physiologic pathways to ensure that our weight stays the same.[7] Our bodies' internal system for managing weight compensates for conscious actions like reducing calorie intake. For example, dieting triggers a reduction in the hormone leptin. Less leptin binding to receptors in the hypothalamus, which tracks that sort of thing, triggers a cascade of reactions, including an increase in neuropeptide Y. What does neuropeptide Y do? It increases your appetite and decreases your metabolism—the opposite of what you're shooting for if you're trying to lose weight!

Chronic dieting results in chronically lower leptin release, spiking hunger and slowing metabolism, which could easily explain why most people with a history of dieting gain weight over time. Our bodies are (deliberately) overriding the "dysregulation" of our weight-loss efforts.

Check out what happened to contestants on TV's *The Biggest Loser.* Six years after their hyped weight loss, most contestants had not only regained almost all their weight, but a study found that their metabolisms had also slowed dramatically.[8] In other words, changes in their brain circuitry meant that, for them, eating less now resulted in weight gain. They had employed what are often called extreme weight loss methods, but even "normal" dieting could have led to the same result. Hypothalamic control exists to resist change (bringing us back to homeostasis), so as extensive research demonstrates, the same process happens any time body fat stores are reduced, regardless of how the weight was lost.

If you've dieted, think about your own experience. You reduced your calories and maybe you also started or amped up an exercise routine. Whether you went low-carb, low-fat, or low-sugar, the beginning stages probably were pretty heady as you watched the needle drop on the scale. But then it probably got harder to maintain. Most likely, you found yourself thinking about food all the time. You started to feel desperate, and even foods that never appealed to you before were suddenly calling out to you.

What diet plans don't tell you is that biology lies behind that drive to break your diet. It's not your "lack of willpower" that derails you. Your body's physiologic mechanisms underpin every one of the symptoms you've felt.

Even your taste buds are affected when you diet, as your leptin drop inspires you to find a wider than usual range of foods appealing. Biology can be powerful, and no matter how much willpower you think you have, it may be no match for the biological mechanisms triggered by your diet.

If you gave in and went off your diet, don't blame yourself. It doesn't mean you're a glutton or a weakling. In fact, most dieters show extraordinary self-restraint, persistence, and determination. You didn't fail; the diet did.

Maybe you had great willpower. I was at times a great dieter, able to "just say no" despite my gnawing hunger. I even found that after a while hunger signals dissipated and dieting got easier. There was physiology behind that, too, as my body turned off the appetite signals rather than waste the energy if I was ignoring them anyway. So your willpower is fine. But that still doesn't mean you're going to lose weight if you diet. To compensate, your body could slow your metabolism, burning fewer calories over time. This explains why some people actually gain weight in response to cutting those calories. And that anxiety that triggered you to break your diet? What you thought of as "emotional eating" was more likely a response to a normal biologic regulatory drive.

Bottom line: Diets. Don't. Work.

Or maybe another way of saying this is that diets do work, remarkably well, triggering your internal weight management system to kick into gear and protect your precious energy stores.

Don't fall for the hype about exercise as a means to sustained weight loss, either. Research shows that while we can influence our size in small ways, for most of us, our size doesn't change dramatically when we engage in regular exercise. Steven Blair, an exercise physiologist who has served as president of the American College of Sports Medicine, the American Academy of Kinesiology and Physical Education, and the National Coalition for Promoting Physical Activity, likes to say, "I was short, fat, and bald when I started running, but after running nearly every day for more than thirty years and covering about seventy thousand miles . . . I am still short, fat, and bald." Blair's extensive study of the research leads to the inevitable conclusion that one's conscious mind can rarely outwit hypothalamic control.

Your body is enormously powerful and successful in managing your weight, thanks largely to the hypothalamus. So don't fight it. Revel in it. You can relax about eating and enjoy your food. Let your body do what it does best. Trust yourself, pay attention to helpful signals like hunger and fullness, and everything will be okay. The best way to win the war against fat is to give up the fight. Let your body guide you to a weight that's right for you.*

This isn't about giving up. All you're giving up is an ineffective way to get what you're really looking for. It's about moving on. It's about body respect and body trust, not body shame. These are what help you make better choices about what to eat and how to eat and other self-care practices.

THE SHORT SUMMARY

The human body has self-protective mechanisms in place to help us survive. Our fight-or-flight survival response is designed to mobilize our brain and body to fight an enemy or run from danger. We also have a freeze response that can help us hide from a predator. Both fight-or-flight and freeze can also be triggered by social stress.

A fight-or-flight response starts when a brain structure known as the hypothalamus senses threat and initiates a sequence of events that results in the release of neurotransmitters and hormones like epinephrine and cortisol into our bloodstream. These trigger dramatic changes: Our breathing rate increases. Blood is redirected away from our digestive tract and into our muscles and limbs, which require extra energy. Our awareness and vision sharpen, impulses accelerate, and perception of pain is blunted. We become prepared for fight or flight, both physically and psychologically. We also become hypervigilant and distrustful, on the lookout for the enemy.

When activated, our fight-or-flight system triggers us to perceive everything around us as a potential threat to our survival. It's built to bypass our rational mind. This alertness causes us to interpret almost everything and everyone in our world as a potential threat. As a result: We may overreact

---

* Body trust isn't something you intellectually understand and then quickly implement. It takes time, effort, and practice to dump diet culture thinking and regain body trust. That's why I wrote an entire book about it, *Health at Every Size*, with more updated ideas in the coauthored *Body Respect*.

to the slightest comment. Our fear is exaggerated. Our thought process is distorted. Our focus is narrowed to things that can harm us.

When we're stuck in survival mode, our heart shuts down, our rational mind is disengaged, and we're focused on fear. This prevents us from making thoughtful choices and recognizing the consequences of those choices. We can no longer relax and appreciate the moment. Relationships suffer.

Chronic activation of our stress system also increases our allostatic load, which ups our risk for a long list of conditions and maladaptive behaviors, including anxiety attacks, metabolic disorders, and yeast infections, to name but a few.

BRINGING IT HOME

Being treated poorly, being oppressed, is painful not just materially and emotionally, but also physically. Being excluded, rejected, insulted, demeaned—or, in my case, misgendered—contributes to a physiologic stress response, making stress not just biological, but inherently political.

Reading this stuff isn't easy, is it?

The good news is you always have opportunity to rewire your brain to better support you. Just as stressful events can forge neural pathways, so can healing practices. You can harness this phenomenon—called neuroplasticity—to build new and better neural pathways in your brain and come out stronger and better for the adversity you've weathered. We'll learn how in chapter 10. But first, we should talk more specifically about trauma and how it alters your brain.

Chapter 3

THIS IS YOUR BRAIN ON TRAUMA

Do you:

- persistently feel that there's something wrong with you, that you're ugly, stupid, or out of the loop?
- often feel distant or cut off from other people?
- prefer to stay home, curled up in the fetal position?
- have trouble sustaining relationships?
- experience frequent mood swings?
- have persistent sadness and depression?
- feel easily overwhelmed?
- trigger easily, experience explosive anger?
- feel hypervigilant, super alert or watchful, on guard?
- experience a sense of dread?
- feel numb or disconnected from your body?
- frequently have bad dreams or nightmares?

- startle easily?
- have trouble sleeping?
- have trouble concentrating or getting things done?
- have physical reactions when you get anxious (heart pounding, trouble breathing, or sweating)?
- suffer from disturbing memories or thoughts of a stressful experience from the past?
- get lost in rumination that you just can't shake?
- engage in addictive behaviors (drugs, alcohol, food, shopping, etc.) to stave off feeling overwhelmed?

These are all common symptoms experienced by traumatized people. While most of us can check off "hell, yeah" to a number of these questions, not all of us would qualify for an official trauma diagnosis. Regardless of whether we meet the criteria for a trauma diagnosis, we can all benefit from trauma-informed care.

Trauma-informed care recognizes that mean, harmful, or antisocial behavior usually arises from a person's harsh experiences rather than from malicious intent. In other words, a trauma or a trauma-like experience triggers your survival system and sets your current behaviors in motion.

Consider the above behaviors from a survival perspective. If your life is threatened, you're going to want strategies in place to protect yourself and survive. This means you want to be hypervigilant, you want to avoid situations where you're not in control, you want to react quickly to events or unfamiliar noises, you want to sleep lightly and be awakened easily, you want to have intense memories of specific painful events in your life so you can watch for them again. Distrusting others is extremely helpful. After all, people have let you down and you're not going to allow that to happen again. Being angry at times helps you protect yourself. Being depressed at times stops you from being too active—and putting yourself out there spells more danger. You're going to avoid making yourself vulnerable. Substance abuse? That, too, is adaptive, allowing you to temporarily escape your circumstances when you don't have other coping skills.

Understood in this way, those behaviors are brilliant responses intended to help you take care of yourself. They are good skills to cultivate in dangerous times. Yet these adaptive behaviors become maladaptive over time and contribute to difficulties with regulating emotions and connecting with others.

Even those of us who don't think of ourselves as traumatized go through times where our brain pattern mimics a trauma response: our prefrontal cortex goes offline and we get caught in the grip of reactivity. Fortunately, you don't have to stay stuck in these conditioned responses. You can rewire your brain to have more beneficial "default" functioning. But before we talk about rewiring, let's unpack what trauma is.

WHAT IS TRAUMA?

Sometimes we experience something that so violates our sense of safety and rightness that we feel overwhelmed. We feel shattered. The mind freezes in that moment and can't let go, can't just integrate it and carry on. The jolt could have come from an event, such as a natural disaster, terrorist attack, sexual assault, being in a war zone or car accident, seeing someone murdered, even a messy divorce. Even if it doesn't involve physical harm, any situation that leaves us feeling overwhelmed and isolated can result in trauma.

Trauma can also stem from not just a singular event but an accumulation of ongoing stressors, such as growing up in a crime-ridden neighborhood or an environment that was unpredictable or dangerous, being bullied, or suffering partner abuse or childhood neglect.

It's also traumatizing to grow up surrounded by cultural messages that say you are worthless because of who you are. This is the trauma of oppression, and it's the experience of most people with marginalized identities. Having a supportive and loving family or community may not be enough to protect you from internalizing toxic cultural messages.

Most of us carry trauma in our bodies to varying degrees. For example, we've all experienced gender-based trauma, but the difference is in the degree. The trauma experienced by cisgender folks, if not often labeled trauma, is real. Consider men who lack full access to their emotions (because they were taught that "real men" shouldn't cry) or women caught up in the pursuit of beauty ideals (because they were taught that beauty is currency). We can all remember being shamed for stepping outside those gender boxes or silently fearing that others will see our gendered shortcomings.

When you feel ashamed of or feel the need to conceal aspects of yourself in order to survive or find belonging, then what you're experiencing isn't true belonging. Instead, you constantly hustle for your worthiness (to use shame researcher Brené Brown's language). That's traumatic.

Although we talk about the catalyst as the trauma, in fact trauma is about an individual's response—it's one's subjective experience that defines whether an event is traumatic, not the nature of the event itself. Then it extends beyond the story of what happened to become the imprint of how your past lives on inside you today.

The invisible nature of some traumas can leave us confused. To an outside observer, an emotionally deprived child might appear fine, since their basic physical needs such as clothing and schooling are fulfilled. The lack of external recognition makes the invisible scars more damaging. The child feels unloved and unworthy, all the while hearing from society that they are well taken care of. This disconnect can create confusion, guilt, and shame.

Unfortunately, too many traumatic encounters go unrecognized by typical diagnostic criteria. This is unfortunate because people may then feel ashamed that what they experienced isn't *really* trauma and thus is unworthy of attention.

As you can see, there's a lot more that causes trauma than the usual stories. Consider this humiliating story from my life. It may not contain a "classic" traumatic event—there was no rape, bomb explosion, or earthquake—but, the impact was traumatizing.

A few months after my bat mitzvah, when I was about to enter high school, my mom was pressuring me even harder to act like my assigned gender. Enchanted by the Barbizon Modeling School advertising slogan—"Be a model, or just look like one"—she'd convinced herself that I could be taught to be a girl. I protested as she signed me up for the program. But the truth was, I wanted it. I wanted to learn how to pass. I was willing to endure modeling school if it let me escape the misery of feeling inadequate and wrong.

Predictably, modeling school only reinforced my feeling of wrongness and inadequacy. Applying mascara meant poking myself in the eyes.

Walking in heels was painful and awkward no matter how much I practiced. I left each day more ashamed, brandishing smudged makeup and limping from twisted ankles, reminded in the most demoralizing of ways that I was not the "girl" my parents hoped I'd be. Indeed, I was more certain than ever that I would never be that girl.

Ever the problem solver, I made a deal with the program director behind my mother's back. After she dropped me off each day, I would hang out in a back room reading. Just before pickup, the Barbizoners would hastily apply my makeup to convince my parents I'd been in class all day. Everyone was happy. I could lose myself in books, the Barbizon people could dispense with struggling to train me, and my mother believed I was getting closer to becoming the girl she had always wanted me to be.

That is, until graduation day, when I had to parade my newly taught femininity down a catwalk. The program instructor dressed me and applied my makeup, but as I walked down the lighted catwalk, my (unpracticed) heels were markedly unsteady. When I stumbled, my heel caught in the string of lights attached to the painted backdrop. It came crashing down, managing to hit every model in training. One girl was taken to the hospital with a broken arm. The wreckage ruined the evening for all the hopeful young models and their proud families.

My attempt at passing had failed—and failed big-time. My parents were heartbroken. Even the professionals couldn't make me a real woman. The air was thick with our mutual shame.

Of course, these classes were not an adequate or even accurate description of "girl," but they focused on what was, then and still now, expected of women: to be thin, elegant, and beautiful and to walk constrained. In the car riding home that evening with my parents, I knew that I was supposed to want these things for myself. I also knew, as clearly as ever, that I didn't.

The event stands out for me as a day on which my life was forever and dramatically changed. Much deeper than the awareness that I could not succeed at this particular construct of femininity was a nagging feeling that threatened the integrity of my understanding of self. It would, however, take decades for this awareness—that I wasn't a girl—to fully surface.

While I can laugh as I tell the story today, I can also remember what it was like to be that awkward teen, feeling the shame of not being a Real

Girl—and having it so publicly revealed. To feel my parents' disappointment in who I was. To know my parents felt ashamed, believing they were negatively judged because of who I was. I mark that day, as with the bat mitzvah, as one of the turning points that pushed me into an outright war on my body—an eating disorder and later drug addiction were just two of the many ways I found ways to comfort myself from the shame.

For many of us, showing our authentic selves at some point proved unsafe. The inauthentic self we learned to show the world as armor kept us protected. "Passing" as a girl allowed me to survive my childhood, but it also contributed to my feeling isolated and alone. And it strengthened my conviction that something was wrong with me, which only magnified my shame. Healing required that I recognize that the problem wasn't in me, but in the environment that didn't treat me well. I did what was necessary to survive a toxic environment. That was smart, a sign of remarkable resilience at the time.

As an adult, I have more agency and I can make different choices that allow me to heal. I can find and create safe environments where I can shed my armor, where I can be seen, and where I can feel love and belonging. This last point is key: It's belonging rather than self-love that helps me live as my authentic self. This is not a solo journey.

POST-TRAUMATIC STRESS DISORDER

The diagnosis of post-traumatic stress disorder (PTSD) applies when the response to trauma takes over our lives, causing our brains to live in the past in a way we can't control. When someone has PTSD, the nerve connections between the amygdala, hippocampus, and prefrontal cortex are weakened. The hippocampus becomes hypoactive and can't store the memory, while the amygdala becomes hyperactive, keeping you in a fearful state. The prefrontal cortex isn't able to override the hippocampus and soothe the amygdala when there is no danger. It's as if you're stuck in the traumatic experience.

This closely resembles what happens in chronic stress, except that in traumatic stress, memories of the traumatic event dominate your thoughts, sending you into fight-or-flight mode at the slightest provocation. Therapists describe this as being "reactivated." In the short term, people may avoid the pain provoked by the memories through disassociating—that is, they cut off from their bodies, so much so that they often cannot describe their own physical sensations and may have difficulty recognizing normal sensations like cold or hunger.

About 20 percent of people who experience a traumatic event go on to develop PTSD, which is defined by the following diagnostic criteria:

- Reliving the event through intrusive thoughts and/or recurring nightmares
- Avoiding things that remind one of the traumatizing experience, such as people, places, thoughts, or other activities related to the trauma
- Having negative thoughts or feelings that began or worsened after the exposure to trauma
- Being hypervigilant or hyper-aroused, which may include feeling irritable or quick to anger, having difficulty sleeping or concentrating, and/or being overly alert or easily startled

Other criteria include that the symptoms last for more than a month, create distress or functional impairment, and are not due to medication, substance use, or other illness.

Proper diagnosis can be powerful. Those four little letters mean that symptoms are more likely to get taken seriously and not dismissed as someone being "too sensitive." People who don't fit the stereotype, like people with marginalized identities whose trauma comes from oppression, are less likely to get the diagnosis—and therefore less likely to get help and accommodations. They are also vulnerable to thinking their trauma responses mean there's "something wrong with them."

TRAUMA-INFORMED PERSPECTIVE

What happens when we see ourselves through a trauma-informed lens? The National Center for Trauma-Informed Care articulates this paradigm shift as moving from asking "What's wrong with you?" to "What happened to you?" It means reexamining the stories you've told about yourself in a more compassionate light.

For example, maybe you lack the energy to clean your house or go grocery shopping, but that doesn't mean you're lazy. Few people are. More likely, if you consider yourself lazy, you just don't have energy reserves to draw on because you're so busy surviving, or you've devoted all your energy to hypervigilance. Perhaps you have such fears of inadequacy in front of others that you are frozen and can't get anything done.

Don't like exercise? Maybe there's a reason. For example, the emotional trauma of being known as the fat, clumsy kid in gym class may prevent you from becoming interested in sports. As burlesque performer Fancy Feast describes, "I wasn't bullied, but I didn't have to be. Being last to finish the mile run, being chosen last for dodgeball, not fitting into child sizes for my school uniform—all made it easy for me to absorb the message coming in: none of this was designed for me, exercise was a form of punishment, and I would be less of an inconvenience if I would just shrink myself."[1]

When viewed through a trauma-informed lens, the behaviors we think of as counterproductive or destructive instead get understood as survival. For example, adolescents are often perceived as being purposefully hostile, rude, or disrespectful when, in reality, they may be unconsciously trying to protect themselves from additional trauma. In other words, they are emotionally traumatized and have a deep sense of shame, and antisocial or unkind behavior is a way of pushing people away and protecting themselves. They may become emotionally shut down to the point where they are no longer sensitive to their own needs, and carry this into adulthood.

A trauma-informed lens requires ongoing openness to reexamining what you think of as your own bad behavior, and others' behavior as well. It asks us to consider that everyone is doing their best given the circumstances, and that our behavior is usually an attempt to regulate ourselves so that we feel safe and comfortable. Consider this example. A former colleague and friend altered some of our joint work without informing me or seeking my collaboration. When I discovered that she had done this, I initially experienced it as a profound violation of trust. However, lightening up on my judgment enough to ask why helped me to learn that she was reeling from the hurt brought on by the ending of our personal relationship, and those feelings resurfaced more viscerally every time we did business together. (That was my experience too.) She altered our work because she thought it needed updating and that I would be in support of the update; she did so without collaboration to protect herself from the pain our interactions surfaced. This understanding was a game changer for us. We realized that we were continuing to hurt one another in our efforts to avoid more hurt—which motivated us to realize that we needed to either repair the relationship or set better boundaries. There's a lot to be learned when you open to looking behind "bad behavior."

These days, healers are putting less attention on diagnostic criteria and instead recognizing the value of offering trauma-informed care to everyone. We're all at least a bit traumatized living in a world with so much injustice, whether we are on the receiving end or bear witness to it. Of course, this is not to say that all trauma is the same or has the same impact.

TRAUMA AND BLAME

If you experienced a traumatizing incident, it's helpful to remind yourself that you didn't have control of the situation—it happened to you. Whatever you did or didn't do in the moment was in large part mediated by your reactive reptilian brain, with little input from your rational "thinking" brain. Your response—to fight back or not—was derived from a history embedded in your body, recorded from your own life experiences and that of your ancestors.

Too often, traumatized people blame themselves or think that if only they had reacted differently, they could have controlled the outcome of the situation. Neglected kids often believe that if they were more lovable, their parents would have paid more attention to them. Part of healing is letting go of that, recognizing the limited power you had, and acknowledging that you did the best you could at the time. Trauma is not a personal failing. Trauma happens *to* someone, whether it is the result of a singular traumatic event or ongoing microaggressions.

Self-blame is particularly poignant in the example of rape. Most people who have been raped blame themselves in some way. Perhaps you offered a friend of a friend a ride home and blamed yourself when that person forced themselves on you in the car. However, giving a friend's friend a ride home is a perfectly reasonable, kind thing to do. The ending to the evening was not your fault.

Or, perhaps you "submitted" to sex, not fighting back or saying no, even though you didn't want it. Maybe you were drunk or unconscious. There are so many reasons that explain why you acted the way you did, some of which have to do with your own belief in your power or worthiness. These are definitely traits worth exploring, but the bottom line is: No one has the right to your body without your affirmative consent. What you were wearing, how drunk you were, whether you were on a date, whether you are a sex worker, and what your gender is are irrelevant to the boundaries of what constitutes rape. But they may contribute to self-blame and to whether you experience the violation as trauma.

People become more vulnerable to abuse, assault, and discrimination when they are dependent upon others who hold individual or collective power over them. Kids, for example, are dependent on their adult caregivers and may not have the resources to escape their situation. Adults may depend on others for employment or basic needs, such as food, shelter, and clothing. Or, they may believe they are dependent as a result of social conditioning. This is why many people stay in abusive relationships: they lack the resources, power, or confidence to make choices to protect themselves or to pursue their own self-interest or protection. But their dependence makes them more vulnerable to inequity and exclusion, and to many other forms of violence.

CHILDHOOD TRAUMA

Childhood is a particularly critical time for brain development. When the process of development is disrupted by trauma, the results can be profoundly damaging. Our brains develop over time to enhance our ability to survive. When you are raised in a traumatizing environment, your brain develops in a way to ensure your survival in that setting. The neural pathways that optimize your ability to survive in that dysfunctional environment become overdeveloped, while development of other pathways may be stunted.

Adverse childhood experiences (ACEs) can include things like physical and emotional abuse, neglect, caregiver mental illness, and household violence. A survey called the Adverse Child Experiences Study[2] asked people if they had experienced any of three categories of childhood abuse before the age of eighteen: psychological (being frequently put down or sworn at, or living in fear of physical harm), physical (being beaten, slapped, burned, cut, etc.), or sexual (being forced into various acts). The survey also asked about four types of household dysfunction: if someone they lived with was a problem drinker or user of street drugs, if mental illness was pervasive in their household, if a household member had attempted suicide, if there was violence or criminal behavior in the household.

The findings were dramatic: The more forms of adversity a child experienced, the more prone they were to depression and attempting suicide as adults (when compared to those who reported no adverse experience). People with four or more different types of ACEs were five times likelier, in the previous year, to have been in a depressed mood for two or more weeks, and twelve times likelier to have attempted suicide. Experiencing more types of adversity in childhood was strongly associated with alcohol and drug abuse. It was also associated with higher incidence of diabetes, chronic obstructive pulmonary disease, stroke, and heart disease.

This study wasn't a fluke. A meta-analysis of 124 studies verified many of these links.[3]

Scientists use the term "toxic stress" to explain how ACEs trigger biological reactions that lead to those outcomes. If a child is subjected to multiple ACEs over time, particularly if they lack supportive relationships with other adults which can buffer them, a long-lasting stress response ensues which increases allostatic load and results in excessive "wear and tear" on the body.

Another disturbing finding in the ACEs research is that fully half of the adult perpetrators of intimate partner violence had been abused as children. In other words, victims of childhood abuse are highly vulnerable to passing their traumas onto others. Also chilling is that half of the victims had also been abused as children.[4] Being victimized as a kid makes us vulnerable to continued victimization as an adult.

OPPRESSION *IS* TRAUMA

The National Scientific Council on the Developing Child made the important decision to expand its definition of ACEs beyond the categories covered in the initial study to account for community and systemic factors, including violence in the child's community and experiences with racism and poverty. The body experiences the same stress response regardless of the type of adversity.

Oppression lives in our bodies. It is an ideological system and its effect is deeply physical.

TRAUMA, BODY HIERARCHY, AND THE HEALTH CARE INDUSTRY

This oppressive culture tells us that some bodies are better than others, that some bodies are more worthy of respect than others, and that those of us in marginalized bodies should strive to achieve normative oppressive ideals as a prerequisite to being treated well. Health professionals, who fall prey to the cultural myths just as others do, are (often unconsciously) complicit in imposing and enforcing this oppressive ideology.

Doctors are tasked with curing or helping us manage disease, not caus-ing disease, right? Yet, this mandate goes by the wayside when consider-ing fat people and bariatric surgery. The surgery's intent is to intentionally damage healthy, functioning organs and have patients voluntarily assume the risk of death and "complications." (Bariatric surgery refers to opera-tions that help promote weight loss. It's among the highest-paying surgical specialties, which perhaps partially explains why accuracy and integrity in research and reporting are suspended.)

People are misled about the health risks associated with being fat and told that bariatric surgery is a solution to all that ails them, from sickness to singleness and even diseases they do not have. As speaker, author, and "real-life fat person" Ragen Chastain recounts, "I've been told by doctors that I should have the surgery to cure my Type 2 Diabetes (which I do not have), my high blood pressure (which I do not have), my mobility prob-lems (which I do not have), and just to make things easier 'dating-wise'— which is not an issue since I'm in a long-term relationship with someone who loves me as I am, and not based on how my body could look after surgical manipulation."[5]

Bariatric surgery is more appropriately labeled high-risk, disease-inducing cosmetic surgery than a health-enhancing procedure. Its goal is to intentionally induce malnutrition, and post-surgical nutrition deficien-cies are the norm. A critical mind is essential in evaluating the research, as you have to parse the data rather than trust the bias-laden conclusions. Consider, for example, what's not being named, tallied, or reported. Why is there so little long-term follow up? Why are so many patients left out of follow-up analysis and how does this skew reported results? Why aren't potential harms being sufficiently investigated, like disordered eating, body-image distress, suicide, bone loss, falls, substance abuse, and heart failure, to name but a few?

We're not getting the full story. People who have had poor results from surgery may not return for follow-up evaluation, admit the painful side effects publicly, or acknowledge that the quality of their lives is far worse after surgery. As one post-surgery client explained to me: "We're ashamed to talk about the negatives. After all, we've failed all our lives and now we've failed again. So we pretend that it's all rosy. We accept the compliments and quietly soil our pants, quietly tolerate the hours of excruciating pain that results from one poorly chewed piece of food, the ongoing hospital visits to treat our nutritional deficiencies. But what scares me most is the denial. Scratch a 'success story' and you find someone having numerous complications, but they are so brainwashed to believe they were going to die from fat, and so desperate for social approval, that they actually believe they are healthier and better off for having the surgery."[6]

The health care mandate "Do No Harm" also goes by the wayside when considering short people. The idea that height is important for all things, from finding love to earning higher paychecks,[7] to succeeding in life and being taken seriously, is well documented in the scientific literature. It didn't surprise me to learn that to become a fashion model, a woman must be at minimum 5'8", though the average American woman is closer to 5'4". But I do admit to being surprised that even sperm banks discriminate; many have a 5'10" height requirement for donors, despite an average male height in the US of 5'9". Short kids who are healthy and not low in growth hormone but might wind up shorter than their peers can now receive an official diagnosis—idiopathic short stature—and qualify for synthetic growth hormone shots. These shots don't confer any health advantages, but they do come with a long list of potential contraindications. The psychological distress associated with being very short (in other words, distress resulting from being victim to stigma and discrimination) is used to justify treatment.

I have compassion for why fat people and short kids (and their parents) consider or choose to undertake medical intervention. The idea of escaping a stigmatized and discriminated against class, however false or health-damaging the method, provides hope, while managing or ending the stigma or discrimination can seem out of reach. Consideration of these ideas really drives home the message of this book: We must work to end the stigma and discrimination at their root, support one another, and develop our individual resilience to manage the stigma and discrimination while it persists.

TRAUMA RESILIENCE

We humans are a resilient species. If we are around people who love us, take care of us, dive deep into compassion for us when things are particularly hard, we can do well despite horrible things happening. If someone with a marginalized identity, for example, was raised in a loving family and belongs to a strong supportive community, they may be less scarred by systemic trauma.

Various protective experiences can mitigate the harms of ACEs and make us more resilient. These include having access to adequate food, living in a safe and clean home, and attending a high-quality and well-resourced school. We can also gain protection from unconditional love from adults, whether a parent, caregiver, teacher, or other ally, or even from mere contact with an adult we trust. Having a close friend to confide in likewise bolsters us. Other sources of support include involvement in civic organizations such as service clubs, religious organizations, or social groups; participating in an organized sport; doing charitable work; or having an artistic or intellectual passion. What each of these experiences have in common is that they remind you that others value you, which helps you learn to value yourself. Humans are remarkably adaptable, and compensatory factors that we accrue later in life can often help us transcend a traumatic childhood. Each protective experience makes us better equipped to compensate for a high ACEs score and improve our health and well-being.

This means that a bad start in life doesn't seal a negative fate. We can even grow stronger for our pain. As an example, there is some research that supports the idea that people with a history of child abuse develop enhanced abilities to sense threats in the environment and learn new things, which are excellent traits to hone.[8]

HOW NOT TO TRAUMATIZE KIDS

My parents did the best they could, given the resources they had and what they knew. Their efforts to make me gender-conform came from good intentions. They wanted the best for me. What they didn't understand was that conformity wouldn't make me happier. It was a short-term plan to avoid the pain of stigmatization, with long-term consequences. It sent a message that I was the problem and failed to call out the real problem, which is our discriminatory culture.

Life is painful. We can't protect our kids from every insult and injury, nor should we try to. What we can do is sit with them as they experience it, help them to know they aren't alone, and model that we can handle suffering as a part of being human.

The best you can do is love your child, as they are. The template for healthy brain growth for a kid and for healthy emotional development is a nurturing relationship with caring, responsive adults. Children can't handle an attachment void. Without loving support at home, kids may rely more on peers and need more outside validation. They may also become more vulnerable to absorbing cultural messages of how they are supposed to be.

Rethink common parenting practices. If your kid throws a temper tantrum, the last thing you want to do is impose a punitive "time out." Time to cool down may be valuable, but not when it is perceived as punishment or withdrawal. That sends a message to the kid that when they're in pain, you're withdrawing from the relationship. You are teaching them that the relationship is unreliable and conditional, that they are acceptable only if they please you.

My kid is at the brink of adulthood now, and I think of the ways I've failed him. I didn't know how to act around a young child. I was waiting for him to grow older so I could engage with him intellectually.

I used the excuse that because my partner was the primary caregiver and was competent and loving in that role—she was the one with so-called maternal instincts—it took me off the hook. It didn't. All the loving attachment our kid got from her didn't cancel out the messages he received from my distraction and detachment, although it did help him develop the skills to offset it.

Now, I understand that intellectual engagement, words, activities, or common interests aren't the basis of a true relationship; real closeness is about *being with*. "I welcome you to exist in my presence. Being with you brings me joy." Presence. It can't be cerebrally understood, but you can feel it. What was it like for my kid when he was aware I was not really present with him? For kids, that detachment gets translated into "I'm not important enough." They read it as their inadequacy. It's traumatic.

I had to work on that, to learn not to let my mind wander off into work. To just be there. My active presence could give him the security he needed to feel independent enough to play on his own, to give him space.

Many parents worry that they failed their kids, especially parents who are traumatized or engage in addictive behaviors. We are all imperfect. We all make mistakes. Please show yourself some compassion for your inadequacies. You're just being human.

Incidentally, upon reviewing this self-criticism, my partner (and co-parent) commented that I'm being too hard on myself, exaggerating my disengagement. I suspect she may be right; perhaps my writing reflects a skewed reality influenced by my harsh inner critic. Are you tough on yourself, too?

HELPING GENDER-NONCONFORMING KIDS

Gender-nonconforming kids are at a higher risk than the general population for being teased, bullied, and shamed. Caring parents, of course, don't want their kids victimized in this way. My parents knew that if I wore my brother's suit to my bat mitzvah, I'd be met with negative judgment and ridicule. Shaming me for gender nonconformity was their misguided way of trying to protect me (and themselves). But of course, it didn't work. I fantasize about what they could have said that would have made my life a whole lot easier:

> We know that femininity isn't your thing and that you prefer to express yourself in a suit. We love you for that. We support you in all that you are. But we also want to help you understand that the world you are growing up in has judgments about gender and is going to be hostile toward you when you express your gender. So we want to help you decide how to handle that. Do you want to wear your brother's suit to your bat mitzvah and face potentially hurtful reactions? Or would you

rather wear a more socially acceptable dress? Or, perhaps we could work together to find some compromise. We love you and support you whatever you choose.

It's too late to make that happen for me. But hey, we can make our parenting fantasies happen for the next generation, right?

These strategies are important not just for parents, but also for teachers and other caregivers and influencers. All of us can cultivate space in a child's life where they can walk in and hang up their armor. Don't underestimate how valuable that is for a kid. You may not be able to change the conditions of their life, but it is still hugely important that kids feel seen and valued. One person can make a difference. I honor all teachers and caregivers who use their considerable power to positively influence the next generation and inspire a more just future, where all kids are valued and supported.

INSTITUTIONALIZED TRAUMA

In a society organized around inequality and systemic oppression, it is inevitable that people will experience the powerlessness, violation, and suffering associated with trauma. Institutionalized trauma, also known as systemic trauma, refers to the ways people are harmed by systems such as the criminal justice system, educational system, health care system, etc. In the United States and many other countries, these systems better serve people with dominant identities, at the expense of those with marginalized identities. Consider the "school to prison pipeline": A low-income Black boy suffers from trauma in his home and community, which results in little time or support for studying or completing assignments and a short fuse. He then gets labeled as a troublemaker in school and is pushed on a trajectory that will most likely lead to juvenile detention center, jail, and prison.

Or consider a non-neurotypical person who gets labeled as not bright at school, though the issue is really that they are processing information in a way that is not recognized by the school. The label gets internalized and they come to believe that there is something wrong with them.

Or consider the People of Color who have experienced trauma resulting from abusive police practices or know others who have.

Or consider the fat people who are denied routine health care, like access to life-saving transplants or gender-affirming surgeries; are subject to contemptuous, patronizing, and disrespectful treatment by health professionals; denied care for their symptoms because their health issues (like sinus infections!) are attributed to excess weight; or prescribed damaging weight-loss treatments.[9] It's not surprising that the majority of fat people report avoiding or delaying medical care as a result of a history of traumatic interactions with health care providers.[10]

Or consider the communities that face higher risk of cancer because their water, soil, and air are toxic, victims of polluting factories that tend to be located in low-wealth neighborhoods rather than affluent ones.

Systemic injustice is traumatizing and runs deeper than any of us can imagine. Many people who are more privileged under these systems may be insulated from the reality that what they take for granted isn't accessible to a lot of people. For example, as an able-bodied person, I never have to think about whether I can access the toilet paper in a bathroom. (I use this example because it surprised me when a colleague I had invited to guest-lecture in my class informed me of the indignity of not being able to wipe her butt in my workplace bathroom because she couldn't reach the toilet paper dispenser.) Another example is when I hosted a workshop in a venue that billed itself as accessible for people with disabilities, though it didn't have a bathroom stall wide enough for all of our participants. I didn't learn that until it was discovered by a fat person who wasn't able to use the facilities. Structures were designed for people like me and I have been able to take that for granted.

Identifying systemic trauma can help to relieve the shame and self-blame of the victims of these systems and can also help those who benefit from the systems to become aware of their privilege and leverage it to advance social justice rather than their own self-interest.

INTERGENERATIONAL TRAUMA

Trauma isn't isolated to an individual. It also blows through one generation and on into the next.

My dad could be a nice guy—generous (always) and kind (often). He was also an alcoholic with an explosive temper. A functional alcoholic, he was sober and productive during the day, with the martinis and meanness surfacing at night. I stayed out of his way in the evening and grew practiced in the art of stealth living, learning how to be in a room without anyone noticing my presence. My mom and sister absorbed the brunt of his rages. My mom tried to placate him and avoid his temper, but simple things, like clinking dishes while unloading the dishwasher, were enough to trigger an outburst. If he had had a bad day at work—as was often the case during my adolescence—she could do nothing to fend off his rage. My sister, on the other hand, pointedly provoked him. My brother must have been good at stealth living, too, because I don't even remember where he was during these moments.

Trauma spreads between people. My dad had his own stories of a painful childhood, including having a distant mother and an absent father. He received little warmth or nurturing. I have compassion for why his mom may have shown so little warmth. She was trying hard to make it as a single parent. Ironically, the time she spent away from him was in effort to create a better life for him. In the absence of a nurturing mom, though, my father never developed emotional skills for coping with discomfort or anxiety or sadness. His rage ran on pure instinct. His reptilian brain leaped into action without progressing through the logical thought process of the cortex, which might have been able to suppress the minor irritation of hearing rattling dishes.

Sometimes, he'd apologize afterward, in his awkwardly ineffective way. "I told her to empty it before I came home," he'd say, as if that justified his abusive tirade. He was as disappointed in his temper as we were. What he did not see was that they were signs of his unresolved trauma.

That was his legacy, and now it's mine. Part of my trauma was feeling helpless to protect my mom and sister. I stayed "safe" behind my books, clinging to Tiggy, my stuffed tiger and confidante. The trauma made me vulnerable to "reptile brain" activity, too—leaving me, like him, with a short fuse.

I managed to avoid following my dad in taking my anger out on others, but unfortunately, I took it out on myself instead. Rather than rages, my vulnerabilities had me using substances—like food and drugs—to stave off negative feelings. I also learned to fear human connection and to be vigilant, suspicious, and mistrustful of bonding, always alert for signs of betrayal.

These are some of the legacies of trauma.

Tiggy was an important component for me surviving childhood, a point I'll return to later. Having an outlet is one of many effective ways to help manage hard times.

HISTORICAL TRAUMA

So often in history we hear about a dominant culture perpetrating mass trauma in the form of colonialism, slavery, war, or genocide. What we hear less about is that the affected group, tribe, or nation passes on their physical and psychological symptoms to later generations, who inherit those pathologies.

The Cherokee Indian tribe's experience provides a potent illustration. When the Europeans colonized Mexico, they brought germs that wiped out over half the Cherokee population. The Cherokees who were still alive were forced to leave their homes and to walk more than a thousand miles, to "Indian Territory" in what is now Oklahoma. More than four thousand people died on the way and were buried in unmarked graves along the "Trail of Tears." Their children were kidnapped, sent to assimilation boarding camps, and forbidden to use their own languages and names or practice their religion or culture. They were assigned Anglo-American names, pressured to alter their clothes and haircuts, and forced to abandon their way of life because it was supposedly inferior to white people's. Many were beaten and sexually abused.

Not surprisingly, the Cherokees now live with high levels of fear, grief, anger, and a persistent feeling of powerlessness. With that as legacy, is there any wonder why they experience such a high incidence of substance abuse and disease? The Cherokee Nation is typical of Native American* populations in rates of diabetes running 35 to 40 percent. Trauma, not just genes, drives that painful statistic (more on this in chapter 4), and trauma explains why mental health challenges and substance abuse run high among Native Americans and why they are the racial or ethnic group most likely to commit suicide. Health inequities are especially severe in the Dakotas, where Native Americans' average life expectancy is twenty years less than that of white Americans.

Native Americans are still subject to racism and lack of opportunity, and that trauma is passed on from one generation to the next. This is a classic case of historical trauma, a term that links people together based on a group identity, like race. Historical trauma can be seen as a subset of intergenerational trauma, which, as we saw, is characterized by family transference of trauma through generations.

The transference of trauma manifests not just in how we treat one another; its effects are also physical. A common misperception says that the genes you get from your parents came from your grandparents and nothing your parents did or do can change them. Yet research in epigenetics shows something quite different. Epigenetics studies show trauma passes down through generations through more than just learned behaviors (the "nurture" part of the old "nature versus nurture" debate). Parents do indeed pass on their chromosomes, but the condition these chromosomes are in when a child receives them—and how they are then activated or suppressed—can be improved or diminished by events and experiences

---

* There is no consensus on the terminology most respectfully applied to people with ancestry indigenous to the Americas. Some people suggest that because the term Native American includes the word American, it describes people within the frame of their colonizers and should be avoided. Others appreciate that using the word American affirms that they are also Americans. The term American Indian is favored by some, although criticized by others for its misinformed origins, which date back to the 1490s, when Christopher Columbus and other Europeans referred to all of Asia as "India." Assuming they had reached Asia, they referred to the inhabitants they encountered as "Indians." I chose to use Native Americans as it appears to be the term most commonly accepted among Indigenous people, though I recognize that it is not uniformly accepted.

in the parents' lives. And not just traumas—even mundane matters, like where you live, who you interact with, how you sleep and age can all eventually cause chemical modifications that will alter those genes over time. These modifications can be passed from parent to child.

Historical trauma gets triggered without our knowing. The legacy of slavery is in North Americans' blood. Time and again it's been shown that North Americans of all races and genders tend to go on higher alert when they see a Black person, even if they may not consciously consider Black people dangerous. This is what literary scholar and cultural historian Saidiya Hartman calls the "afterlife of slavery,"[11] which is characterized by the continued presence of slavery's racialized violence within modern society.

This is why police brutality and the state-sanctioned murder of Black people is so enduring and prevalent to our modern reality in the United States. If you think someone is dangerous—even if that perception is below the level of conscious thought—you're going to be quicker on the trigger.

I remember watching a Black man pop a car door lock with a file and assuming he was breaking in. If he had white skin and wore a suit, I expect I would have guessed the truth, that he had locked his keys in his car. I'm glad a friend stopped me from calling the police. She reminded me that while police may make me feel safe, they probably have the opposite effect on the People of Color who predominated in the neighborhood.

First reactions like these, based on instinct, don't express who I want to be, but they do reveal primal traits and anti-Black legacies at work. Education and intellectual awareness alone can't purge racism from your system, because trauma doesn't just live in our thinking brains. Our rational brain can't entirely stop it from occurring, and it can't talk our body out of it. That makes it deadly for Black people, as their mere existence becomes a setup for victimization in our racist culture.

STOPPING THE CYCLE

Trauma has a dual nature, living inside of us individually and collectively. Individual healing and social justice are intertwined, because what oppresses us externally has also made us suffer internal trauma and its accompanying fallout. We cannot separate the paths when talking about individual healing and social justice work because our well-being depends on the interconnectedness of all communities. Likewise, we can't truly see the collective picture without thinking about the individual impact.

To stop the cycle of trauma passing through generations, we need to change the conditions. We must be committed to active decolonization from systems of oppression. Consider Jewish survivors of genocide. When my family escaped pogroms in Poland by emigrating to the United States, they did much better economically and socially (more on that later), largely supported by opportunities provided only to white people. While some trauma was passed from my grandmother to my father, the trauma was lessened in my generation. (Anti-Semitism, of course, still abounds. "Better" doesn't mean "problem solved.")

That's quite different from the African American experience. Many African Americans are descendants of those who were enslaved and have been harshly victimized since: stripped of resources; lacking access to education, employment, and housing; subject to discrimination, incarceration, violence, or death. The trauma persists because the ideology of white supremacy, used to justify slavery, persists. The damage to African Americans continued long after the abolition of slavery in 1865. Efforts to subordinate and economically exploit Black people have extended through sharecropping, Jim Crow laws, redlined Black ghettos, and mass incarceration.*

---

* Sharecropping refers to a system where a landlord allows a tenant to use the land in exchange for a share of the crop, which resulted in trapping many people who were formerly enslaved in a new system of economic exploitation. Jim Crow laws were laws that enforced racial segregation, denying Black people the right to vote, hold jobs, get an education, or other opportunities. Redlining refers to the denial of services to residents of specific, often racially associated, neighborhoods—for example, banks denying mortgages, mostly to People of Color in urban areas, preventing them from buying a home in certain neighborhoods.

Long before many of us were born, Black scholars began writing, archiving, and creating work around the legacy of slavery, the intergenerational trauma from slavery, and the blueprints for building a world without those cages. In our modern age, scholars continue to shape and influence this work by viewing body liberation through the lens of anti-Blackness, striving to stop the cyclical machine of anti-Black death. Rachel Cargle, Tressie McMillan Cottom, Brienne Colston, Da'Shaun Harrison, Samantha Irby, Myles E. Johnson, Kiese Laymon, Ijeoma Oluo, Ilya Parker, Hunter Ashleigh Shackelford, Sabrina Strings, Sonya Renee Taylor, Melissa Toler, and thousands more are doing this work to deepen the possibility of a future without white supremacist imperialism and a world that affirms the abundance within us all.

THE TRAUMA OF TRAUMA

One of the greatest casualties of trauma is our weakened ability to trust people and allow ourselves to be vulnerable. The trauma of social injustice requires us to face the world with our armor on and carry that through the day, no matter how heavy it is, because we do not feel safe in the world. Later on we'll look more at shame and vulnerability, and the importance of connection, as well as tools for coping.

We can acknowledge and even honor the past, but we don't have to stay stuck there. We don't have to live our lives forever defined by damaging things that happened to us and a culture that invisibilizes or tries to confiscate our personhood.

I don't like to talk about "recovery," as the term implies coming back to something you were before. In that sense, you never recover—you are changed forever by your experiences—but your trauma *can* be transformed into strength. Neuroplasticity and trauma go hand in hand. Just as traumatic events can forge neural pathways, so can positive and constructive experiences help you cope and heal, establishing new neural pathways. Many people experience positive transformation after trauma, like a fresh appreciation for life, a newfound sense of personal strength, or greater empathy, so much so that psychologists coined the term "post-traumatic growth." I am a better person because of—not in spite of—the trauma I've endured. Now, for example, when I tell that Barbizon Modeling School story, I no longer feel the pain. I can even laugh at the absurdity. When others laugh, too, it's an avenue of connection. Not only do people see and empathize with me, but it also allows them to view their own traumatic histories in a more hopeful light.

If all we ever do is focus on the pain of oppression, we lose sight of our individual and collective agency. Broadening our lens to view not just the pain, but the stories of resistance and transformation, allows us to see that a very different future is possible—and that we can call it into being.

HEALING

Healing starts by acknowledging trauma's effects on our lives. Deep and enduring pain arises from the knowledge that your childhood and past experiences have damaged you in significant ways. It doesn't have to stop us from growing and developing, having fulfilling relationships, find a career that we're passionate about, and living a meaningful and satisfying life. To the contrary, feeling pain can be a good thing. It can remind us of the critical importance of creating love and connection in our lives and make us more empathetic to others, thereby deepening relationships.

To start, forgive yourself. Forgive yourself for survival behaviors you picked up to manage or endure your trauma. Forgive yourself for being who you needed to be. Show compassion for your own wounds. The traumatic stress reactions you experience—the behaviors and emotions you don't like—are responses to surviving trauma. They are normal reactions to abnormal situations, and reflect your strength, your determination, and your will to self-preservation. You are a resourceful, resilient survivor.

Recognize your trauma and how it fuels the behaviors that disappoint you. Acknowledge that it's not your fault. Your emotions (housed in the limbic system) are in charge of your body, causing the instinctive fight-or-flight response behind those behaviors. The trauma has hijacked your brain, blocking your prefrontal cortex (rational brain) from regulating your emotions and helping you make good choices. That prefrontal cortex also takes the lead on sensing what's going on with other people and their feelings—empathy, in other words. So, if your trauma has impaired your empathy, it's because it makes you distrust and disconnect from others.

Since trauma robs you of your sense of safety and trust, a crucial part of healing consists of learning who to trust and reestablishing safety in connection with others. In order to relax, you need to believe that you can rely on others, to know that no one will hurt you in a certain space or relationship, and to feel protected. But connection is elusive for traumatized people. We are cut off from the very thing that can help, and this alienation invariably leads to shame. We blame ourselves for our relationship problems, for the ways we self-soothe or avoid.

Shame surrounds trauma. The emotions you experience and the behaviors you've adopted—anxiety, depression, dissociation, reactivity, intrusive thoughts, avoidant behaviors, substance abuse—are all ways of coping with your pain, and yet you may feel shame for "choosing" them. And a hallmark of shame, what allows it to fester, is secrecy. This is why speaking your truth and connecting with others can be such an important part of healing. To stop the self-defeating loop you are stuck in, you need compassion and love—from yourself and others. Name your pain to friends so they can bolster you, find support groups, get professional help. Help yourself by letting others help you. You are not alone. Know, too, that overcoming shame is hard; in chapter 10 we will look at some tools to amp up your resiliency and help you break out of this shell.

Healing doesn't mean that you escape your pain but rather that you expand your window of tolerance for emotion. Healing means that you're not always focused on soothing your pain (by means of drugs or sex or gambling or whatever your pattern is), nor are you running away from yourself (by cozying up to the internet, for example). You're not trying to please people just so they'll like you. Instead, you are considering what you want, what you need, what you feel—not in a selfish way of ignoring others, but in a way that is true to you and consistent with your values. Ironically, accepting your discomfort is the best way to make it go away. It gets easier over time—and with community.

Remember, too, that trauma is lodged in your body. As a protective response to trauma, people often learn to turn off the parts of the brain that produce unpleasant feelings. Yet those exact brain areas are also instrumental in enabling the entire spectrum of feelings and sensations that mold the very core of our identity and our conception of our place in the world. This leads to the ultimate tragedy of trauma: we become disconnected from ourselves.

Trauma is rarely something we can think ourselves out of. Much of it has to do with unconscious parts of the brain that keep interpreting the world as being dangerous, frightening, and unsafe. When you tell a traumatized person "You're not a bad person" or "It wasn't your fault," it's common to be met with: "I know that, but I *feel* that it is." Traumatized people know we "shouldn't" feel that way, but we do. Our brains go on autopilot to try to manage the difficult feelings, fueling behaviors that may be maladaptive today.

Reconnecting to our bodies is a critical aspect of healing. Almost anything that can help you reconnect to your physicality is valuable—running, dancing, karate, to name just a few. A wide range of physically-oriented therapies, such as EMDR, neurofeedback, yoga, and somatic therapy, have shown well-documented success in helping us push beyond our cognitive limitations to heal trauma.

BRINGING IT HOME

Trauma forces us to see that people are vulnerable to their environment, providing a conceptual framework for understanding how oppressive social and political conditions get inside us and cause personal suffering and dysfunction.

In a society organized around domination, it is inevitable that trauma will be pervasive, both because the systemic oppression itself is traumatizing and because the power differential that is an aspect of oppression supports individual acts of domination. Calling out structural injustice shifts the blame off individuals, similar to how a trauma-informed approach shifts the question from "what is wrong with you?" to "what happened to you?" This shift acknowledges and destigmatizes the challenges we face and empowers us to engage in personal and community healing.

Unresolved trauma doesn't just harm individuals—and drive self-harm—but also drives a cycle wherein victims become perpetrators, harming and traumatizing others. Among those who have committed serious crime, the vast majority have also suffered trauma. Few death row inmates have not suffered lives that read like a case study of extreme abuse, and it is the rare juvenile incarcerated for rape or murder who has not endured a cruel childhood. Abusers are humans with stories, just like us. Absorbing our culture, we all become perpetrators—perhaps not as explicit abusers, but in the unconscious bias that lodges in our mind and bodies, fueling the microaggressions that slowly and cumulatively traumatize, a topic of considerable discussion later in the book. Understanding this helps us generate compassion for ourselves and others, even as our actions do harm, and instills us with the responsibility to unlearn the lies we have been taught.

Trauma lives in the body and sets our behaviors in motion, but we can heal, and even come out stronger. All trauma can disconnect us from our bodies, and the cultural body hierarchy can have the impact of disconnecting some of us even further, deepening our body shame and making us believe our bodies do not belong to us. It takes active work to reclaim your body—to stay with it, trust it, and care for it. But it can be done.

To begin, we must recognize that our traumas are not our fault, and that we are not alone in our woundedness. We are all suffering from the individual and collective traumas of injustice and finding our way in a world that doesn't give equal access, opportunity, or respect.

What connects us to one another is our human vulnerability—our need for belonging, for feeling valued and connected to others—and the distress we feel without it. This realization of our shared humanity can move us to seek connection with empathetic and understanding others. Connection with others, in turn, can help us feel safe enough to wade into our pain and vulnerability, rather than trying to escape it through disconnection or other coping behaviors. Stay tuned for deeper discussion of connection and vulnerability in chapters of their own.

We can also cultivate our self-compassion and learn to give ourselves a break when we engage in behaviors that we're not so proud of—like the ones described in the next chapter.

Healing from trauma helps us to claim our bodies as our own and experience what it means to live in them, themes also explored in future chapters. We can't fully move our way out of trauma because oppression and other structures of domination are ongoing, but we can learn to treat bodies—our own and others—with the respect and caring they are due.

I wish for all of us safety and the opportunity to fully inhabit our bodies. I wish for a future where body sovereignty is a birthright.

Chapter 4

THIS IS YOU TRYING TO COPE

This chapter is for the people who are tired of thinking they are messed up for what they do, tired of feeling they just need to "get over" themselves, or tired of blaming themselves for bringing on their dis-ease. We'll view behaviors, disorders, and diseases through a compassionate lens, seeing their original value as safety devices and lifeguards, however maladaptive they may be, and give you a new way to conceptualize coping. By the end of the book you'll also have a game plan for healing.

Whatever's going on for you, I want you to know: you're not stupid, you're not lazy, you're not "too sensitive." You may have mental health challenges, but hey, I worry more about those who don't have mental health challenges. I'm not sure it's such a great trait to be well adjusted to this sick world. I'd rather we move away from the stigma associated with mental health challenges and see their value.

I'm not going to tell you to suck it up and try harder. I'm going to explain how you got to this place and offer compassion for how difficult it is. We'll keep our focus on putting you back in control, so you have choices and stop feeling commandeered into behaviors that don't serve you.

THE COUNTERINTUITIVE WISDOM OF SUBSTANCE ABUSE AND MORE

My name is Lindo Bacon and I am a human being who suffered so much that I turned to drugs, alcohol, food, shopping, workaholism, perfectionism, and other behaviors to soothe or distract myself from my pain.

I am grateful I found ways to temporarily cope with my circumstances. I recognize that these behaviors also cause pain and I would like to cultivate other skills that let me sit with and manage the challenges of being human.

Imagine how starting with this introduction changes the conversation on addiction and coping behaviors. Consider the contrast to the more typical treatment program self-introductions: "My name is Lindo and I'm a drug addict."* In my version, my identity is rooted in my humanity, not in my reactive behavior. It also acknowledges that pain is part of the human experience and that we all need coping strategies.

Our coping behaviors come from wisdom and allow us to manage in a difficult world. Consider substance abuse, which allows you to temporarily escape your circumstances. It's a brilliant response if you need to take care of yourself in the moment. However, it can also keep you stuck, worsen problems, and create new difficulties—and it doesn't help in the long term.

---

* Please don't misunderstand. I'm not dissing 12-step programs outright. Many people receive value from them, sometimes life-saving. That said, I do have concerns about certain aspects of these programs.

THE BIOLOGY OF EMOTIONAL REGULATION

Earlier we learned about the prefrontal cortex, the brain area that helps regulate the limbic system (the "emotional center"). A well-developed prefrontal cortex allows you to consider your emotions and make choices that are beneficial (even if they go against instinct), that are harder, or that fail to give immediate gratification. With a poorly developed prefrontal cortex, emotions rule.

Our brains are wired to make essential behaviors pleasurable to increase the odds that we will repeat them. Scientists call this "reward-based learning." Eating and sex are examples of essential behaviors. As both are required for human survival, it's not surprising they are biologically wired to trigger a potentially pleasurable response. If there's no reward, why go to the trouble of eating or having sex?

The main chemical that mediates this process is a neurotransmitter called dopamine. When you have a pleasurable experience, an influx of dopamine signals that something important is happening that needs to be remembered. The memory is recorded by the hippocampus and the amygdala creates a conditioned response, making it easier to repeat the activity again and again without thinking about it. This leads to the formation of habits.

See food. Eat. Feel good. Repeat. Trigger, behavior, reward. Simple, right? See attractive human. Have sex with attractive human. Feel good. Repeat. Trigger, behavior, reward. (Of course, food and sex only have the *potential* to make you feel good. Negative experiences and associations are certainly common, too.)

You're smart. You've figured out that you can use reward-based pathways for more than essentials like acquiring nourishment. You recognize that when you feel like crap, this same eating pathway can help you feel better. So you reach for the chocolate when you get that credit card bill. Can you stop getting down on yourself and recognize how brilliant this is? The chocolate works in the short term!

This natural tendency to usurp biology's pleasure pathways also comes to the fore when we use methamphetamine and other drugs. Some drugs can stimulate the release of double or even ten times the amount of dopamine released by food or sex. The resulting neuro-flood causes the "high" that occurs with drug use. I still remember the first time I tried cocaine and the feel-good burst that came along with it. I felt joy. My sadness disappeared. I then, of course, wanted to repeat the experience. I didn't know how to access that soothing or joy on my own, so I was vulnerable to craving drugs.

It's a simplification, though, to consider dopamine to be purely about pleasure and reward. Dopamine is really more about anticipation of reward, and even more precisely about the effort you're willing to expend to get that reward. As neurobiologist Robert Sapolsky describes it, "Dopamine is not about pleasure; it's about the pursuit of pleasure."[1] What the dopamine is really doing is motivating you to do whatever is necessary to feel good. It increases your general level of arousal and your goal-directed behavior.

Another neurotransmitter pivotal to this reward system is serotonin. While dopamine brings feelings of pleasure and provides a happiness boost, serotonin is more of a mood stabilizer, contributing to feelings of contentment, happiness, and well-being, and inhibiting the compelling motivation of dopamine.

Most people realize that substances can trigger this pleasure pathway but are less aware that behaviors can as well. Consider shopping. The notion of "retail therapy" is not just a cliché. When you're thinking about buying a treat for yourself—expecting a reward, essentially—dopamine surges. Actually buying something results in an even harder dopamine kick.

In one insightful study, neuroscientists scanned people's brains as they contemplated buying items. The researchers noted extra activity in the nucleus accumbens, described as the pleasure center of the brain.[2] That's to be expected, but it's the next step where this study got interesting. When the research participants were told how much the items cost, there was more activity in the part of their prefrontal cortex responsible for executive functioning and decision-making, as well as the insula, which processes pain. Those with the most active insulas were most likely to decide not to buy the product, which points to the fact that sometimes the joy of holding on to your hard-earned cash beats the thrill of getting new stuff.

The take-home message is that you are biologically wired to pursue pleasure—this gets stimulated through substances and behaviors—but you also have biological wiring to keep pleasure in check so it doesn't turn into pain.

How well these pathways support healthy functioning differs for each of us. For some people, for example, shopping's immediate gratification always seems to outweigh the consideration of suffering (by overspending, say). Others allow their budgets to keep them in check. That's not unlike substance use. Some people may feel driven to drink away their problems, even as they know they'll pay a price the next morning. For others, knowing they need to be "on" for work in a few hours supports them in calling it a night.

Why are some people more vulnerable to problematic behavior? Recall our discussion of the high allostatic load imposed by stressful lives. One hallmark of bearing a high allostatic load is weak functioning of the prefrontal cortex. Another is decreased secretion of dopamine and serotonin. For those reasons, a person with a high allostatic load just isn't so good at bringing their rational mind online to help regulate emotions, making them vulnerable to anything that increases dopamine and serotonin levels, such as substance use or other reward-based coping behaviors like gambling, shopping, or compulsive internet use.

YOUR COPING STRATEGIES

Whether you're struggling in your romantic life or falling behind at work, healthy coping skills can be essential to getting through tough times. We all have go-to coping strategies, not all of which serve us well. What's yours? Do you click too many items into your online shopping cart? Work overtime, to avoid creating a life outside of work? Consume a nightly bottle of wine to settle down? Do you dissociate from reality so that it can't get to you? Or maybe you have an unrelenting drive for everything to be perfect? Perhaps you're prone to blaming others when things go wrong, which allows for distraction from the pain of what's really going on? Or prone to blaming yourself and feeling worthless?

Some people cope in more socially acceptable ways. Yet even if they sound less problematic—there's obviously a huge difference between heroin addiction and perfectionism—these behaviors stop us from living with a deeper sense of presence and love. If a habit is hurting you, change helps, regardless of the degree of the problem.

Whatever your issues, whether shopping, reactive anger, perfectionism, workaholism, or substance abuse, it's not easy to break conditioned responses. They're wired into you and it takes effort to disrupt the pathways. But science and history show it is possible.

I don't want to label all coping behaviors as bad. We need ways to manage our emotions. We need downtime and distraction. Sometimes zoning out is the best possible thing you can do for yourself. Netflix can be good therapy. A settling glass of wine may be therapeutic.* The trick is figuring out when your behavior settles you and when it hijacks you. Giving yourself permission to escape now and then makes you less vulnerable to feeling driven to escape.

In the next section, we'll unpack a few examples of maladaptive coping. I'll start with perfectionism and workaholism, two behaviors that are front and center for me, and then cover aggression. Then, we'll apply that same lens of understanding maladaptive coping to disorders and diseases like depression and diabetes.

PERFECTIONISM

Perfectionism is my go-to tool when I want to control difficult circumstances. It surfaced when I first tried for attention and love in my family. The hope of perfectionism is that if I become smart enough, or acquire whatever other trait I think others value, they will care for me. That sure puts a lot of pressure on me to perform, and it relies on my (false) conviction that I can control others' appraisal of me.

---

* This is not true for everyone! Some people need to avoid alcohol entirely. Please take care of yourself.

It also trips me up, making me believe that I need to be perfect in order to deserve love. I don't. I make mistakes. But my mistakes don't make me undeserving of love.

Being perfect isn't human. Pretending we're perfect inhibits connection. People connect across vulnerability (a point important enough to merit its own chapter later). Love and respect emerge between imperfect and messy human beings.

WORKAHOLISM

Sometimes I get so focused on work that I can't let go of it. The word *driven* applies, as I'm no longer in the driver's seat. Even when I turn off the computer and am with my family, I'm distracted. I drive for the dopamine surge I get from a focus on work. The fallout is that I don't give my partner and kid what they need. Nor do I end up getting what I need.

It's easy for me to fall into workaholism because I get so much reinforcement that my work is making a difference. This outside validation feeds me, whether it's a standing ovation or the "likes" I get on a social media post. It's that need for external validation and the great satisfaction I gain from it that sometimes diminish my connection with others and time spent with my family.

Why is workaholism my particular shtick? I was raised in a family where I felt valued for my achievements more than for who I was. My success as a student was a ticket to getting the attention and pride I desperately wanted from my parents. That started me on the endless drive to achieve—Who really needs three postgraduate degrees?—but, much professional accomplishment later, I have finally come to realize that this endless drive for achievement is never going to satisfy or serve me. What I'm really craving is acceptance for who I am at my core, not what I can achieve. In some ways, the attention I get for this work I currently do—writing and speaking—is very hard on me because it reinforces the value of my professional identity. But in the process, I'm not sure I always get seen.

Others have a very different experience of workaholism. Some people use work to distract themselves from traumatic thoughts. It can be effective for that, too—in the short term, of course.

Working hard, like most behaviors, is not inherently problematic. But workaholism is quite distinct from working hard to make ends meet. It's what's driving the behavior that determines its effect. There is a clear difference, too, between a hard worker and a workaholic. A hard worker is emotionally present for family, coworkers, and friends. A hard worker can put their work aside and tend to other things. A hard worker can recognize they are more than their work. A hard worker may have periodic bursts of overworking to meet a deadline or an emergency, but they can also follow up with a reduced schedule or days off to restore depleted resources.

And to be clear, workaholism doesn't work. A meta-analysis (summary analysis of multiple investigations' findings) of eighty-nine primary studies found that workaholism was related to lower satisfaction with job, family, and life and diminished physical and mental health.[3] It doesn't help you succeed at work either. That same meta-analysis found that not only does workaholism fail to improve productivity, but it also strongly relates to increased job stress and burnout.

Clearly, workaholism is damaging, but it's important to remember that it is a biologically driven strategy (thanks, dopamine cycle!) that we construct to manage our fears and cope with our circumstances. Originally it was a smart strategy when you lacked better skills to help you manage. But, in the long run, it doesn't serve you. What does help? You'll get a detailed explanation in chapter 10. Short, simple answer, for now: It's about acceptance. Believing you're okay as you are. You don't need to prove yourself. And don't worry, I'll be providing strategies to help you get there.

AGGRESSION

Why is aggression so common? One reason is because it's a very effective outlet for temporarily mitigating pain and relieving stress. You take it out on someone else. The scientific term, "displacement aggression," refers to those times when you take out your tension on an innocent bystander through physical or emotional violence. Like a steam valve, you've got all this pressure building up and you have to let it out somewhere. You take control over your life by taking control over someone else's life. Rat studies make the concept easily understandable. Research shows when a rat is shocked, it activates a stress response. The kicker is that the response is lower in a shocked rat who can then bite the hell out of another rat.

Dad gets yelled at by a client and comes home, trips over his daughter's scooter, and proceeds to smash it to smithereens. Follows up with a rant at his husband about not cleaning up after the kids. That's displacement aggression.

Dumping your emotions on someone else, while it may give you an outlet and provide temporary relief, can really throw you—and others—for a loop.

I was recently victim to painful displacement aggression. Believe me, it's no fun to be on the receiving end. (Trigger warning: intense fatphobia soon to be named.) I received an anonymous email that read, "You killed my daughter. My daughter died of diabetes because people like you make it okay to be fat." Whoa! Of course the woman was extremely upset—her daughter was dead—and offloading her anger may have lightened the sting for a bit. But I doubt that soothed her for long. I hope she can eventually find peace and direct her emotion where it belongs. My clarity that I didn't deserve this blame, plus my compassion for why the woman lashed out, helped me manage the insult.

Distressingly, displacement aggression is one of the most efficacious things humans can do to feel less stressed. Particularly if you are low on the social scale, or don't have other ways of feeling your power, displacing aggression onto those even lower in the pecking order is a reliable way to reduce cortisol secretion. We see it all too often when domestic violence plays out. Boss unfairly lashes out at employee, who then brings it home and takes it out on an even less powerful child or spouse—cruelty, spitefulness, physical abuse, however wrong, may seem momentarily like the only way to blow off pent-up steam. This explains why, when inequality fuels violence, it is mostly disadvantaged people preying on other disadvantaged people. This also contributes to rates of child/intimate partner abuse increasing dramatically during times of economic duress.

Cisgender men control a disproportionate share of resources and thus are disproportionally offenders of displacement aggression, while women and people of other genders are frequent targets.

Interestingly, in researching "air rage" (a passenger losing it on a commercial flight), scientists found a substantial predictor. On planes with first-class sections, the odds of a coach passenger going ballistic goes up almost fourfold.[4] Further, if coach passengers board through first class, meltdowns are even more frequent. Researchers assume that's because you start the flight by being reminded of where you fit on the class hierarchy. The coach passengers take out their rage not on first-class passengers but on people directly around them. So you get the dude lashing out at the woman and baby sitting next to him or the hapless flight attendant serving his row.

Don't avoid your own pain by giving it to someone else.

If you're the aggressor, take heed. I know you don't want to be a jerk—you wouldn't be reading this book if you did. So, start by honoring that you want to be a good person. Apply some self-compassion. Aggression is a reaction that you were taught. It probably helped you survive a bad situation in the past and so far you haven't found other ways of managing. Then take a hard look at what's driving the aggression. Know that anger is almost always a secondary emotion, meaning that there is also a more primary feeling beneath it like fear, hurt, sadness, or shame. Accessing the primary feeling may help divert you so you don't take your feelings out on someone else. Be accountable for the ways your words and actions hurt others.

If you're victim to someone else's angry outburst, as in intimate partner violence, try to keep perspective. The problem is not you, the problem is their inability to manage their emotions effectively. That understanding can help mitigate your downward spiral into unworthiness. I wish you safety. Both of you need help, separately (and then perhaps together, if safety permits).

Remember, too, that when you are higher on the social scale, you have more opportunities for outlets, whether it's negative outlets like taking it out on lower-ranking people (like your kids or service employees) or positive outlets like getting a massage now and then or taking the time for a walk outside. For those lower on the social hierarchy, it may take more creativity to find outlets. Regardless, it helps to have compassion for why you do the things you do—and put the effort into finding ways to cope that are less harmful to you and others.

ADDICTION

Some coping behaviors cross a line into addiction. Conflicting definitions of addiction abound. I'm going to use the term *addiction* to refer to habits and actions we continually repeat despite adverse consequences. Addiction rests on a lack of control, where you are driven to do something even though you know it's not benefitting you. It goes beyond drugs. It could mean continued use of anything: hours on social media at the cost of work, school, or family commitments, or continued shopping despite the damaging drain on your bank account. From the point of view of brain physiology, the workaholic and drug addict are trying to release the same brain chemicals. It's the same process.

THE BIOLOGY OF ADDICTION

What's going on biologically in addiction? Earlier, I discussed the *trigger, behavior, reward* pathway wherein you discover that implementing a coping behavior gives you some relief, and the more you do it, the more it gets hooked into your brain. Neural patterns take hold, becoming habits. After a while, you don't even consciously have to think, "Oh, this will make me feel better." When things go wrong, your brain is wired to automatically go to that behavior to get you out of that bad place. Turning on autopilot like this frees your prefrontal cortex for other thoughts.

Over time, your body comes to depend on the drug or behavior to stimulate your reward system. When you're not doing the drugs or behaviors, your dopamine levels decline, leaving you with painful withdrawal symptoms and intense cravings. You may feel compelled to keep taking drugs or doing the behaviors to avoid these negative emotional and physical withdrawal symptoms. The brain doesn't function normally without the drugs (or whatever addictive substance or behavior you're hooked on).

Addicted people usually have low serotonin levels. When serotonin levels are low, the reward-seeking effects of dopamine become amplified. In other words, the needs and cravings you have become much more compelling. If you're already hungry, for example, that candy bar ad you usually ignore may sound suddenly convincing; next thing you know you're detouring to the 7-Eleven. Depression and anxiety can also be triggered when serotonin is low.

An addicted person, like someone with depression, may feel flat, lacking in motivation and unable to enjoy things that were previously pleasurable. A vicious cycle ensues wherein people need to keep taking drugs—or continue with their addictive behavior—to feel okay, which only makes the problem worse. They may also need to take larger amounts of the drug to get that same feeling, an effect known as tolerance.

HOW BIG INDUSTRY HIJACKS YOUR BRAIN

As an aside, know that Big Industry also studies neuroscience—and for more than idle interest. They're using brain hacks to hook you on their products. Their profits, and their very survival, depend on it. It turns out that when a reward is intermittent or unexpected, it stimulates a bigger dopamine release than you get from regular, consistent satisfactions. It's why so many of us love a surprise party (not me!) or unexpected gift (hint!). It's also why gambling can be so addictive, where people throw the dice based on the possibility of an intermittent reward. In fact, slot machines work on algorithms that allow people to win just enough times to get them to keep playing, even though on average everyone loses money.

Corporate America exploits this. They know that this intermittent reinforcement extends to anything that is new or unexpected. That's why social media platforms like Twitter, Instagram, and Facebook—and your email provider—love to buzz you with "alerts." Turn off those alerts so you're less vulnerable.

Here's another example of corporate America hijacking your brain: our vulnerability to instant gratification. If you act quickly, you don't have time to adequately run it through your prefrontal cortex and consider the big picture, like whether buying those new shoes now may get in the way of paying your rent next week. One-click shopping has been quite a money-maker for industry, as is the instant availability supplied by a drive-through fast food restaurant. My advice? Don't fall for the "buy now" hype.

The more we learn about our emotional reactivity and triggers, the better we can defend ourselves against manipulation like this. Marketers and corporations depend on us to respond in the short term, to react by instinct and "addiction" rather than after reflection when our long-term interests are front of mind. This book can help you not only curb your impulses to binge on drugs or food or anger, but to resist marketing come-ons that play on the same trigger-reward mechanisms and can likewise deplete us more than they help.

ADDICTION IS ABOUT WHAT'S ALREADY HAPPENED

Oppressed people and those who have otherwise suffered hard lives fall prey to addiction more readily. History shows that addiction can be rare in a population but become widespread when social circumstances worsen. (Genetics play a role, but not as a primary driver of addiction.)

Consider again the Native American experience.* Native American people had access to addictive substances like alcohol and peyote before colonization. However, we don't hear stories of addiction from that era. If addiction were purely genetic, it couldn't explain the disparity between the high rates of addiction among Indigenous people today relative to the low rates among early Native Americans. Instead, the high levels of addiction in Native American groups today reflect trauma and disempowerment.

---

* Not all Native Americans have the same experience. It is helpful to use a generalization as a starting point, with the awareness that it may not apply to individuals. In this case, the generalization about high levels of addiction in Indigenous peoples helps us understand the impact of colonization, even if it may not describe any one individual's experience.

Colonization and its follow-up deprived people of access to meaning and dignity. The trauma is passed on from one generation to the next both because the conditions persist and because coping styles are passed down.

This sociohistorical perspective does not deny that differences in vulnerability are built into individuals' genes and experience. It shows the relative unimportance of individual differences in the face of societal determinants. Addiction is much more a social than an individual problem.

Addiction theory for decades relied on the now-discredited assumption that drugs—or behaviors—themselves are the problem. Researcher Bruce Alexander conducted a study that on first look suggests that exposure to cocaine leads to addiction for rats.[5] He gave his rat subjects access to both pure water and cocaine-laced water. Almost all rapidly became addicted to cocaine to the point of death, which seems to suggest that the coke itself was problematic. Then Alexander considered the rats' circumstances. They were in tiny, individual sheet metal cages without much stimulus. They couldn't even see one another. He set out to test whether their living conditions influenced the outcome.

He created a study space he called "Rat Park," filling it with rat delights like climbing platforms, tin cans to hide in, wood chips to strew, and exercise wheels. He also allowed the rats to be together rather than isolated and alone. This time, when given the water choice, the rats shunned the coke version. The difference was dramatic: from a rate of almost 100 percent for isolated rats in dreary conditions, overdoses fell to almost zero in socially connected and comfortable living conditions. The real issue seemed to be the conditions of the rats' lives.

If you're bored, lonely, or dissatisfied with your life, coke is a good distraction. If you're living a good life, your body's natural cocaine-like chemicals usually work, making cocaine less interesting. Human experience seems to bear this out. Consider the Vietnam War, where a fifth of American troops used heroin. Detailed research later showed that 95 percent of them stopped when they returned home.[6]

Such studies led Professor Alexander to revise his understanding of addiction. It's the cage, he learned, not the chemical. Addiction is simply a response to your life circumstances. This is true, too, for imprisoned people. Many incarcerated individuals become addicted to drugs while in the bleak conditions of prison. Certainly, the cage here matters more than the chemical.

We need to take responsibility as a culture for the conditions that lead so many to addiction. If we want people to give up their addictions, we need to make their lives easier, to support them in making the changes they need. Easy enough to say, you might think, but how to make it happen? What kind of happy juice or universal lever could make everyone's lives suddenly easier? In fact, ordinary human tools—no divine intervention needed—can help minimize addiction, starting with legislation. Raising the minimum wage, for instance, and providing affordable housing and health care. Social tools that build community and address the spiritual void that arises from materialism, like drum circles or community gardens, can also make a difference. When we focus on the financial, mental, emotional, and physical well-being of people with addiction, we can improve their living situations.

In previous chapters, we discussed how shame can dog people, particularly if they have marginalized identities. They see themselves as failures, as flawed. They internalize societal stigma. Addictive behaviors allow them to get away from this experience of themselves. Reassigning the blame to the culture and addressing the shame is an important aspect in healing. We'll talk more about that later on.

WHO SUCCUMBS?

Of course, privilege and status do not provide freedom from addiction. In fact, some research indicates that teens who are raised in affluent families and attend prestigious high schools are more prone to addiction and substance abuse, relative to the national average.[7]

Kids from affluent families are subject to some of the same vulnerabilities as poor kids, including genetics, neglect, trauma, and so on. They also have other contributors. For example, I had extra money, safer places to acquire drugs, and a car that got me to my dealer's location easily. Because I was doing well academically, people didn't suspect that I had a problem.

These made my drug habit easier. Substance abuse is way more than a "poor person problem."

WHO RECOVERS?

Why does one person recover from addiction and not their friend? People will say it's about "hitting bottom," but I don't think so. Some people's addictions expose them to horrible pain and yet they still won't give them up.

What prevented me from descending into severe addiction was faith in my future and my conviction I had something to contribute to the world. Academic success allowed me to experience my worthiness and helped me set boundaries: no coke during the school day, abstaining when I needed to focus for an assignment or test. Not everyone receives that kind of external validation.

INJUSTICE CONTRIBUTES TO ADDICTION

Discrimination and disparity in income result in inequitable access to opportunity, achievement, or hope for a better future. The same conditions that keep us from acquiring education or wealth or family happiness often steer us toward more immediate rewards—short-term stimuli that turn into addictions. Combine this with home environments that tell some kids they aren't valued and addiction almost seems like a foregone conclusion.

LOVE IS THE ANSWER

We all need supportive resources and opportunities to create a meaningful life. In particular, we need people who believe in us. "The opposite of addiction is not sobriety. The opposite of addiction is connection," concludes author Johann Hari in his convincing TED Talk, "Everything You Think You Know about Addiction is Wrong."[8]

We have so many distractions available to us, and without healthier sources of connection, they're easy to grab on to. Consider smartphones. I remember the days when people attended my workshops and, during breaks, talked and got to know one another. Now, everyone's using that "downtime" to check email or "socialize" with people far away, ignoring the real folks right in the room with them. When I ask my students to put their phones away, you'd think I was denying them access to their drug.

Given how often we call ours a "connected" society, it's ironic to talk about disconnection as a cause of addiction. But the modern notion of connectedness feels more like a parody of human connection. My Facebook and Twitter followers didn't sit with me when my parents died. It was my flesh and blood friends and family in the hospital room with me—people with whom I have deep, nuanced, and textured relationships.

For too many of us, our society resembles a barren rat cage far more than a stimulating and supportive community.

Helping addicts demands that we deepen connections. Rather than the tough love approach of "I can't be with you because you're using," we need to say, "I love you regardless of whether you're using. My love is unconditional and if you need me, I'll come be with you. I don't want you to feel alone."

This doesn't mean that bad behavior is tolerated or goes unchecked. Heartbreaking accounts abound of parents whose kids stole from them or were violent toward them, and intimate partner abuse is a devastating and chronic problem across all demographics in the United States. Protecting yourself and enforcing appropriate boundaries are necessary and appropriate. The challenge is in loving and accepting someone while maintaining the boundaries that keep you safe.

DEBUNKING OLD IDEAS ABOUT BEHAVIOR CHANGE

I used to believe that willpower was the answer, that my mind was in charge. That since I wanted to lose weight so badly, I could just *think* myself out of eating dinner. Self-control was my thing.

Studies on willpower[9] suggest that's not how it works. "Just do it" might motivate in the short term, but not lastingly. Willpower works, in other words, only until it doesn't.

Why? Stress. We are masters of self-control only until something stressful comes up. Then, our prefrontal cortex, the brain structure doing the thinking and planning, gets kicked offline, and we're suddenly subject to our primitive brain. Those urges we were "willing" away now become more powerful. The doughnuts we resisted all week suddenly own us when we confront the looming threat of a utility bill.

Don't blame yourself. Instead, look for strategies to manage your stress when the storms hit. And show some self-compassion.

CRIMINAL "JUSTICE"

If we wanted to design a system that would worsen problematic behaviors like addiction, we couldn't have come up with anything better than the US criminal "justice" system. We've tried punishing and criminalizing for hundreds of years. Crime hasn't ended, and now we've got the highest prison population per capita in the world.

Nor is shaming people an effective response. If negative consequences or stigma stopped addiction, there wouldn't be addicts.

Racist drug policies are devastating. Communities of Color are unjustly targeted and then funneled through a discriminatory mass incarceration system that irreversibly destroys lives. People of Color convicted of drug possession are often given disproportionately harsh sentences. When released, having a criminal record prevents them from getting the jobs and housing they need to reestablish their lives. To add further insult to injury, those with criminal records are denied the right to vote, robbing them of the opportunity to express how society has failed them and distracting us from addressing how society should and can correct these injustices.

A war on drugs means we are punishing people for being traumatized and abused. What is really needed to address addiction is to remove the barriers between people and connection. I'd rather conceptualize a society that is more compassionate and equitable, where instead of incarceration we helped people find reasons to live, like meaningful work and livable wages. This would remove the need for drugs or damaging behaviors to escape or to get that dopamine surge. When crimes are committed, a system of restorative justice can help us repair the harm and build community (more on this later).*

I'd always subscribed generally to the idea that white people have it easier under our economy and our laws. But it turned out I had to travel—away from home and out of my comfort zone—to learn it in a personal way. While getting to know Atlanta for the first time, I met a Black man about my age. Like me, he was visiting Atlanta. Unlike me, however, he was returning after a twenty-five-year absence to a city he'd known well, having grown up there. We bonded, reminiscing about our teens and early twenties. We found a lot of common ground and shared experiences, including, for example, our drug abuse and shameful behavior while under the influence in our younger years.

In the intervening years, I built my career.

Where had he been for the last twenty-five years?

Prison.

For doing the same crap I had done.

The difference between our adult lives, even though we'd been making the same choices, hit me hard. As a white person living in predominantly white suburbs, I was far less likely to get busted for doing drugs and other illegal activities than a Black man in an economically depressed neighborhood. (Black people are nearly four times likelier to be arrested for marijuana possession, despite the fact that they use marijuana at about the same rate as white people.[10]) I'd also had more access to resources to get the help I needed to create the life I lead today. As a result, I was able to build a career and use my gifts.

He was deprived of that same opportunity. Making the same "choices" I did took him on a very different trajectory. That's how our unjust system works.

---

* "Restorative justice" offers an alternative approach to crime or misconduct. It brings together those involved in conflicts to let them address harms, take responsibility, work through blame and guilt, and make peace with the situation.

Yes, I've worked hard to get where I am, but hard work alone is not what defines outcome. Let's stare directly at this ugly truth. In my youth, I committed (drug-related) crimes equivalent to those committed by the majority of people in prison today. I wasn't criminalized or punished. I was supported. In this man's face, I could see the stark injustice of one American losing decades of his life for stuff that I, another American, got away with and moved on from.

There are many people, perhaps you, who work hard, who have unique talents and dreams for their lives and our world, but don't get supported in developing their talents. People who don't get seen and don't feel valued. Instead, they (you?) get stumbling blocks thrown in their way at every step along their path. They (you?) suffer from this, and so do we all.

As a collective, we lose access to others' talents and all the ways they could contribute to our world. It's burdensome economically, too. We all cover the high costs of incarceration and the lost labor—and taxes and purchasing power—of a huge cadre of (mostly male) citizens, since formerly incarcerated people often can't get jobs. We can't go wrong by committing to social and economic justice—they aren't just charitable and good for us economically, but, as we've seen, also a neurobiological fix that can serve to reduce addiction.

RETHINKING BAD BEHAVIORS

A friend of mine was too angry for rational discussion when her eleven-year-old daughter was caught shoplifting candy, so she asked me to intervene. When I asked her daughter what she did with the candy, she told me she shared it with kids at her school. On further questioning, it became clear that the girl was lonely and didn't know how to make friends. The candy made her instantly popular.

So, what should you do in that situation?

Get to the root. Help the girl develop the skills to get what she's really looking for, which is to feel better connected, all while holding her accountable.

My questions helped the girl see that loneliness drove her actions and allowed us to explore her loneliness and discuss more effective strategies to manage it. We went the "transformative justice" route, introducing her to the eighteen-year-old store clerk who was called on the carpet when inventory went missing.* Hearing that another person was harmed by her actions caused the girl to experience guilt and want to do something to alleviate her guilt, motivating her to apologize and offer restitution.

I was particularly struck that this helped both the victim *and* the thief heal. The store clerk was not only off the hook for the missing inventory, but also working through the incident resulted in a better understanding of trust, power, and privilege for both the clerk and her boss. Contrast this experience to the criminal justice system, which focuses entirely on the offenders and doesn't help the victims—or system—heal.

HEALING

Biology wires us to keep going for the easy, habitual response by default. If dopamine is the juice we all need, how do we get our bodies to produce it in ways that support our health and well-being, rather than depleting them? What promotes our capacity to make independent choices that counter the habitual response?

Compassion and connection.

The more compassion and care we can show to ourselves and to people in difficult circumstances, the more we enhance our ability to make better choices. If we isolate ourselves—or if we ostracize people who are addicts, further adding to their shame—we are just entrenching ourselves and them in the morass.

When we are cut off from others, we lose access to one of the primary healthy sources of dopamine. But we can rewire our brain to get more pleasure out of relationships, to crave human contact instead of unhealthy substitutes. Healing involves reconnecting our dopamine reward system to

---

* "Transformative justice" takes restorative justice a step further, using a systems approach to delve deeper into why the crime or misconduct occurred and address the root cause.

relationships. With practice, we can teach our brain to stop searching for dopamine in all the wrong places and, instead, to reach out to another safe human being.

Connection isn't just being nice. It's the wholesome flipside of addiction: it both stimulates our biological reward systems and makes for a kinder, more loving world.

THE COUNTERINTUITIVE WISDOM OF "DISORDERS" AND "DISEASES"

When we think of coping, our thoughts usually go to behaviors as opposed to psychological and physiological (as if we can really separate the two!) "disorders" and "diseases." We don't usually think of disease as a way to cope, particularly diseases we identify as physical, like diabetes or cardiovascular disease, yet disease can act like a drug or a bad habit in that it's a way you respond to and try to deal with stress. The difference may be that your body imposes disease with less conscious control or participation from you.

Consider type 2 diabetes, in which insulin resistance limits the body's intake of glucose (sugar) by the muscle and instead stores it as fat, which can be deposited on the liver. It can wreak havoc and make people really sick, and yet it evolved for a reason, serving an adaptive purpose. During cycles of feast and famine, when early humans couldn't be sure of their next meal, these sugar-rich fat cells could help people survive. This "thrifty genotype" hypothesis, proposed by geneticist James Neel in 1962, still holds sway in the scientific community. A consequence is that today's dieting behavior may encourage diabetes, because dieting mimics the historical famine experience—after all, your body may know it's being deprived of food energy but it can't guess at the cause.

Think about that. Dieting, a commonly prescribed solution to diabetes, is actually part of its cause. It makes you wonder what other disorders we misunderstand by focusing too much on behavioral cause and effect at the expense of our bodies' (natural) fundamental needs.

Framing disorders and disease as a response to experiences, rather than contextualizing them in specific organs in isolated human bodies, lets us understand suffering within a pathological environment and avoid the victim-blaming that often accompanies diagnosis. In other words, it's not your fault. Science has established that people's physiology belongs inextricably to the environment in which they live, work, and play.

Typically, when we hear the word *disorder* or *disease*, we think of individuals who need treatment. We're going to reframe that to consider a troubled society needing transformation. Most illness is socially distributed, meaning certain social groups are more likely to develop the condition. Their vulnerability usually tracks differences in social class and opportunity, even when genetics has been accounted for. It's not that genetics or behavior don't matter in disease incidence, just that social determinants also play a role—and in most diseases, population-wide, often a much larger role. As an example, the Centers for Disease Control and Prevention estimates that social or societal factors contribute over 55 percent influence to population health, compared to about 5 percent genetic and biological contribution.[11] Health behaviors, all told (including diet and activity habits), account for about 20 percent.

DETERMINANTS OF POPULATION HEALTH[12]

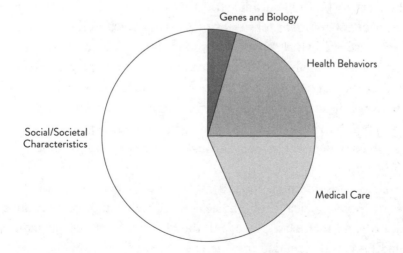

Genes and Biology

Health Behaviors

Social/Societal
Characteristics

Medical Care

Relative influence of the four determining categories of population health: rough approximations

Chronic diseases like diabetes or heart disease are mislabeled "lifestyle" diseases, when in fact behaviors aren't the central problem. It's the difficult lives those behaviors are in that cause disease. Marginalized people have worse health and worse health behaviors, yes, but their health problems don't come from those behaviors alone. Studies show that in the higher levels of illness among low-income people, only a small percentage comes from behaviors like smoking, poor nutrition, and lack of exercise. Those studies find that stress and the environment play by far the bigger role.[13]

We get sick, in other words, not predominately because we do or eat the wrong things, but because our lives are hard, our environments toxic, and the resources that would empower us are beyond our reach. Health improves as the conditions of life improve, not only because stressors fall away but also because better conditions lend power to respond to our environments and shift to healthier, more positive behaviors.

CHRONIC STRESS TRANSLATES INTO DISEASE

By examining the biology of chronic stress, we can better understand how it can create an environment for disease. As discussed earlier, stress stimulates the release of cortisol, which helps flood your bloodstream with glucose, providing immediate fuel for large muscles. Cortisol may also cause insulin resistance, "freeing up" the glucose for instant use. Cortisol additionally narrows the arteries while epinephrine increases heart rate, forcing blood to pump harder and faster. All of this is great for fight-or-flight situations, sending energy coursing through your blood and priming your muscles for action.

But that's not something today's bodies often need. Most modern stressors are psychological, not physical threats demanding strenuous muscle activity. All that extra glucose in the blood doesn't get burned up by the muscles it was intended for. Instead, the high glucose levels are a setup for an array of diseases. For example, high glucose levels cause the pancreas to go into overdrive, releasing excessive insulin. Over time, the overworked pancreas can become permanently damaged. And arterial constriction and high blood pressure can result in vessel damage and plaque buildup, making heart disease a likely outcome.

So when stress is occasional, it's a biologic safeguard; when chronic, it explains why virtually every disease appears more often among stressed-out individuals. Our stress system doesn't care about our long-term health because if you can't survive the present, there is no long term. For the same reason, stress shuts down our immune system; no need to repair your body or fight disease if you've got a crisis going on. But for people with hard lives, the crisis is never over.

To understand this better, let's turn to diabetes as an example.

DIABETES: A SOCIAL—NOT LIFESTYLE—DISEASE

Diabetes is said to be an epidemic. We're told it's a lifestyle disease brought on by bad eating habits and laziness, and that the cure is willpower and self-control.

This perception, however, doesn't jive with what we know from science. Type 2 diabetes can best be described as a disease of oppression. It may be individuals who suffer the symptoms, but it's their environment that largely causes the problem. Diabetes mainly singles out those who are most vulnerable: those lowest on the socioeconomic ladder and with the least power.[14] (Reminder: statistics describe averages, not individuals. Resist the temptation to dismiss this section if you or someone you know is socioeconomically privileged and has diabetes.)

The Pima tribe illustrates this point. Diabetes was virtually unknown among these Native Americans before the increasing incursion of Europeans into what is now Arizona. Around 1900 the Europeans diverted the Pimas' water supply, disrupting their way of life. Unable to water their crops, the Pimas shifted from the physical labor of farming to lives of little labor. Famine, rare in their past, grew chronic.

The timing of this significant change in lifestyle coincides with the introduction of diabetes among the Pimas. At the turn of the nineteenth century, there was only one recorded case of diabetes. In 1937, twenty-one cases of diabetes were documented, making the prevalence of diabetes among the Pimas similar to that of the general US population. By the 1950s, however, the prevalence among the Pima had increased tenfold, and has now ballooned to the highest reported prevalence of diabetes of any population in the world.[15]

Though genes played a part, the near total prior absence of diabetes in this population (and its continued rarity among less-stressed Pima tribes in Mexico) shows that something more than genetic heritage accounts for the disease's surge. Trauma is largely to blame.* Few people have genes that could protect against what the Pimas have endured. The Pimas lost their culture and self-determination and what they got in return were conditions that support disease.

The Pima are an extreme case, but in their isolation, they prove the larger picture. Type 2 diabetes prevalence accurately gauges status in society. In general, in industrialized countries, the less power, money, and status of a group, the higher the incidence.[16] For example, people with less education, lower wealth, and less prestigious jobs, and People of Color, all have higher incidence than their more privileged counterparts. Childhood trauma—like being an abused child, or having a parent who was incarcerated, mentally ill, or abusing substances—is also associated with higher risk for diabetes later in life. Trauma also plays out in the much higher incidence of diabetes among military veterans, in whom the rate is more than twice that of non-veterans.

The most common narrative blames diabetes on behavior, or, to be more specific, eating too much, eating the wrong foods, or sedentary behavior. It is true that people who exercise regularly and eat nutritiously are healthier, no matter what stress they're under or what genes they have.

---

* Selective reproduction may be another contributary cause. Those who did not have the ability to become insulin resistant and conserve calories died of starvation and did not reproduce. Those who were insulin resistant were able to use calories more efficiently, as the insulin resistance increased their ability to survive the starvation and reproduce. Over generations, a higher percentage of the population became insulin resistant.

On the other hand, it's also true that people who do those things often have power to begin with, giving them time and resources to exercise and to buy and prepare healthy foods. It is harder to adopt such healthy behaviors when you have little power.

So while it is true that disadvantaged people, on average, display less healthy behavioral "choices" and worse health than people who are more privileged, their health problems don't come strictly from those behaviors. Stress and environment play much bigger roles. It is also true that people's health behaviors are influenced by the conditions of their lives. I put "choices" in quotes to make the point that while they do have different lifestyle behaviors now—less activity and eating more processed foods, for example—the Pimas' behavioral "choices" were foisted on them by the changing conditions of their lives. By ignoring the context, the concept of "choice" is often used as a weapon against marginalized people.

The context of people's lives determines their health, which is why blaming them for poor health or praising them for good health is harmful and misses the point. People usually can't directly control the most significant contributors to their health.

It is also true that poor people are often too busy making ends meet (striving to feed their family, protecting their right to food stamps against means testing, finding and keeping housing, working multiple jobs, and so on) to spend time on the relative luxury of gym workouts and fresh home-cooked meals. They're often necessarily preoccupied working on very basic survival needs.

To be clear, the scope of diabetes is not limited to people with low power. There is a range of contributory factors beyond the social determinants. Regardless, if you have diabetes (or any disease!), please don't blame yourself! We're all born with challenges in our genetic code and our life circumstances that make us vulnerable to disease, and this is one of the challenges you were dealt. Your body was genetically vulnerable to challenges with glucose regulation and some combination of factors triggered that genetic propensity.

We can't get away with blaming diabetes on fatness, either. While type 2 diabetes is more common among heavier people compared to those in the "normal weight" category, the vast majority of "obese" people don't have diabetes.

We're at the brink of a paradigm shift in diabetes care. The old and still-entrenched paradigm focuses on high weight, poor diet, and lack of physical activity as the causal factors for the high incidence of diabetes and fails to raise sufficient awareness of the impact of stress and the political, environmental, and social structures that have created and continue to feed the prevalence of diabetes.

To help you challenge the current paradigm, let's examine one of the most misguided beliefs: promoting weight loss for treatment and prevention of diabetes. The American Diabetes Association, for example, recommends, "Diet, physical activity, and behavioral therapy designed to achieve and maintain >5 percent weight loss should be prescribed for patients with type 2 diabetes who are overweight or obese."[17] So convinced that thinness is the preeminent solution, they extend the weight loss recommendation to those who fall below the criteria for diabetes diagnosis, in hopes of preventing diabetes, even recommending a specific program: "Refer patients with prediabetes to an intensive behavioral lifestyle intervention program modeled on the Diabetes Prevention Program (DPP) to achieve and maintain 7 percent loss of initial body weight." They denote their recommendations as Evidence Category A, meaning there is "clear evidence from well-conducted, generalizable randomized controlled trials that are adequately powered." The National Institute of Diabetes and Digestive and Kidney Diseases, which conducted research to examine the DPP, corroborates the value of recommending DPP, declaring that "the DPP showed that people who are at high risk for type 2 diabetes can prevent or delay the disease by losing a modest amount of weight."[18]

Is that really so? On the next page is the actual data, drawn from their report.[19] In the chart, "lifestyle" refers to those who were in the DPP/DPPOS group; "metformin" refers to a comparison group who took metformin, a diet drug; and "placebo" refers to a comparison group who did nothing.

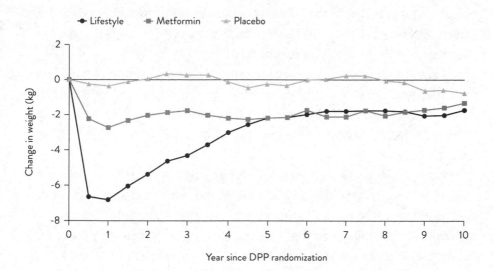

I suppose the word "modest" regarding weight loss was well chosen. The change in body mass index (BMI)* was less than 1 unit after ten years! This is well below the 5 to 7 percent weight loss goal they deem desirable. In other words, they demonstrated that they were not able to achieve the recommended goals. And truth be told, would you have rather endured the ten years of dieting, or been part of the placebo group that did nothing but had similar results? You can see that those who took a diet drug didn't fare any better either.

The weight loss was minimal, and there were multiple interventions that could have caused the outcome (changes in diet and exercise, for example), so it's a stretch, too, to attribute the health improvements to that tiny weight change as opposed to changes in lifestyle. Calling it a stretch is overly generous; let's name it for what it is: unethical reporting. A better

---

* Body mass index (BMI) is a person's weight in kilograms divided by the square of their height in meters. Though adopted by the World Health Organization for assessing health, BMI has long been recognized as a flawed tool for measuring health outcomes. Critics (including me!) assert that the BMI category of "normal" does not reflect a normative or optimal value; "overweight" falsely implies a weight over which one is unhealthy; and the etymology of the word *obese* mistakenly implies that a large appetite is the cause. Current use of BMI not only doesn't serve its intended purpose, but it results in a health-damaging stigma.

argument can be made that the interventions they studied are damaging, given the known deleterious health effects of the weight cycling and stigma induced by this study and others of its ilk.[20]

Many other investigations *do* demonstrate very compelling evidence that behavior changes benefits health, with or without weight loss, my own government-funded study included.[21] Studies that separate weight loss from health behavior show no correlation between weight loss and benefit to health.[22]

Data from the also government-sponsored Look AHEAD (Action for Health in Diabetes) trial was significant because it was the largest and longest randomized trial evaluating whether weight loss and lifestyle modification could reduce deaths from cardiovascular disease in people with diabetes.[23] It was terminated early due to "futility of results," meaning the trial failed to reduce deaths from cardiovascular disease.[24] The average weight loss? Again, less than 1 BMI unit.

When we actually pay attention to data, even a quick glance at the research shows that despite decades of trying, there is no evidence that efforts to prevent or reverse "obesity" are successful.[25] What the evidence does tell us is that this lack of success is biologically mediated,[26] not a failure of willpower or a character flaw. The scientists are failing, not the people following their recommendations. Much evidence suggests that the prescription for weight loss is more likely to result in harm, promoting weight stigma and, ironically, worsened health behaviors, health, and well-being.[27]

It is true that most people with type 2 diabetes fall into the BMI categories of overweight or obese. It's also true that insulin resistance, one of the main underlying problems in type 2 diabetes, encourages weight gain.[28] In fact, weight gain may actually be an early symptom, rather than a primary cause of the path toward type 2 diabetes.

Even if high weight contributes to diabetes, what is clear is that its role is exaggerated and, more importantly, the focus on weight is not just unhelpful, but damaging. Dropping the weight focus allows other (evidence-based!) possibilities to emerge. For example, a study published in the *New England Journal of Medicine*[29] examined health outcomes over the course of ten to fifteen years for women initially living in stressful, low-income housing projects. They randomized them into three groups:

one got a voucher for better housing and help moving, one a voucher for moving to any area without help, and the control group got neither. Both groups who got housing assistance had lower prevalence of diabetes compared to the control group, with the group that got the most housing assistance having the lowest prevalence. None of the participants got a drug prescription or advice on lifestyle changes. This is one of many studies providing evidence that diabetes prevalence can be reduced through social policy, without weight loss or behavior change prescriptions.[30]

The new paradigm starts from affirming the individual's worth, value, and cultural traditions, and recognizes the physiology of oppression: that one's environment (economic, political, and social factors) and individual stress response trigger biological reactions within the body, like diabetes, and affect lifestyle behaviors. It acknowledges that while behavior change is valuable, it can't remove the stressors one faces, and supports systemic solutions in tandem with individual change. This approach moves away from the stigmatization of weight and avoids the metabolic dysregulation and other fallout of dieting. It also enables us to integrate clinically meaningful data about social determinants, stigma, and stress as we consider strategies for individual change. Chapter 10 provides more details on what this might look like in practice.

BRINGING IT HOME

There are smart reasons you do the things you do and smart reasons your body has developed a disorder or disease. It's all about a self-protection system that's gone awry. Substance abuse helped me cope with a difficult world when I didn't have other skills. When I was a thirteen-year-old trans kid with no role models and no explanations for how to manage a changing body that I couldn't relate to, dieting and exercising to lose the hips that betrayed me helped me feel I had a sense of control and the possibility for a body that felt more like me. My focus on body manipulation didn't solve my problem, but it temporarily distracted me from it and gave me a sense of hope.

I've reframed my thinking over the years. When I learned to see my substance abuse and eating disorder as gifts, strategies that helped me survive difficult times when I didn't have better skills, I could be appreciative of how they served me as I searched for other ways to take care of myself that didn't bring along painful side effects. When I read my anxiety as an alert that I'm dealing with a challenging situation, rather than spinning off into hopelessness and helplessness, I can pay attention to and honor my fear, perhaps amp up my self-compassion.

Understanding this helps us lighten up on the self-blame and transfer the blame to where it belongs, which is on an unjust world that doesn't always treat us well. It also helps us appreciate the wisdom of our bodies, hidden in our maladaptive behaviors and diseases. This reality check also helps us refocus our attention on a turnaround of healing and transformation.

Chapter 5

FEAR IS BIOLOGICAL

Fear was a frequent companion as I wrote this book. My head told me that I suck at writing and would never get my point across in a compelling way. That no publisher would want the book. That, if published, no one would find the book. That it would get no respect.

Why should you trust that I can help you through fear, knowing that I, too, am a victim of it? Precisely because I own my fear and normalize it. Fear is human. Wanting to give up in the face of fear is human. (Besides, apparently my fear didn't stop me: I did publish the book!)

Fear may just be one of the most beautiful and adaptive aspects of who we are. If we don't feel fear, we're not cautious. If we're not cautious, we're not safe. Without fear, we might walk into oncoming traffic or unlock the door for the intruder brandishing a knife. Without fear, we don't have our defenses up when discrimination rears its head, allowing it to permeate deeper into our psyche.

Last week, I accompanied a fat friend to her doctor's appointment. She has a history of being traumatized in health care settings, with the medical community dismissing her problems and treating her to yet another weight loss lecture (even when she had the flu!). No wonder she feels fearful every time she books an appointment. In the past, she gave in to her fear, postponing medical care and not getting the help she needed. When she was able to listen to her fear, on the other hand, she was empowered to put a strategy in place to help get the care she needed.*

Let's stop glorifying fearlessness. Instead of running from our fear, we can listen to it and find the wisdom. We can use our fear to validate that yes, sometimes the world is unsafe and we are treated in harmful ways. That awareness will help us build our resilience and make thoughtful choices about going forward. When we don't listen to our fear, on the other hand, we lose its protective benefit and the potential for harm worsens.

Fears about this book and how it would turn out alerted me to the manuscript's deficiencies and the need for continued editing. It led me to share the manuscript with others and get feedback. It helped me create a better book. How can you harness your fear for your own moment of greatness?

THE BIOLOGY OF FEAR

When we describe fear as being in our "heads," I don't think many of us imagine physical structures. We should. Fear is acutely physical.

As we saw in chapter 2, the amygdala, part of the limbic system (your "emotional" brain), is often referred to as the fear center. The amygdala's job is to attach emotional significance to objects or events to form what are essentially emotional memories. Connected to numerous other parts of the brain, the amygdala can provoke a quick response, so quick that no conscious thought can outrun it. In fact, in less than a tenth of a second it can stimulate a surge of epinephrine, causing a racing heart, muscle

---

* That included bringing me and also asking her doctor to read an educational letter from the appendix to my book *Health at Every Size*, freely downloadable from the book's website, on providing sensitive care to fat patients.

tension, and sweating. When your anxiety feels out of control, blame it on the amygdala.

Your amygdala is on the lookout for potential harm, and as you go about your day, it pays attention to sights, sounds, and events that you may not be consciously focusing on. If it senses danger, it can trigger the fight-or-flight response.

It's late at night, you're home alone, and you hear a noise at the front door. Maybe it's the wind. Or maybe it's a burglar trying to get in.

There are two pathways that activate simultaneously when your brain senses you are in danger, as in the above scenario.

The first path is immediate and almost entirely autonomic, meaning that it's on autopilot, not filtered through the "thinking brain." We don't consciously trigger it or even know what's going on until it has run its course.

Your ears send nerve impulses to the thalamus. The thalamus then quickly forwards the message to the amygdala. The amygdala receives the message and takes protective action. It signals the hypothalamus to initiate the fight-or-flight response that could save your life in case that noise was in fact an intruder. This process happens quickly, well before your brain has been able to determine if in fact there is an intruder.

The second pathway has a longer, slower course. This process considers the options.

Your ears send nerve impulses to the thalamus. The thalamus then sends this information to the sensory cortex, where it is determined that the information needs to be interpreted. The cortex sends the information to the hippocampus to establish context. The hippocampus considers questions like "Have I heard this before? What did it mean in previous instances? What else might help me know if it's the wind or a burglar?" It might pick up on other data, like visual clues that it's windy outside. It then puts all this together and makes a determination. It could, for example, conclude that the noise is most likely the wind and thus that there is no danger. It then alerts the hypothalamus to shut off the fight-or-flight response.

In sum, you probably had a moment or two of terror spurred by the first path, and then, through the second path, your "thinking brain" helped you calm down.

If you can't bring your thinking brain online, you get stuck in fear.

ANXIETY

Fear is the emotion—and biological response—that arises in response to a perceived immediate threat. Anxiety is the emotion—and biological response—that arises in response to an *anticipated* threat that things might go wrong. One of our most valuable evolutionary gifts is to be able to anticipate what's ahead, and anxiety keeps us attentive to possible danger lurking there. If you feared a predator, you would take steps to avoid one, perhaps traveling by daylight and with others, and this might keep you safe. So you can see how even anxiety has biologic roots and is part of a healthy protection system. That's a good thing. But not when our anxiety rules us.

Most of us have never experienced a plane crash, but that doesn't stop us from sitting on a plane and imagining it happening. Anticipating a fearful stimulus can provoke the same response as actually experiencing it.

However, *anticipated* threat means it hasn't happened. It's just a mind game you're playing out. The trick is to use our anxiety to discern which thoughts to pay attention to and which are unnecessary—so we don't get hijacked by an anxious mind.

Fear and anxiety have the same physiological stress response. When anxiety is prolonged, this response causes the same emotional and physical damage discussed previously. Anxiety can easily become chronic and wired into us, so we move through life with generalized anxiety. Our minds are constantly looking for things to worry about. We're so worried about the future that we lose sight of the present and don't realize that the thoughts aren't real—they're just thoughts.

NEGATIVITY BIAS

We are naturally wired for what scientists call a "negativity bias." I bet you have experienced what I'm talking about even if you haven't heard the term before. It's that tendency to give more attention or weight to negative experiences over neutral or positive experiences. You get six compliments on your haircut, but when one person doesn't mention it, you're convinced it must look awful.

The negativity bias is biologically built into us, another remnant of a well-developed survival system. Think about our prehistoric ancestors. To pass on your genes, you need to find food. You also need to hide from predators. Miss out on that potato and you may have a chance at finding something else to eat tomorrow. But if you don't avoid that tiger today, there will be no tomorrow. The negative stuff usually has more urgency and impact. So, it's not surprising that our brains evolved to be more alert to danger—and that this process is even more acute in those of us with trauma-impacted brains.

The amygdala uses about two-thirds of its neurons to look for the negative. Negative events and experiences go straight to the mind's memory bank, unlike positive events and experiences, which usually need to be held in awareness longer if they are to transfer to long-term memory. As neuroscientist Rick Hanson is fond of saying, the brain is like Velcro for negative experiences but Teflon for positive ones.

This hard-wired tendency toward fear means we often overestimate threats and underestimate opportunities and resources. In a day in which a hundred small things happened, ninety-nine of them neutral or positive, my negativity bias means I tend to focus on the one thing that was negative. I then try to remind myself that the tendency toward the negative is just me being human. By accepting that a negativity bias is an inherent part of the human experience, we can adopt strategies to manage it.

CONFIRMATION BIAS

Negativity isn't the only assumption our brain sometimes puts in our way. Humans are also wired with what scientists call a confirmation bias, the tendency to search for or interpret information in a way that confirms our preconceptions. It's a painful, stuck place to live, and it only amplifies our sense of fear and self-doubt.

As an example, I fix on stories of past rejections. This makes me nervous going into social situations as I look for the rejection that I expect to happen. Maybe that's true for you, or maybe your experience is more like my friend's. They reflect on the fact that they have never been thought attractive enough to be placed in situations where rejection is a possibility, causing them to expect that same invisibility, again and again.

Looking at this from an evolutionary perspective can help us make sense of why a confirmation bias is wired into our brains. Evaluating evidence requires a great deal of thought. Our brains prefer shortcuts. This saves time, especially when we're under pressure. For most of human history, people experienced little new information during their lifetimes, and decisions tended to be survival based. That's not the case anymore. To stave off overwhelm, we tend to take shortcuts, so we give more power to information that allows us to conclude what we want and confirms our current beliefs. We're less likely to take in information that may threaten our worldview.

A functional magnetic resonance imaging (fMRI) study shows where the confirmation bias arises in the brain and how it is unconscious and emotion-driven.[1] The study was conducted in the run-up to the 2004 presidential election; thirty men—half self-described as "strong" Republicans and half as "strong" Democrats—were asked to evaluate statements by both George W. Bush and John Kerry in which the candidates clearly contradicted themselves. Both groups let their own candidate off the hook yet were critical of the opposing candidate. Interestingly, the researchers didn't see increased activation of the parts of the brain normally engaged during reasoning (the cortex); instead, circuits in the emotional center (the limbic center) were activated. As this demonstrates, confirmation bias also explains why two people with opposing views can see the same evidence and both come away feeling validated by it.

FEAR TRIGGERS

We believe the things we believe about ourselves because at some point we were taught they were true. For instance, if you are regularly made to feel inadequate, that conviction gradually wires into you, teaching you to be fearful and to expect to be confronted with your inadequacy on an ongoing basis.

Fear and what triggers it are as diverse as each person's lived experience. Consider how different it is to wake up with plenty of money than to wake up wondering if you have enough to buy food today. Or sleeping in a safe, quiet neighborhood versus living on a crime-ridden block. Or waking up in your safe, well-appointed mansion full of luxuries and wondering if your spouse will attack you today. Many of us, regardless of social class, face threats to our safety and well-being that trigger our fear response—things like abuse, intimate partner violence, and war. Also common are social fears triggered by rejection, personal failure, and concerns about our adequacy or lovability. Fears of wrongness and not belonging are universal.

Though fear feels very personal, it may be harder to understand that social forces (poverty, racism, weightism, ableism, and so on) also trigger fear and a feeling of unsafety. But they do. Imagine you are a parent raising a Black son and you know how vulnerable he is to be a target for violence or poor treatment. The ongoing awareness of our vulnerability wears on us every bit as much as the individual and discrete acts of injustice that we experience.

Historically, the police have weaponized, enforced, and implemented racism. The police force as an entity began as a collective of slave catchers. This historical and generational fear that Black people and People of Color experience is valid and also another reason why Black people have different hurdles when it comes to healing trauma that is ongoing and daily. This reality challenges how fear shows up and how we navigate our own survival.

If fear plays a central role in your life, please have some self-compassion. There are valid reasons why you are fearful and why many of us struggle with survival within a system that is not designed for thriving. Many things are out of your control. Know, too, that there are things you can do to increase your control and your ability to manage fear.

AGENCY: THE SECRET TO MANAGING FEAR

"Agency" refers to the sense of control you have over your circumstances. It is one of the central factors that can influence how we experience fear. When we feel in control, we can channel our response rather than being sucked into a fight-or-flight reaction. Having greater agency is one of the largest reasons why people with advantaged lives live longer and with less disease than oppressed and marginalized peoples. Understanding why can help all of us protect our health.

Let me explain why agency is so important by discussing a few issues separately, and then I'll show you how they come together.

FEAR AND CONTEXT

How we experience fear can run the gamut of emotions. I probably don't need to conjure up images for you to understand that fear can instill terror, but let me remind you that some people, in certain situations, find it fun. Think rollercoasters and scary movies. North Americans even have an entire holiday devoted to the celebration of fear, Halloween.

Context determines how we experience fear. If we feel safe, we can then shift the way we experience a situation. When you are in a haunted house, for example, and a zombie drops from the ceiling, your rational mind (cortex) comes online and tells you it isn't a real threat. In contrast, if you're walking down a dodgy alley in the middle of the night and encounter a stranger with a gun, your rational mind teams with your "emotional mind" (limbic center) to perceive danger and activate the fight-or-flight (or freeze) response.

Our fear response is not so much about the event itself, in other words. It's about our interpretation of the event. You would have a very different response if you came across a tiger in the wild than if you saw it behind a fence in a zoo. The hippocampus and the cortex process the context and, if the tiger is behind a fence, dampen the fear response.

Past experience affects how you react. So if you were attacked by a pit bull when you were a kid, you are more likely to tremble when you see one. By contrast, my childhood best friend had a pit bull named Sweetie, who was the cutest, cuddliest doggie imaginable. To this day I don't tense when I see a pit bull the way many others do.

Even if they're not events you remember, memories lodged in your brain can unconsciously play into your reactions. Your cortex stores *event* memories, while your amygdala stores *emotional* memories—and the memories in the amygdala can last longer than those in the cortex.[2] This means that you may have emotional reactions that puzzle you. My friend Marco is terrified of birds. He didn't understand why until, in his mid-forties, he reunited with a childhood friend who was with him, in his teens, when their friend was murdered. His friend told him that they were in a field swarming with birds. Apparently, the association lodged in Marco's amygdala, but the explicit memory had disappeared from his cortex.

FEAR AND DISTRACTION

If your head is tripping out on fear of losing your job, that's a great distraction from the project due tomorrow. Give in to the fear and it may become a self-fulfilling prophecy. Yet the distraction is compelling. After all, it *is* effective at taking you away from your present-tense pain.

FEAR AND SOCIAL LEARNING

We learn about fear socially. Babies learn to fear unsafe aspects of their environment, such as a hot stove, by following cues from their parents. Social learning is not exclusively positive, however. It can also breed a damaging level of fear. Consider the current media context where multiple news outlets and social media networks compete with one another by exploiting bad news and constantly pushing out alarmist and sensationalist stories about violence. At times news and social media (our social environment) teach us that the world is a scary, dangerous place, and without well-developed skills at media literacy and the ability to put what you read into context, it's easy to spin out into fear and anxiety.

TYING IT ALL TOGETHER

As psychiatrists Arash Javanbakht and Linda Saab explain, what ties together these factors—context, distraction, and social learning—is our sense of control.[3] When we can recognize what is and isn't an actual threat, we can put it into context, stay focused on the present, and feel like we are in control. That perception of control is critical to how we experience and respond to fear—and how the fear lodges in our body. How much agency you have just may be the key factor explaining how injustice gets under your skin. The more control we have over our lives, the lower our risk for disease.[4]

Social hierarchy and the stress response have inspired much research demonstrating that where you stand in society can govern how triggered you are by stress. One investigation examined the role of executive stress[5] by studying full-time workers in either business or the military who were taking executive education classes at Harvard Business School. They classified the participants as either leaders, defined as those whose job required them to manage other people, or nonleaders. The leaders in both business and the military showed substantially lower levels of stress than the nonleaders, as determined by surveys of anxiety and biological measures of cortisol.

These results echo a massive research study of British government employees that has been collecting data since the 1960s.[6] The British civil service is a hierarchy with clearly defined job grades. People in this study are all insured under Britain's national system, so no differences in their access to health care can cloud the results. The data indicates that those in higher-ranking jobs have better health and longer lifespans. Each pay grade down the hierarchy is associated with more stress-related health problems.

When we describe executive work as "stressful," we ought to put that into context. Executives may have more emails in their inbox than they can get to or work longer hours, but in most cases they have power over when and how to deal with challenges. They can take bathroom breaks when they want. They can take a cab when their car breaks down. They can hire a nanny when their kid is too sick to go to school. They have much more control over how their time is spent than the administrative assistant who schedules their appointments or the janitor who cleans their office.

Understanding the importance of being able to exert control over our lives is the key factor in understanding how to protect ourselves. There are always ways to find more agency within the context of your life. We are active in our lives, not merely shaped. For example, you may not be able to call the shots at your fast food job, but that doesn't mean you can't captain your pickup basketball team. You could even organize a political fundraiser to enhance your sense of agency in your life. How can you seek out more agency in your day-to-day?

HOW WE REACT TO FEAR

There are four common reactions to fear: anger, shame, judgment (blame), and dissociation (avoidance). Let's discuss each and explore how we can use them to our advantage.

ANGER

If you feared a predator, you would do what you could to avoid it, right? What happens, however, when that predator is a human who sexually molested you and you can't avoid them? What happens when you see the police officer who didn't believe you? Fear would be a natural response, as would be the anger that may follow. Anger with the predator, and with the fact that the world creates and protects these types of predators. Anger for so many other reasons.

If your anger is reactive and unthinking, it protects you from fully feeling the discomfort of the injustice. In the long run, though, that anger amps up your allostatic load, damaging your body.

Anger isn't always a bad thing, however. If you couple your anger with a recognition of your own value and awareness that the problem is the circumstances, not you, you can use your anger to set boundaries and stand up for yourself.

If you have a history of woundedness—and most of us do, particularly if we have a marginalized identity—our on-button may be jammed for fight, even pushing away others who care for us. In chapter 10, we'll discuss ways to help you sit with the uncomfortable feelings instead of instantly reacting. By sitting with uncomfortable feelings, you open yourself up to more connection—and probably a lot less road rage too!

SHAME

Sometimes fear activates a shame response. Shame emerges when we confront the difference between who we are and who we think we should be. It's such a deep and primal feeling that I'll devote the next chapter to it. But for now, here's a quick story about one of our most common fears, the fear of rejection.

Imagine you get up the guts to swipe right and soon you're going on a date. Fifteen minutes after you meet, your date takes a phone call, then tells you they have an emergency and need to go. Your brain creates a story. They had arranged for that incoming call so they could bail if they found you unattractive. Dang, that hurts.

You call your best friend for support. What does your friend say? "Of course they walked out on you. You dress like a schlump, honk when you laugh, and can't carry a conversation. What do you expect?"

Do you really think your hypothetical best friend would be that cruel? No, of course not. But the situation is much worse because this, or something similar, is probably what you said to yourself. Our feelings of inadequacy are easily triggered by these types of situations. When rejected, most of us will start thinking bad thoughts about ourselves, what we wish we were, what we wish we weren't.

Please, don't do this to yourself. I want you to be kinder to yourself. For now, a simple approach to consider: Think about what you might say to a friend in a similar situation and direct that loving energy towards yourself. I know it's in your wiring to go to that "I suck and I'm ugly" placc to varying degrees; that's probably true for every reader. But you can change that—not just the short-term response, but the biological wiring that sends you on that path of self-denigration in the first place. (Keep reading!)

JUDGMENT

Judging others or ourselves can be a way of shifting attention from the pain. Consider this the next time you are critical of someone's actions—or your own. Being overly judgmental of ourselves and others is often a sign that shame is lurking nearby.

This was my self-talk recently: "I'm so stupid. I should have known that when he said he grew up in Georgia, he was referring to the country, not the state." Then I got down on myself for how unaware I am in general. It was no longer a simple mistake but a judgment about my character. It went deep, sparking memories of previous shameful experiences, serving as further confirmation that bolstered my insecurity about my cultural illiteracy.

We'll come back to this in the next chapter, but for now remember that when you are harshly judging yourself or others, it's helpful to stop long enough to consider whether you are blaming and shaming yourself for beliefs you have absorbed from our culture, or if you truly agree with them and choose to own them. With so much important stuff to fill our brains, is it reasonable to expect that everyone needs to know that Georgia is both a country and a state? I'm not dissing the importance of cultural literacy, but what I am suggesting is that we give ourselves a break.

You can turn it around: "I'm so stupid. How could I have said that?" becomes "We all mess up at times. It's okay to make mistakes or to not know everything—it's part of being human. Not knowing something doesn't mean I'm stupid. Making a mistake does not mean I'm a jerk."

Often our judgment about others tells us much more about ourselves than about the person we're judging. It helps to get curious about what's really going on and see what, if any, shame is being displaced in ourselves by judging others.

Say you walk into an ice cream shop and see a fat man eating a large sundae. What's your immediate thought? At the risk of triggering some readers, I'm going to name a common judgment in order to debunk it and arm you with a reframe: "Ugh, he's so fat. Why doesn't he just lay off the ice cream?"

For the fat people, I'm sorry people are so ignorant, mean, and uncompassionate. It's understandable if you're uncomfortable eating in public or even food shopping, and if the looks you get cause you to spin off into common self-judgment: "I eat too much. I shouldn't be eating this ice cream. My body is too fat, telling others that I'm messed up." Anger is also understandable, whether it's at yourself, at the judgmental person, or at a culture that supports this.

My advice is to breathe. Reground. Remind yourself that the problem is in the culture, not your body. Anger you may be feeling toward that person and toward the oppressive culture is warranted. You don't deserve that disdain, even—and especially—if you are prone to binge eating. (After all, the drive to escape pain is a helpful human trait and binge eating does help you achieve that, albeit temporarily.)

Next, offer yourself some compassion. (More on that later in the book.) As blogger, cultural commentator, and soon-to-be author Your Fat Friend writes, "When some bodies are held up as examples of what not to look like and who not to be, all of us suffer. It creates a culture of judgment and rejection, which leads to a world of hurt and shame."[7] She continues:

> Every aspect of fat hate feeds into this machine. So, for that matter, does exclusion of bodies with disabilities, bodies of color, trans bodies, old bodies, and more. From overt harassment like shouting names at fat people walking down the street, to seemingly benign diet recommendations, or dwelling publicly on the parts of our bodies we hate—it all teaches us that our bodies are wrong, that they're shameful reflections of the worst of our character. It's a system that rejects all of us at one time or another.
>
> And it leads to worse health. When I feel disconnected from my body, I don't take care of it. When I embrace my body, when I appreciate what it does for me, I do. Learning not to hate our bodies isn't a matter of feeling good or appeasing the self-esteem of fat people, it's a matter of our physical health and emotional survival.

For the fat people, for those of you who feel the judgment of others—it isn't easy publicly eating as a fat person—I feel your pain. I wish for more kindness and acceptance in this world. I offer you compassion, the awareness that you deserve better, and release from your shame. I offer you love. You can't control how others view you. But you do have some power to control your response and how much power you give them to affect you. Please give yourself a break when those negative judgments penetrate you; it's going to happen sometimes. Put some energy into developing the skill of offering those gifts of love and compassion to yourself. May continued reading support this process.

For those who leap into judging others, know that you are being hurtful not only to that person, but also to yourself. Exhibiting that disdainful look is shame-inducing. Is that who you want to be? You are also flattening a complex person into a stereotype and missing someone extraordinary. Stop long enough to ask yourself if what you are judging others for are beliefs that you have swallowed from our culture, or if you truly agree with them and choose to own them. You'll likely find that your judgments tell you more about you than about them. When you judge others for their looks, odds are it's because you've bought into an oppressive value system and that you don't feel great about how you measure up or you are burdened by the pressure of trying. It may be, too, that you are clinging to a need to feel deserving of accolades for your body, for you've put hard work into self-restraint around food or an obsessive exercise routine. If so, know that this isn't healthy behavior, it's self-righteousness. Also, it's time to re-educate yourself about fatness. Challenge the assumptions behind your judgment. For example, if you believe that fatness is simply about overeating, lack of willpower, or laziness, you are ignoring decades of research and misleading yourself. And if people need to meet your definition of healthiness before they're entitled to being treated with respect, this again indicates a problem on your end, not theirs. Challenge yourself to learn more and use this as opportunity to look deeper into your own values.

DISSOCIATION

Dissociation refers to losing touch with awareness of our immediate surroundings. We've all experienced dissociation: daydreaming, highway hypnosis, or getting lost in a book or movie are all examples of our brains dissociating from our current surroundings. So, too, are denial and depression. During a traumatic experience, dissociation can be particularly valuable, helping a person tolerate what might otherwise be too difficult to bear. Many people also dissociate so they don't have to feel fear. Understanding dissociation as a badge of survival helps us find solutions.

As you increase your tolerance for rejection, loss, disappointment, shame, conflict, and uncertainty, you decrease your reliance upon defenses that maintain dissociation from painful feelings. Increased awareness also brings increased choice. For myself, I know it is helpful when I can recognize it is happening so I can practice bringing myself back to the present.

On a simple level, my partner is very effective at helping me through my minor dissociative moments. "Seems like you spaced out, where'd you go?" she asks me on occasion. I appreciate the gentleness and caring expressed in the question, and it can often help me to reflect, talk, and gain insight.

For those who have experienced childhood neglect or abuse, your fallback orientation is that of threat, fear, and survival. You may not know what a trusting and loving relationship looks like. Dissociation, once a helpful survival mechanism, means that you are withdrawn from others. Learning to find trustworthy people and open the path to loving relationships is a scary challenge, but a necessary part of healing. People can and do learn how to trust and find love.

Severe traumas or repeated traumas may result in a person developing a dissociative disorder. Individuals with dissociative disorders are frequently misdiagnosed because the symptoms can be confused with many other problems—symptoms like depression, mood swings, difficulty concentrating, temper outbursts, memory lapses, substance abuse, and even hearing voices, or psychotic symptoms. Be open to exploring these symptoms through professional help, and do make sure that your caregiver is trained in trauma-informed care. Proper diagnosis can do wonders in getting you the help you need.

HEALING FROM FEAR

In order to step out of being hitched to our fear, we need to feel safe. After you identify what you're scared of, it's valuable to reflect on how realistic it is. Is your fear legitimate? Are you safe? If you aren't safe, what can you do to protect yourself?

Being scared when you have a predator living in your house is perfectly reasonable and can help you try to protect yourself. Being scared that others may not like you, particularly if you have a history of past rejections (we all do!), is also perfectly reasonable, though usually less useful. Most of us carry a basic sense of inadequacy—that we're not good enough, that others will see this, that we'll get rejected, and most deeply, that we won't be loved. If we can accept our feelings, we can better examine their veracity and how best to manage them.

So how do you undo the grip of fear?

First, it's helpful to honor why the fear is there. Think of fear as your friend, one who intends to keep you safe and protected. Fear is good—you just need to learn how to listen to and manage the insight your friend offers.

Next, recognize how much suffering comes from not acknowledging the fear that's there. That helps motivate us to stay with our fear. Start by noticing the fear and just recognizing that you're avoiding it.

I've got a friend who hasn't spoken to me in months. I assume it's because she didn't follow through on something she committed to, knew how important it was to me, and felt horrible about disappointing me. That she couldn't follow through makes sense to me. She's overwhelmed with survival needs—working long hours to support her family and caring for several kids. Yet she doesn't give herself a break. Instead of having compassion for her own hard situation and accepting that she can't do everything she'd like to in order to help her friends, she feels inadequate and ashamed that she can't be the person she wants to be. By avoiding me, she can avoid seeing the disappointment she imagines that I feel and thus avoid her feelings of inadequacy.

Yet I imagine this keeps her up at night, triggering a deeper shame because now she blames her bad behavior on the fact that she's a bad person, and has a concrete story that, at least in her mind, affirms this for her. By trying to avoid the discomfort of disappointing me, she is experiencing much more pain than if she had just allowed herself to lean into the fear.

The next step to managing fear is acknowledging how normal it is. When I see fear come up, I can just say, *Oh yes, I'm human.* We're all working on it. This helps me sit with it, knowing it's just a fact of life to manage.

Next, it helps to insert a pause for reflection, before you get hijacked into reactivity. Stop running. Pause. Face your fear. If we can learn to pause, if we can slow down even a little and be with each other, we can shift from fight-or-flight to tend-and-befriend. This is our evolution.

Stay in that vulnerable state. Offer tenderness and compassion to the hurt place in yourself. That's much better than focusing on why you're so messed up. If you're having trouble offering tenderness to yourself, maybe you can bring to mind compassionate others who do accept you.

Next, sit with it. I've found a ritual that works great for me. I invite my fear to tea. Seriously. Tea warms me, comforts me. I use it to make the environment a little safer, to make it easier to explore the hard feelings. This great idea came from radical dietitian, spoken word poet, and scholar Lucy Aphramor.

When I sit with it, I notice the physical sensations. I usually feel fear in my throat, as if fear itself is choking me. We all have different physical sensations of fear. Try to figure out what it's like for you.

Then, I just watch it. What I inevitably notice is the sensations wash over me and change form. Over time, they have less power over me. I am less attached to my pain narrative as I recognize how ephemeral it is. (I've learned this habit and gotten better at it over time through practicing meditation, as we'll explore in chapter 10.)

Does anxiety get in the way of your participation in life? Breathe and feel the fear. Let it be there. The anxiety may still be there, but it's not in control. Stop running from fear and instead allow yourself to grow comfortable with its existence, with the fact that it is present, and that it is another part of human emotion. You'll find there's room for it and it doesn't need to control you. In fact, it only controls you when you try to avoid it. Only by feeling the fear can you examine the story that's beneath it.

In my case, that story is the fear of rejection, which is an almost universal human experience. Let me share an aha moment I had that has helped me immensely in going forward despite fear. Fear of rejection was spinning out of control for me. Why did I have so few close friends? I wondered if something I bring to the table blocked me from finding the intimacy I wanted. I have felt rejected frequently in the past, leading me to believe something about me makes me unlikable, an unlikability on display for everyone to see. So I did something brave. I reached out to a few ex-friends (all of them therapists!) who I felt had rejected me and I asked for feedback to help me sort this out. What I got back was enlightening.

In one case, I got "It's not you, it's me." Now, you don't usually fall for that line, do you? Well, what I learned is that sometimes it actually is true. That friend told me she stopped calling because she had a ton of things going on in her life—single parenthood, stressful job, divorce—and the only way she felt she could handle her responsibilities was to shut out everything other than work or family responsibilities. She knew I had been hurt but just couldn't take on the time and emotional work of helping me understand that she needed to prioritize taking care of herself. Her rejection really had nothing to do with me and everything to do with surviving her circumstances. That our friendship has been reestablished confirms her explanation—and shows me the "I'm unlikable" story I run is not always true.

This happens to all of us, and it's always hard to believe that it's not about you, particularly if you have repeated experiences. All I can say is it's helpful to push through it. Sometimes the stories we choose to believe about ourselves aren't true.

Other useful responses from my former friends helped reinforce the idea that the friendships didn't persist because of a mismatch of needs, not because of my inadequacy.

And keep in mind that fearlessness isn't a good thing. Your fear may be accurately identifying that a situation isn't safe for you. For example, you may never feel comfortable meeting with your social worker. Perhaps they're homophobic and have the power to take your kids away from you. Knowing that, you can see the basis for your fear and be thoughtful about how you can best protect yourself in an unfair situation.

TRUST YOURSELF

True healing grows out of a deep sense of self-trust. In order to step out of being hitched to our fear or to others' ideas of ourselves, outside measures of what's acceptable, we need to trust ourselves and support each other in seeing our intrinsic value.

Most people feel they are imposters. Our fear is that somebody is going to find out. We'll be exposed. That openness is frightening for so many of us. We are often not socialized, or taught, to be vulnerable. The threat of being exposed as imposters keeps us afraid.

Mindfulness and compassion—more on these later—allow us to, over and over again, recognize when the imposter fear comes up and to sit with it. We investigate and get in touch with our vulnerability. Odds are you'll discover that what you really need is to feel your intrinsic value.

BRINGING IT HOME

Fear is not an enemy to be conquered. It is a normal and healthy response to potential threats. Treat it as a friend who intends to keep you safe. You can harness the wisdom in fear and make sure that it doesn't unnecessarily take you over.

Sometimes you'll find that fear alerts you to potential danger. Learning to distinguish real threats from unlikely ones is helpful in ensuring fear and anxiety don't disrupt your well-being. And increasing your sense of agency goes a long way to helping you mitigate the potential damage fear exerts.

Sometimes you'll find that running into your fears head-on can transform those fears into something beautiful and nourishing. This book is a direct testament to me jumping into my fears and coming out stronger.

Future chapters will help you use fear to your advantage so that it doesn't stop you from living the life you deserve. For now, try this: "I thank you, fear, for all you've done for me."

Chapter 6

SHAME IS
BIOLOGICAL . . .
AND POLITICAL

We are biologically wired to experience shame—and for good reason. From an evolutionary perspective, our survival once depended on close cooperation with members of our group. Violating certain codes of behavior made everyone less safe. Life was too harsh for an individual to survive alone, so being ostracized from your tribe usually amounted to a death sentence. An internal mechanism that alerts us to this danger—the danger of ostracism—therefore serves an essential purpose. That mechanism is shame. Its function is to protect us, to motivate us to act in accordance with community values, preserving both the community and our personal safety. Mental and social isolation are even today a sort of death sentence, though no tigers are involved.

Today, shame also serves the unhelpful role of maintaining our culture's inequitable social structures. It acts as a form of social control that regulates our behavior to conform with cultural values and punish nonconformity. It is both imposed by others and absorbed by us, motivating a drive toward conformity to avoid shame.

This means that people with marginalized identities are set up, to a greater degree, with shame triggers. When we step outside the gender boxes, for example, we are shamed for it. Almost every person raised as a boy has had the experience of knowing they were expected to "man up" and hide their emotions. Almost every person raised as a girl has the experience of knowing they were expected to be accommodating and nurturing. When we don't fit into those binary boxes, we are teased, bullied, or otherwise punished for breaking the rules.

Communal norms police not just our behavior, but our bodies, too. Most of us feel the weight of beauty expectations and shame for not measuring up. Even if we think we do meet the bar, we may fear we can't maintain it (explaining the rise of Botox injections among younger users) or that we're not seen and valued for more meaningful traits.

Shame feeds on the very human need for acceptance and love. We care about what other people think. We want to look good in their eyes. We can all recall experiences of feeling rejected, diminished, and ridiculed. We learned to fear those feelings. We learned to change our behaviors or hide aspects of ourselves to seek approval and avoid shame.

Our shame usually benefits someone. We weren't born being ashamed of our bodies. We weren't born wanting big breasts or a large penis. We learn those inclinations from our culture. If you thought your body was the perfect size, would you need the diet industry? The more you hate yourself, the more vulnerable you are to thinking that buying stuff will help you gain acceptance. The fact that shame is so lucrative entrenches it only more deeply in our culture.

Sitting with our shame, by contrast, rather than reacting to it, lets us see the chasm between who we are and who we think we need to be in order to belong. When we acknowledge shame and its sources, we can develop the critical awareness to have compassion for our vulnerability and to understand what it is saying to us. We can develop shame-resilience, move through it constructively, and grow from our experiences.

WHAT IS SHAME?

At its heart, shame is linked to a fear of being disconnected. Shame is the notion that if people knew me, they'd realize I'm flawed, a bad person, unworthy of love or appreciation. It's about thinking I'm not enough. Fill in the blank: not thin enough, not attractive enough, not smart enough, not rich enough. Shame is inherently social in nature as it is about our discomfort with being seen in a certain light by others. When shamed, one's sense of belonging is negated.

It's human to experience shame; we all do. In fact, most people feel it to varying degrees almost every day. Any time you think you've done something wrong or feel uncomfortable in a social situation, like you don't measure up, you may be feeling a version of shame. It's what drives us to hate our bodies and to fear rejection—and stops us from connecting with others.

Shame can spring from serious events that are laden with cultural judgment, like affairs, incarceration, childhood abuse, sexual assault. But ordinary doubts and struggles can trigger it, too, like insecurities about our appearance, adequacy as parents, money, work prestige, mental and physical health, and our very identity (race, sexual orientation, gender, etc.).

We all have basic stories we keep returning to about what we are ashamed of. How deeply we are mired in it differs, as does the ease with which it surfaces. Our families and our culture(s) teach us early in life that some people have value and that how others look and act is inferior. If you believe you are not good enough, there is a reason.

SHAME VERSUS GUILT

Shame is deeply rooted in how we feel about ourselves. It's different from guilt, and understanding the difference can help us work through shame.

While shame is a deeply held belief about our unworthiness as a person, guilt is a feeling about our behavior. In other words, shame manifests as "I am bad," while guilt manifests as "what I did was bad."

Guilt can be helpful as it can show us what we did (or failed to do) that means we didn't live up to our values. My guilt over not inviting my wheelchair-user friend to dinner was productive learning that helped me take responsibility, apologize to my friend, repair the rupture, and change my behavior in the future. The ability and willingness to view something we've done and hold it up against who we want to be is incredibly adaptive. It can be uncomfortable, for sure, but it supports us in becoming better people.

Guilt can be unhelpful if it's about living up to unrealistically high standards. For example, I forgot my neighbor's name. My difficulty accepting my mistake kept me mired in self-judgment, condemning me to feel bad rather than to change my behavior. It was only when I accepted my inadequacy that I could consider strategies that allowed me to manage it. Eventually, I found a helpful practice: hitching names to associations. I now make it a practice to repeat someone's name when I'm first introduced and mentally link the name to a descriptive word starting with the same letter. (I'm fearful that if others use this strategy, "Little Lindo" might be an obvious choice. Let me prime you: How about "Lovable Lindo" instead?)

SHAME AVOIDANCE

Shame hurts, so we want to escape the feeling. Shame can make me want to hide away by myself and disappear. I want to avoid returning phone calls, back out of social plans, or call in sick to work. Some people's shame stops them from leaving the house altogether. For years, I worked with a virtual assistant. She knew all sorts of personal details about me and took care of so many daily needs that I grew to depend on her as a partner and almost a friend. That's why I was so sad to realize I would never meet her. Every time I visited her town and arranged to meet, she would cancel. I suspect her body shame was so intense it overrode her strong desire to meet me. I'm told by many fat friends that body shame has all too often kept them behind closed doors. Of course, body shame is not unique to fat people, and many people fear leaving the house and exposing themselves, even without that added layer of cultural approbation.

THE BIOLOGY OF SHAME

The discomfort of shame triggers our protective sympathetic nervous system, taking the prefrontal cortex (the thinking brain) offline and letting the limbic system (the emotional brain) run wild. Your response is thus unlikely to be "rational."

Our fight response, when triggered, may make us angry about the person or situation that shamed us. Our flight response may make us want to disappear. If our response is to freeze, particularly in traumatic situations in which we lack power, we may feel trapped. With our prefrontal cortex offline, we also think less clearly, leaving us believing that we are powerless and stuck because something is wrong with us.

Reactive anger and defensiveness commonly tag along with shame as secondary emotions, often coming on so quickly we can't even recognize that shame underlies them. All we feel is the heat and aggression.

All humans experience shame. Even babies display some of its recognizable tics—identifiable bodily changes like a lowering of the eyelids, lowering of the head from a reduction of muscle tone in the neck, and cocking the head in one direction.

I recently witnessed a parent-child interaction in a busy restaurant, two tables over from mine. A baby was sitting in a high chair with a cup of milk in front of her. Her parents were engaged in conversation and not paying attention to her. The baby picked up her cup and spilled some of the milk. The spilled milk fascinated her, so she splashed some more, laughing as the milk spread and running her fingers through it with obvious joy.

Then the mom noticed. "What are you doing? Look at this mess!" she said, clearly irritated.

The girl's interest and enjoyment were suddenly interrupted, and she immediately lowered her eyes and head, dropped her shoulders, and averted her face. She was showing shame.

Mom was unintentionally conditioning her to be neat and controlled and shaming her for the joy she experienced in spontaneous playful expression. The baby, who naturally wants approval from her parents, was learning to suppress her playful urges. Experiences like this from childhood biologically imprint on us and get stored in implicit memory in the amygdala. Repeated experiences reinforce one another. These have lasting impact, making it likely that the girl will be more controlled to avoid feeling shame.

Shame is an important aspect of child development as it can teach us appropriate responses to danger. A good example would be running into the street as a child. If your caregiver screams at you to stop, you feel shame for your action, your sympathetic nervous system gets triggered, and hopefully you can run to safety. If your caregiver immediately comes to you and holds you, this reassurance activates the parasympathetic nervous system, calming you. In that case, shame is teaching you good street-safety lessons.

But what happens if the caregiver is always screaming at the child to stop, even if there's little or no danger, and rarely offers reassurance that the child is okay? The child's sympathetic nervous system is triggered, but the parasympathetic nervous system isn't called into action to calm them down. The body becomes like a car spinning its tires but unable to move forward. This gets registered in the hippocampus, the part of the limbic system responsible for consolidating memory. The caregiver is using "toxic shame" to control the child. Toxic shame is the shame that gets internalized and becomes part of our self-image. It differs from ordinary shame, which fades over a shorter period of time.

Our experiences in childhood are internalized into memory by the hippocampus, creating a blueprint that helps our body know how to respond to future situations. If we were mistreated, the hippocampus internalizes negative messages about ourselves and what we can expect from others. Later in life, when we encounter uncomfortable situations, our hippocampus thinks it's like what we encountered in childhood, triggering feelings of shame and fear and getting in the way of openness to new relationships.

SHAME IS A FEELING, NOT A FACT

When you feel shame, it doesn't mean that you did anything wrong or shameful. Rather, shame is a *feeling* that you are somehow in the wrong. A child abused by their father did nothing wrong yet commonly feels ashamed and at fault for the abuse. People have no power over their penis size, yet beliefs about size inadequacy can trigger painful shame, inhibiting sexual relationships and even comfort in locker rooms.

Shame takes on nuanced meanings based on other identities. For example, anti-Black sexual racism and white supremacy means that Black people with penises* are already hypersexualized and forced to feel shame should they not "live up to" the sexual standards assigned to them. As another example, trans men and transmasculine people are often subject to others' constraining beliefs about penises/penis size defining masculinity, and shame about their penis size may be tinged with the fear that a small or nonexistent penis impedes their ability to be seen and respected for their true identity.

We may also feel shame for the things we do to try to get people's approval—things related to money, sex, work, status, appearance, whatever it is—and then feel ashamed about *that* for being inauthentic. Then we often add insult to injury by feeling ashamed of being ashamed.

The more you're ashamed of, the less comfortable you feel expressing yourself and the more your creativity is inhibited. Shame inhibits full development.

REFLECTED SHAME

You can feel shame not only about your own flaws, but also about other people's behaviors, particularly those closest to you, like your partner or child. Psychologists call this reflected shame.

---

* Are you stumbling over the language here? I refer to "people with penises" rather than "men" to include trans women who may have penises.

A poignant example of reflected shame is the shame my parents felt when I stumbled on the modeling runway. In their minds, they were publicly humiliated for raising a child who failed so magnificently as a girl.

Let's give my parents a break and consider another example that can help flesh out this idea. Imagine your teen daughter regularly gets into trouble. She's gotten suspensions from school, abuses drugs and alcohol, and is rude and disrespectful to you and other adults. Other parents try to keep their kids away from her for fear of her influence.

When your child is making poor choices and acting out, it's easy to consider that a reflection of your poor parenting, to wonder where you went wrong, and to fear what others may be thinking. You may feel many painful emotions besides shame. It's likely you're angry with her, that you're worried she could hurt herself, that you fear for her future, and that you feel guilty about your parenting decisions.

Here's the deal: your child's behavior is not a mirror reflecting how you did as a parent. You can influence your child, but you can't possibly control or be responsible for your child's choices. Nor can you control what others think about you. You can only control how you think about yourself and how you respond to others. So, give yourself a break, okay?

Similarly, when our partner embarrasses us, it feels like a reflection of who we are—after all, we picked this person. Everyone does something hurtful or embarrassing once in a while. The question is really not whether our partners or friends will ever embarrass us or induce our shame—they will—the question is how we manage that shame.

Let's look at some examples of reflected shame in action to see the learning experience.

I was at a party recently, composed of social justice activists and their plus-ones (and in one case, their plus-two),* and a colleague's partner unwittingly made a racist joke, an offense that those who were directly invited to the party just wouldn't have committed in this way. My colleague's face

---

* A "plus-one" refers to a person's invited guest at a social function, usually a significant other. This term is a great example of how social normativity feeds our language and customs, in this case legitimizing couples as the norm. Yet, there are many ways people can thrive in relationships, including polyamory, that get left out of this normativity. And of course, people can thrive without primary relationships too.

flushed red. (Oh, how I feel for those vulnerable to wearing their emotions so viscerally!)

In the example described here, it offered my colleague a great opportunity to use their shame to an advantage and to gently educate. Their partner, having sensed that they made a mistake, took in the feedback and apologized. The shame was used to transform the situation, and the story had a happy ending.

Another friend has a spouse whom she feels, to put it kindly, lacks "social finesse." This is due to a "disorder" that he can do little about called autism spectrum disorder. He's also extremely intelligent, another frequent hallmark of being on the spectrum. It was a bit hard for me and my friends to roll with his social gaffes when we first met him, as he inadvertently insulted several people, much to his partner's chagrin. Over time we've come to accept that it's simply part of his makeup. When he says or does something that seems hurtful, we consider that it was likely not intended the way we think. We love that he's so smart and knows so much about a wide array of topics. His presence always makes for much deeper conversation.

Through having a relationship with a man on the autism spectrum, my friend has learned to resist the inclination to see her partner's behavior as the problem, and to instead see that the problem resides in others' not understanding that their partners' actions mean something different than a stranger might assume. My friend has also learned to better tolerate her shame when she sees his social awkwardness, in part because our friend circle models acceptance. As a couple, they discuss these challenges openly and have learned to make choices about when to engage socially, aware that they won't always get this acceptance in other social groups.

Part of dealing with a partner's oddities is challenging ourselves to be more accepting of difference, even if the people in our lives will never be the "perfect" social animals we might want them to be. If a pattern emerges from your partner's or friend's embarrassing words and actions, dig deeper and have those difficult conversations. How often we feel reflective shame can also give us good information in assessing whether a relationship is right for us. Everyone deserves to feel safe and respected in a relationship, and if you can't offer that, stepping back may be valuable.

As an aside, the biology behind autism-related idiosyncrasies could come down to the fact that social and nonsocial thinking involve separate areas in the brain. Nonsocial cognition, such as general intelligence and problem-solving, activates mostly the brain's lateral regions. Social cognition—thinking about our relationships with others—activates mostly the medial regions. Typically, when one form of cognition is active, the other is inactive. The two compete with each other, so a deficit in one area could lead to stronger influence from the other.

This discussion also highlights the value of considering autism—and other conditions commonly considered "neurological disorders"—as yet another form of diversity (neurodiversity), a viewpoint that brain differences are normal, rather than deficits. This concept can help reduce stigma around learning and thinking differences.

SHAME AND POVERTY

As Dolly Parton famously said, "The worst thing about poverty is not the actual living of it, but the shame of it." We live in a culture that measures success by how we fare competitively with others. Judgmental competition sets us up to believe that some people are more worthy of love and belonging than others. Our world is built around social stratification. At an early age, children pick up from adults around them that you sort the smart from the dumb, the beautiful from the ugly, the wealthy from the poor. They are taught to know which kids live in big houses and which don't. There is so much shame associated with poverty.

When experiencing poverty, researchers found, individuals typically exhibit a "scarcity mindset."[1] The need to focus on short-term survival narrows their attention span, weakens their decision-making ability, and distracts from long-term planning. This means that instead of saving and planning for the future, for example, those living in poverty may spend their limited money on items less essential than a rent payment due in a few weeks.

Shame and feelings of low self-worth may also make people experiencing poverty more vulnerable to spending money on status symbols instead of basic necessities. In other words, shame about poverty may lead to behavior that actually can perpetuate poverty. Individuals who are stig-matized for their poverty and shamed for their misery are therefore being pushed to fulfill the prophecies forced upon them.

Poverty also makes us vulnerable to choices that don't align with our values, further triggering shame. For example, a friend of mine wrote a book that assumed a gender-binary framework, which made it a painful read for me, triggering my feeling of difference, wrongness, and unbelong-ing. This seemed so uncharacteristic of my friend, who understands that gender is not binary.

When I told her I couldn't endorse the book, she understood. She was ashamed of that aspect of the book. She explained that she wrote the book the way she did under duress from the publisher because she desperately needed the book's advance. (Trace it back further and it's also clear that her poverty was structurally induced. She is a brilliant person and a hard worker, but she hasn't had the opportunities that would let her monetize her tal-ents.) The book is out in the world, and she will always have to manage her discomfort. It's also unfortunate to see how one effect of systemic injustice (in this case, poverty) is to set marginalized people against one another.

As another example, a homeless kid has limited options for making money, leaving them vulnerable to feeling like they need to perform sex work. Then they feel ashamed for the things they do to survive. To add further insult to injury, they are then punished with judgment and legal sanctions, as if it's their fault. It isn't their fault, though. The blame rests in a culture that provided no better options for survival.

Cultural commentator, blogger, and community organizer Da'Shaun Harrison poignantly makes this point when describing their sister's death by suicide as "murder by the state."[2] Poverty left her unable to see another option. When I first read Harrison's moving piece, "When Marginalized Folk Take Our Lives, It's Because the State Already Has," the wording "death by suicide" felt awkward and uncomfortable. But point well-taken: the language more familiarly used, "committed suicide," conveys shame and wrongdoing, and implies that the person who died was a perpetrator rather than a victim. Viewing suicide as a byproduct of a social (or health) condition, on the other hand, removes the victim-blaming and can also help us better envision avenues for prevention.

One particularly strong cultural narrative says that people experience poverty because of their own failures; that people are poor because they are lazy, irresponsible, averse to work, criminally inclined, or simply stupid. This explanation locates the causes of poverty in the individual and ignores surrounding social structures.

For example, conservatives rail against funding for food assistance programs, suggesting they create "dependency." What they are really saying is that people in poverty are lazy and must be forced to fend for themselves, denying the possibility that people would like to provide for their own welfare but cannot, for entrenched structural reasons. Many people believe that poverty results from moral weakness instead of recognizing the economic and social structures that hold people there. With this as a dominant narrative, it makes sense that impoverished people internalize those messages and believe that the problem is in them.

The problem is not in the individual. The solution is not that the individual needs to try harder. As Mary O'Hara astutely writes in *The Shame Game: Overturning the Toxic Poverty Narrative*, "The people in desperate need swallowing their pride to turn up on the doorsteps of foodbanks in the fifth richest nation on earth [Britain] or relying on food stamps in the richest nation on earth [United States] are not doing so because they are flawed, failed people."[3] The problem is in the system. The solution is to create an economy defined by opportunity and the chance for anyone to thrive.

SHAME AND EDUCATIONAL STATUS

Educational status is yet another loaded example of a shame-inducing way we stratify one another. My friend, for example, tells me that she always dreads the inevitable "Where did you go to college?" question at social and professional gatherings. Revealing that she went to a community college makes her vulnerable to the stigma of being less intelligent and worthy than others. Hearing that question can be even harder for someone who never attended post-secondary school.

The skills one gains in school are not necessarily what makes us smarter or better people. I studied mitosis, the process of cell division, in high school and aced that exam. Am I a better, smarter person for it? No, but it did help me get a degree. It's time to end education stigma and acknowledge the value that comes from education outside of the class-room or in less-revered institutions.

We also need to be thinking about better conversation starters. I see this repeatedly when I'm in gatherings of people with more money: the get-to-know-you questions are about work or pedigree, whereas in less mon-eyed crowds, questions about current events or pop culture are more likely.

SHAME, ATTRACTIVENESS, AND DESIRABILITY

Bcauty standards parallel systems of oppression. What gets posited as attractive is rarely referred to as disabled or fat, and often reflects cis-normative masculinity and femininity. Light skin is prized over dark, young bodies prized over old bodies. As a result, many of us feel unattractive—and undesired—leading to tremendous shame.

When you don't measure up to arbitrary social constructs that allow you to be seen as attractive, it can be very challenging to hold onto the awareness that the problem is in the culture, not your body, and to avoid internalizing your feelings as shame.

Conventional beauty is so significant to our lived experience that there's even a whole field dedicated to the study of the economics of phys-ical attractiveness, called pulchronomics. It's well established that "pretty privilege" can pave the way to more popularity, higher grades, higher sal-aries, more positive work reviews, and career advancement.[4] Being pretty even helps when it comes to crime: conventionally attractive people are less likely to be convicted—and more likely to get lighter sentences when they are.[5] Not surprisingly, the pursuit of good looks drives several mammoth industries—Americans spent more than $16.5 billion on cosmetic plastic surgery in 2018.[6]

Dating Katie, a grad school classmate and conventionally attractive model, was an eye-opener for me. Pretty privilege filtered into every social encounter she had. (My lack of it did too, though that only became clear in contrast to Katie's experience.) When we were on dates at bars, guys would insert themselves between me and Katie with their back to me and offer to buy her drinks. I wasn't just unattractive to them—I was invisible. They never considered the possibility that Katie was attracted to me: sexism, homophobia, and looksism, all coalescing.

Every outing with Katie revealed how different her experience in the world was from mine. It was a regular occurrence, for example, that if Katie fiddled for some change to pay for coffee, the person behind her in line would cover it with a smile, or the barista would take it from his tip jar to cover it. Even straight old ladies had an extra smile for her (and offered to set her up with their grandsons).

Knowing she was considered beautiful didn't help Katie feel better about herself. She never trusted people—which makes sense, as people seemed to respond to her beauty rather than who she was. She was deeply insecure, always questioning whether an invitation or job offer was earned based on merit or merely because of her looks. This distrust and insecurity were so central to her character that they eventually overwhelmed me, making our relationship untenable. Our experience mirrored the lessons learned from research[7] conducted by social psychologist and professor Christine Ma-Kellams and collaborators, who conducted four studies exploring whether physical attractiveness plays a role in relationship satisfaction and longevity. Among their provocative findings: people deemed attractive were married for shorter durations, more likely to divorce, and—get this—more likely to have their relationships be threatened or dissolved due to their partner's poor relationship satisfaction. While conventional attractiveness comes with many privileges, there's a dark lining that's less discussed: it may work against that sustained connection many of us seek, and get in the way of us feeling seen and truly valued.

Culturally constructed beauty ideals also inform how we view others, influencing who we consider attractive. Desire, in other words, is not innate, but deeply political. And desire affects more than who we want to date or have sex with; it also informs how we treat people, like whether we even notice, or are kind to, that stranger; who we choose as friends; and to whom we give jobs and business opportunities. It saddens me how we are all denied full opportunities for love, sex, friendship, and so much more due to people internalizing desirability constructs. I've learned to become vigilant when my behavior mimics oppressive structures, and my desires have broadened over time, though there's still more work to be done.

Writer, activist, and teacher Caleb Luna advises: "It remains important to me to interrogate desire—not to then become attracted to everyone, but to be aware of what powers are informing my desire and what I am upholding with my desire—but also so that culturally ugly folks who remain publicly and visibly undesired can still receive the justice of interpersonal value and appreciation, especially in our most intimate relationships."[8]

In a keynote speech, "Moving Toward the Ugly: A Politic Beyond Desirability," delivered at the Femmes of Color Symposium, writer, educator, and community organizer Mia Mingus pushes us to challenge the exclusionary beauty constructs that erase disabled people, People of Color, trans and gender non-conforming folks, and fat people, and move towards what she calls magnificence, a concept that embraces ugliness and celebrates the diversity of bodies—of every body.[9]

"There is only the illusion of solace in beauty. If age and disability teach us anything, it is that investing in beauty will never set us free. Beauty has always been hurled as a weapon. It has always taken the form of an exclusive club, and supposed protection against violence, isolation and pain, but this is a myth. It is not true, even for those accepted into the club. I don't think we can reclaim beauty," Mingus says eloquently.

Luna elaborates on this point in another essay, "On Being Fat, Brown, Femme, Ugly, and Unlovable": "Under colonial constructions of beauty and desire, being fat and brown and queer and femme means being ugly . . . Ugly is how I move through the world, how I am viewed by strangers, coworkers, potential lovers, employers, family, community members, doctors, professors, service industry workers, et cetera, and this perception affects how I am treated daily. I have been denied job opportunities because of my body. I do not fit into restaurant booths, airplane seats, or school desks comfortably—which serves as a constant reminder that this world was not built to accommodate me . . .

"I do not mean to say that absolutely no fat folks or People of Color are loved or desired. On the contrary, I see many inspiring examples of this in my own community. However, larger cultural systems that inform individual decisions and desires have been sculpted by centuries of intentional privileging of particular bodies and the marginalization of others."

As Mingus explains: "We all run from the ugly . . . What would it mean if we were ugly? What would it mean if we didn't run from our own ugliness or each other's? How do we take the sting out of 'ugly'? . . . What would happen if we stopped apologizing for our ugly, stopped being ashamed of it? What if we let go of being beautiful, stopped chasing 'pretty,' stopped sucking in and shrinking and spending enormous amounts of money and time on things that don't make us magnificent? . . ."

She continues, "I am not saying it is easy to be ugly without apology. It is hard as f*. It threatens our survival. I recognize the brilliance in our instinct to move toward beauty and desirability. And it takes time and for some of us it may be impossible. I know it is complicated . . . And I also know that though it may be a way to survive, it will not be a way to thrive, to grow the kind of genders and world we need."

There's hope embodied in the closing to Mingus' speech: "If you leave with anything today, leave with this: you are magnificent. There is magnificence in our ugliness. There is power in it, far greater than beauty can ever wield. Work to not be afraid of the Ugly—in each other or ourselves. Work to learn from it, to value it. Know that every time we turn away from ugliness, we turn away from ourselves. And always remember this: I would rather you be magnificent than beautiful, any day of the week. I would rather you be ugly—magnificently ugly."

Next time you feel shame for your looks, can you turn it around? Can you toss aside the drive for beauty and embrace your magnificence? It's not easy, but this is the bedrock that revolution is made of.

SHAME RESILIENCE

So, you get hit with a wave of shame. How do you manage it?

First, remember how normal that is. You're human. Reframe your idea of shame. Think of it as an immature friend trying to protect you by revealing how you don't fit in. (A bit like your more mature friend, fear.) You can then honor the impulse and reduce shame's power over you.

It's helpful to shore up your skills at self-compassion. It's not easy to feel good about yourself when messages from the outside tell you that who you are isn't good enough. Heaping self-criticism on top of that makes you complicit in your own oppression. You don't have to buy into the deprecation. Developing self-compassion allows you to sit with your shame, giving you opportunity to defang it. Can you offer kindness to this human in pain? (Yes, I'm talking about you!) Keep offering kindness to yourself as you feel the pain.

Next, build your skills at seeing your inherent worthiness, despite any contrary messages you may be getting. You are worthy of respect, love, and belonging. You are entitled to be valued and loved by others. You don't need someone else's permission or approval to love yourself and you don't need to earn it. This is your birthright.

Are you ashamed of your behavior? If so, this is an opportunity, a time to reflect about how you can do better—and then make that happen. If you've harmed someone, learning how to take responsibility for it and apologize can go a long way to healing shame. The simple act of saying sorry is a great start.

Yes, sometimes it's on us, but all too often, our shame belongs to the culture, not us. Think critically about cultural messages you've received about who is acceptable and who is not. Discard the messages that indicate that you are unworthy. Reinterpret the things people are shamed for, like poverty or race or fatness or disability, to disrupt their narratives of shame, and to learn to appreciate all aspects of ourselves, including those that are stigmatized. If you think you're too fat, for example, as you come to terms with the fact that the problem is not in your body, but in a culture that stigmatizes your body, you lighten your shame about it.

Recognizing that the problem is not in your body can be especially challenging for fat people as there is such a strong cultural narrative supporting the myth that fatness is under individual control. Some research shows that fat individuals have lower group identification and are more likely to endorse stereotypes about their identity than other stigmatized groups, such as racial or religious minorities. Please, resist that.

Anyone can have negative experiences or emotions around their body, but it isn't the same as the systemic discrimination that fat bodies face. Finding fat and fat-accepting community can be life-altering. You can only be so resilient alone.

Recognizing that you're not alone helps reinforce this understanding that the problem is not you. By speaking out and sharing our shame with others, we learn that our personal stories are never ours alone. There are strong connections between what we experience and social, political, and economic influences. Your shame is at once personal *and* political. When we critically examine the big picture, we are better able to reality-check our personal experience of shame and the cultural expectations that fuel it. The #MeToo movement is an excellent example. Started by Tarana Burke in 2006 and popularized by Alyssa Milano and others in 2017, it supported people in coming forward with their stories of sexual violence, giving solace to many.

Speaking our shame in the right circumstances helps strip its power. If we're met with understanding and empathy, we can sit in kindness, helping us tolerate the discomfort. The pain may not go away, but we improve our ability to be with it.

It's ironic, then, that shame pushes us away from people. Human connection is shame's kryptonite, yet shame pushes us on instinct to isolate ourselves. In other words, the place where we can heal is the place we are often too ashamed to go.

Think about what you've done to try to manage shame, whether it's withdrawing, taking it out on yourself, or lashing out at others. Consider the impact it's had on you, perhaps loneliness, disconnection, anxiety, depression, eating disorders, addiction, other self-harm, rage, blame, resentment, grief, loss, damage to relationships. Managing your shame can save you from much of that pain—and from harming others, too.

Have you hurt others, acting out of shame? I watched an interaction recently where someone accused their friend of being self-centered. What really was going on was they felt ignored and disrespected but were too ashamed to have the conversation from a starting point of vulnerability. The blaming transferred the shame to the other person, enabling them to temporarily feel better about themselves. It didn't help the relationship in the long run, though.

While I don't want to add more shame onto your load, it's important to pay attention to the impact of your shame reaction on others. It's not only compassionate, but it might even help you. I, for instance, sometimes find more motivation in attending to others than to myself—and this outward focus motivates me to be a better person.

Healing from shame may require grieving for the love and respect you deserve but may not always get. For example, your parents may never accept your partner with loving arms. Or, to get by, you may have to work a job where you feel disrespected or make choices that go against your values. Painful as it is to accept unfairness, grieving helps you take the weight off your own shoulders and put it outside you, where it belongs.

OWNING STIGMATIZED IDENTITIES

Much shame is rooted in the challenge of appreciating ourselves and over-coming messages of inadequacy about who we are. I had a powerful experience in my early twenties that helped me understand the power of owning my identity.

It was my first year of college and I still didn't even have language that would help me understand my gender identity or sexual orientation. I became fascinated with a woman named Rachel on the edge of my social circle. She was a brash, outspoken campus activist, always surrounded by friends. I admired that supportive community, and Rachel especially, for their social confidence—a trait I hankered for. I suppose I was a bit of a stalker, watching Rachel and her crowd, even following them around campus. Though I wanted to be a part of their energy, I was too intim-idated to talk to them. One night, I saw an opportunity to tag along as they poured into a packed seminar hall. Following, I figured I could blend into the crowd and remain below their radar. I didn't know what was going on in the room but managed to slide into one of the last remaining seats—unfortunately at the front and center.

Although I didn't know anything about her at the time, I was about to hear the famed poet, feminist, and civil rights activist Audre Lorde speak. When she stepped to the podium, she opened with, "I'm a Black, working-class, feminist, lesbian, mother, poet." The word "lesbian" resonated inside me. My mind raced and I felt panic rise. I wanted to run from the room, but there was no way to without being noticed. Then, things got worse. Lorde was pointing at me. She was asking me to stand up. I slid lower in my chair, glancing around desperately, hoping she really meant someone else—or that she'd have pity on me and call on a neighbor. No such luck.

"Stand up," she said. I did.

"Identify yourself," she said.

I stuttered, muttering something about not wanting to limit myself to particular categories.

She wasn't impressed. "Identify yourself," she insisted.

"I'm a Caucasian woman," I offered.

"Is that all?" she asked.

I nodded, mortified. "If you don't own your identity," she said with obvious disdain, "you give up your power. You allow others to control it."

She went on to other people, including Rachel's clique, who easily threw out identifying terms like "lesbian," "gay," "homo," "queer," "socialist," and "anarchist."

Why was I so uncomfortable? If they tagged themselves with identities, why couldn't I? Until that moment, in a room of about fifty people where I had ended up quite by accident, I had never confronted my attraction to women. I had been in denial about it, in fact. Granted, I was also attracted to men. But the attraction to women was hovering right there, always just below the surface of my recognition. Later, I would come to realize that I am attracted to people who do not neatly fit the gender binary, rather than to men or women specifically.

Looking back now with a little kindness, I can gently say I was clueless. I hadn't realized that Rachel and her pals were lesbians, and my intense interest was not just admiration but a full-on crush. When Lorde ordered me to identify myself, she was challenging me to own my identity as a lesbian (or at least bisexual or queer). I couldn't because I was drowning in shame. Having spent so much time in denial, I was helpless to own it.

Lesbian was a dirty word. That couldn't be me. Could it?

I felt humiliated in front of this group of people, even more so because of how aware I was of my shame in the face of their brazen willingness to embrace their stigmatized identities.

Lorde captures this concept eloquently in her book, *Sister Outsider*. "If I didn't define myself for myself, I would be crunched into other people's fantasies for me and eaten alive."[10] That is what had been happening to me in my family. For most of my life, I had been carrying the weight of disappointing other people's fantasies about the "girl" I should be.

After seeing how Rachel and her group boldly owned their identities, even identities that led to their marginalization on campus, I was too ashamed to face them in class or even look in their direction. I was actually too upset even to attend class for a while. I didn't want to be seen as associated with them, for fear that I would be identified as a lesbian.

This was a turning point toward owning my sexual identity—and it contributed to my understanding of the broader issues of identity politics that would follow. Now I can appreciate Lorde's point, that we need to embrace our identities. Failing to, I now see, leads to shame, separation, and oppression—precisely what I was feeling in those miserable first months of college.

The dominant culture stigmatizes lesbians, viewing them as not worthy of the same respect and rights as a "normal" person, a heterosexual. Instead, as Lorde suggested, I could reclaim that identity and see my attraction to women as a positive aspect of who I am, thereby refusing to take on the shame people expected me to feel.

FINDING MY IDENTITY

Not being able to conceptualize your identity causes massive harm. For me, my inability to imagine myself as trans kept me separated from kindred spirits—and from the possibility of finding myself earlier.

Take, for example, my relationship with CJ. I was twenty-five when I met CJ, a person who would become significant in my life and my lover for five years. I felt instant attraction when I saw her for the first time. She was a woman* who crossed over the border of gender, appearing male with few hints of girl.

I appreciated that CJ shared my gender nonconformity. Yet, ironically, she also triggered my discomfort in my gender expression. These were different times, when it was more popular in lesbian culture to reinforce a gender binary, with women in couples assuming "butch" and "femme" roles. Those roles never appealed to me—I was more attracted to people who, like me, didn't gender-conform—but these roles mattered to CJ.

Failing to be the femme girl of her fantasies flowed into my recurring river of shame. Not being appreciated for my gender identity felt all too familiar—how ironic that I was now facing it from someone who had a similar experience!

It was also triggering to witness CJ being seen for her masculinity where mine felt invisible. I was more adept at "passing" (for a girl), even if I didn't want to. But it also helped me see how much more easily I could navigate the world if my gender identity remained less visible or threatening. CJ, by contrast, struggled to find a job where she was fairly compensated for her talents and treated with respect. Gender nonconformity—like most marginalized ways of being—often translates to lower pay, greater stress, and higher allostatic load, along with other associated maladies.

Twenty years after we split up, I decided to track her down. I came to learn that she—he—had medically transitioned and now went by the name Connor. It made so much sense. I was stunned that I had never imagined that as a possibility when we were together. I attribute this in large part to a lack of trans role models, especially transmasculine people; I just couldn't imagine trans at the time.

I found an online interview where Connor recounted a memory of eating out with my parents. My father, who had a problem with Connor's masculine presentation, said, "It's okay that you're gay, but do you have to dress like a man? Can't you wear some nice slacks or a skirt once in a while?"

Connor walked out of the restaurant that night. "I was livid," he told the interviewer, recalling that it was the first time he ever really stood up

---

* I thought she was a woman at the time. Later, as you will read, I learned I was wrong.

for himself, "simply by walking out of the restaurant." He describes that as the pivotal moment where he realized he was trans.

I, too, remember that scene, though I didn't understand its significance for Connor at the time, and he didn't name it. For me, with my lifelong experience of hearing such remarks from my family, it stood out as the first time I'd seen them directed at someone I loved. I remember feeling glad CJ walked out, setting the boundaries with my parents I had never managed. It had never even occurred to me to walk out. I had assumed bearing it was my only option.

I realize in retrospect that although I had been accepting of his masculinity as a butch woman, I hadn't seen him as a man—which meant I wasn't seeing him. He, too, was not able to see my genderqueer identity showing up. It pains me to think of the two of us back then, together but alone, without the awareness that would have allowed us to have this conversation.

I learned that Connor died of breast cancer. How ironic that the breasts that were so painful to him when he was alive eventually played a role in his death.

In a similar vein, more recently, I was contacted by a friend from college. We hadn't been in touch in the thirty-plus years since graduation, until this email: "Hi, Diana here, but you knew me as Doug." The email went on to recount memories of our college days. I had no idea who she was, but her account contained enough details to convince me we'd hung out. (The black Mustang I drove then isn't easily forgotten!) She, as Doug, had apparently accompanied me on many road trips to after-hours clubs in Manhattan.

I remember those clubs, though I thought I went alone. I visited them to meet my cocaine connection, who also happened to be a sex worker. On two occasions, showing up at the agreed time and place, I walked in on her engaged in sexual activity and unwittingly became part of the scene. Apparently, she set me up—it turned her clients on to be seen by someone they took to be a naive girl. Those nights traumatized me, and I've abandoned many of the details, forgetting even that Diana had accompanied me. I felt violated and used, but rather than take it out on my dealer, I blamed myself. Was I so needy for drugs that I would walk into an unsafe and degrading situation? Once again, I felt like I was the one who had done wrong.

Diana, now an accomplished writer, describes our relationship in her memoir: "Something I couldn't name felt familiar about Linda. There was a kind of tribal recognition, creating a space of freedom, which is maybe what friendship comes down to."[11] For Diana, these road trips also left an impact. They gave her her first look at people with "unconventional" gender identities. Another excerpt from her memoir describes our foray into the club scene:

> Every now and then a drag queen or transsexual* would walk into the space from some back area I couldn't see. It was the first time in my life I was in the presence of such people, and I tracked them as I talked to Linda. They were doing ordinary things, talking, sitting with legs crossed smoking cigarettes. It all felt surreal. Every time one of them stood up and walked off, I pictured them retiring to a hidden lair, where they lived a life I could never fathom.
>
> I didn't say a word to Linda about my thrill of being around transsexuals. It was clear we both liked adventure, and departing from the status quo, mixing with freaks and transgressors. At times we tried making conversation with others, but mostly we just sat wide-eyed— two kids, alone together, nursing drinks in an after-hours joint in New York City where anything could happen, though not much did.

CLAIMING YOUR IDENTITY

Each of us is composed of a nexus of identities that connect us to a system of power and regulate how we are seen and treated, shaping the course of our lives. Greater awareness of what our identities mean to us allows us to

---

* *Transsexual* is a term used to identify people who have changed or want to change their body through surgeries, hormones, and other body modifications to have physical characteristics that match their sexual identity. It's an older term that originated in the medical and psychological communities and is not as commonly used today because of its history in pathologizing people. For those of us outside the category, it may best be a term to avoid; instead, we can more respectfully use the term *trans*.

own our own stories and take back the power to define ourselves. Awareness also provides opportunity to reflect on what kind of a person you want to be and how you can be accountable to others.

The ongoing process of claiming my own identity, inspired by that chance encounter with Audre Lorde, has been so life-altering for me that I have since designed tools to help others in that process and regularly conduct guiding workshops for groups and individuals. At the end of the book, I provide reflection materials to help you (and groups) explore your identities and how systems of power privilege or disadvantage you. The reflection exercise is also a tool for learning about others and developing cultural humility.

SOMETIMES CONFORMITY IS THE RIGHT CHOICE

You have a choice between conforming to live in the world as it is or demanding that the world accept you as you are. If you can substitute pride for your shame, embrace it. But sometimes conformity offers the safer and healthier option. When we choose to conform, we also need to pay attention to accepting that we are doing the best we can given the circumstances. We can also build a community to hold us privately.

It is too easy to say, "Drop your shame, embrace your pride, it will set you free." Because shame is often about survival and protection, you cannot be free so long as the cultural threat remains. No matter how comfortable you become with yourself, it's nearly impossible to filter out the discomfort imposed by the wider world. It's painful to recognize that the society you live in does in fact have power over you. Cultural ideas—about queerness, for example—may limit your job opportunities. They mark you for potential violence. They may result in social exclusion. The more you understand that valid reasons underlie the shame you feel, the less it controls you and the better you can choose how to protect yourself in a prejudiced world.

For some, staying in the closet or otherwise hiding your difference may be the healthiest option. Coming out offers incredible advantages like the increased opportunity for being seen and authentic connection, but also may make you less safe.

Of course, the more "outsider" identities you inhabit, the more complex or hazardous these choices may become. For me, as a privileged white person who's also queer, coming out as queer may be relatively uncomplicated. But for trans Women of Color it's considerably less safe. People still get killed for being queer, disproportionately poor Women of Color, in the United States and elsewhere. (In 2017 at least twenty-nine transgender people died from violence. I write "at least" because many cases are unreported. According to the Human Rights Campaign, "It is clear that fatal violence disproportionately affects transgender Women of Color, and that the intersections of racism, sexism, homophobia and transphobia conspire to deprive them of employment, housing, health care and other necessities."[12])

Even while it can be deadly to be trans, I sense a culture shift coming. Genderbending is trending in pop culture these days. Identifying as trans even helps me at times in my role as influencer, giving me enough marginalized status to be viewed as a spokesperson for the marginalized, but with so many privileges that I don't threaten. (This isn't okay. It's important to me to always remember this and to use my privilege to dismantle the unfairness I benefit from.)

Things may be getting better, but that doesn't change the fact that if you're queer and hold hands with your partner at the movie theater, you could meet with violence, whereas when a straight couple holds hands at the movies, people choose to think "How sweet."

But it's also true that that act of holding your lover's hand may empower someone struggling with their own identity, who feels less alone after witnessing it. Or maybe your visibility gives hope to a parent wondering if their child can ever feel pride and enter loving partnerships. You just don't know the full impact of your actions.

For me, there was a tipping point where the pain of not being seen seemed to outweigh the potential risks associated with visibility. This, in part, motivated me to write this book.

THE NORMALIZATION OF SHAME

Some types of cultural shaming are so normalized that we don't even recognize them as shaming. Think about the word *obesity*. "Obesity" is a category based on the body mass index (BMI), which, as we saw earlier, is a mathematical equation derived by dividing a person's weight in kilograms by the square of their height in meters. BMI measures physical appearance, not health, yet the term *obesity* is used to pathologize bodies. When the American Medical Association declared "obesity" a disease, it overrode a recommendation by its own expert panel, which had found that correlations between "obesity" and morbidity and mortality rates established no causality. The panel expressed concern that medicalizing "obesity" would lead to further stigmatization and unnecessary treatments.[13] It did.

Using the word *obesity* is dehumanizing, yet it's so normalized that few people notice. Most fat people can't even name how it bothers them because the health narrative it's couched in makes it acceptable. It can be easy to forget that the word *obesity* is a reminder that the world pathologizes fat bodies and polices all of us.

Shaming also comes in the form of other "health" messaging, like signs proclaiming "Your health is up to you!" What's wrong with that? It assumes a level of privilege and control most of us lack. Few individuals control major factors that influence our health, like genetics, neighborhood, socioeconomic status, access to health care, education, or social supports. Nor can we prevent our exposure to health-threatening trauma such as abuse, racism, or stigma.

GETTING HELP

There are numerous tools you can utilize to help combat the effects of shame, but few are as effective as saying it out loud. In some situations, it may be safer to reveal your shame to a paid professional than a friend. In addition to the chance to understand yourself better through therapy, the simple act of revealing hard truths about yourself to someone and then see them stick with you can help you tolerate and accept yourself. Support groups, especially if committed to confidentiality, can also be valuable. The internet may provide anonymous support, as can a hotline. If you are stuck in the "I am bad" mindset, there are resources out there to help alleviate your discomfort.

Of course, there are many potential practical barriers to accessing resources like these, including cost, lack of insurance, limited time, the difficulty of missing work, inconvenient locations, limited clinic hours, transportation challenges, and child care difficulties, to name a few. Go easy on yourself if you have trouble accessing help. There are so many economic and practical challenges that the act of seeking help can sometimes feel like yet another burden.

BRINGING IT HOME

Experiencing shame is part of being human and thus unavoidable. Please show some compassion for yourself when you experience shame. While you may not be able to make it go away, you can develop the resilience to recognize it, move through it constructively, and grow from your experiences.

One of the most powerful potential antidotes to shame is speaking it. Making yourself vulnerable and showing your authentic self allows you to sit with it and lessen its power over you. When we reach out to others, we can find that we are not alone. We can be met with the empathy that helps us tolerate our shame. We can also find the love and connection we need to survive amid unfairness. That kind of vulnerability is hard, though—and complicated. If we share our shame in the wrong context, it can get exacerbated. That is why we need to exercise care in cultivating relationships, protecting ourselves as we go—enough of an imperative to merit an entire chapter on vulnerability. Keep reading.

Chapter 7

GETTING TO VULNERABILITY

Vulnerability is no easy feat. Our social realities and marginalizations make it hard. How much vulnerability to offer is a complicated decision that depends on our feelings of safety, survival, trust, and belonging.

Our deepest human need is to be seen and valued by other people. We're told that the secret to happiness is to be our authentic selves, to show up. Of course, it's not that simple. Show yourself and you may get rejected. As we have seen, it's easier to show your authentic self when the world tells a story that values that self. Presenting an authentic self is safer for people with privileged identities and personal histories of love and support. There are valid reasons to hide our full and authentic selves, including the reality that expressing them may put us at risk. Think of all the trans women who have been killed for being themselves, or men ridiculed for expressing fear. Our shame about certain characteristics may also hold us back, much of which may be the result of internalized oppression. Hiding aspects of ourselves is often intended as self-protection.

If your coworker doesn't share much about their personal life, maybe there's stigma associated with what goes on behind the scenes. They may not expect the luxury of being met with understanding and respect when they share personally. So don't rush to judgment when you see someone self-protecting—and that includes if that someone is you.

This poses a challenge: if we don't show ourselves, how can people get to know us or accept us? Not revealing ourselves leaves us isolated. Any "acceptance" we may get feels hollow and undeserved. Unless I open myself to being hurt, I am closing myself off to being loved and connected. It is also harder to love ourselves if we don't feel love reflected back from others.

In this chapter we'll look at the question of how to find the sweet spot between protecting oneself and showing up fully, in order to experience love and belonging.

VULNERABILITY VERSUS SELF-PROTECTION

When you show up completely and reveal your authentic self, you run the risk of rejection: nasty looks, social rejection, job loss, physical violence, or worse. It makes sense to want to hide aspects of ourselves that we think will prevent our acceptance, whether they are traits we dislike ourselves or traits we know to be stigmatized or judged harshly by others. We want to put forward our most likable self. I went to a party recently where I was really *on*. I felt witty and smart, like I knew how to play the game socially. Then I came home and felt crappy. I had *performed* friendliness and bonding, rather than really connecting with anyone. I was acting not as myself but as the person I thought they wanted me to be. Acting inauthentically is such a lonely feeling. This inauthentic presentation of ourselves results from being policed all our lives and taught which traits are valued and which aren't.

Of course, this is nuanced, as there are no objective standards to what traits get valued across social identities or locations or time. Boys don't cry, right? And while a tearful girl may be supported by her girlfriends, her crying will hold her back in a corporate setting. Even this line of thinking must be fleshed out further. Lawyer, scholar, and civil rights advocate Kimberlé Crenshaw coined the term "intersectionality" to help explain the oppression of Black women and show how multiple oppressions intersect to form our experience.[1]

As Crenshaw describes, the intersectional experience needs to be taken into account as its influence is different than the sum of its parts. While boys can't cry and girls can't cry in corporate settings, the reasoning behind these things differs depending on race. Black boys don't cry, for example, not just because it threatens their masculinity, but also because they are often taught they can't cry if they want to be valued or seen as credible. And while girls can't cry in corporate settings because they won't be respected, Black girls can't cry because they also face the "Angry Black Woman" trope—forever seen as women who are unable to "control" their emotions.

When you analyze a situation from an intersectional perspective, it becomes clear that generalizations about groups are likely describing dominant group experience and misrepresenting those with multiple levels of marginalization. Sojourner Truth, an African American abolitionist and women's rights activist, explained this in her famous speech "Ain't I a Woman?," bringing attention to ways in which the feminist movement served white women and didn't speak to her experience as a Black woman.

Additionally, the tropes associated with Black people inherently force them into binary gender boxes. Even in addressing Crenshaw's theory of intersectionality, we must remember that gender is more complicated than woman and man. Sojourner Truth's demand for inclusion in a narrative of gender and safety was also an acknowledgment of the failure of gender defined and limited by whiteness. This, too, complicates vulnerability, race, and gender. When Black people are already seen through the lens of failure based on standards of whiteness that are embedded as systemic ideologies, this automatically limits the access Black people have to authenticity, performance, and embodiment.

MODERATING OUR VULNERABILITY

Vulnerability is crucial in friendships, and this section unpacks the vulnerability required in sharing ourselves with friends. I write with an awareness that I don't navigate this area as well as I'd like.

My tendency is to offer up too much vulnerability and then to feel too exposed—what's been called a vulnerability hangover. Seeing others fall into their patterns of oversharing of vulnerability helps me understand mine better. For example, I remember when a friend and I went to dinner with two new acquaintances. My friend told an intimate story of childhood trauma. When she had originally told this story to me privately, there was trust and intimacy, and I could empathize. It helped us bond. I related to the innocent and vulnerable child she was, how painful the experience was, how it shaped who she is today. Sharing the story with me helped her manage the pain, knowing that I didn't blame her or see it as shameful, and that I thought she didn't deserve to be treated that way.

When she retold the story in this new context, however, it was met with an awkward silence. Our companions couldn't engage. They couldn't give her the emotional support she needed in telling that story. It's not that they were incapable of empathy, but rather that the context wasn't appropriate for this deep dive.

I watched this happen and could feel how hard it was for her to reveal herself to this degree and not meet with the empathy and support she needed. She lacked the social skills to see it was, in this setting, an overshare. She left feeling hurt and ashamed; she had revealed a tender part of herself and the tenderness wasn't supported.

Her sharing and vulnerability, rather than offering the intimacy she was after, had come across as a burden, an expectation. I realize I often make the same mistake. I want to get better about boundaries and learn the limits of vulnerable sharing. Rather than give my vulnerability lightly, I need to save it, and offer it in places where it can be honored.

"Using vulnerability is not the same as being vulnerable; it's the opposite—it's armor," writes researcher and author Brené Brown. Brown describes oversharing like my friend's as "floodlighting"—treating vulnerability as a tool to elicit validation. "When we use vulnerability to floodlight our listener, the response is disconnection," says Brown in her book *Daring Greatly: How the Courage to Be Vulnerable Transforms the Way We Live, Love, Parent, and Lead.* Closely linked, she says, is the "smash and grab," in which you "smash through people's social boundaries with intimate information, then grab whatever attention and energy you can get your hands on."[2]

I understand this in theory even if I'm not so good at navigating it. In order to determine when to share or not share, we need to reflect on our expectations and know what reaction we're looking for. If I use my vulnerability to try to reach intimacy, that's unfair to the other person. It's manipulative and usually backfires.

My need to reach out and talk about what's going on in my life can be intense. That makes me vulnerable to dumping it on people with whom I haven't developed the kind of relationship that can absorb that information. Then I feel like crap after, a vulnerability hangover.

I understood this all too well when I was on the other side of the floodlighting equation with a new acquaintance. It was our first time alone socially. It was evident she was nervous and wanted me to like her. I asked a simple question about her background, and this triggered a lengthy description of her abusive childhood. I could tell it was a well-practiced story.

Listening to it overwhelmed me. I didn't want to hear it and didn't want the responsibility of tending to her and providing the empathetic response the story called for. She was trying to fast-track us into being good friends and I wasn't ready. I felt used.

She was also disconnected from the emotion of the story as she was telling it, which felt to me as if it wasn't coming from her heart, in the moment. Vulnerability isn't just about sharing pat or rehearsed personal stories. It's about rawness. We can often sense when people aren't being authentic in the moment. It gets in the way of connection if we can't feel others' presence.

As much as I felt used by this new acquaintance, I could relate to her. I don't want to dump on others, yet I do. It's so hard for me to be alone with my loneliness. I want more intimacy. So I let loose, hoping that will cut some of the pain. I have compassion for why she may have poured out her story like that, and for the likelihood that she's hurt that I haven't followed up to spend more time with her.

It's helpful to see how icky it is to be on the receiving end of this kind of false or unwarranted sharing. Rather than achieve the intended goal of furthering intimacy, it blocked it. Seeing the imbalance in action helped me calibrate for myself what level of sharing is appropriate, and learn to check myself to consider the setting before dumping intimate information.

I wish I had magic glasses to show me only the right people, and a magic wristwatch to alert me to the right times to share, but I don't. I'm learning and getting better at it, though, recognizing that if my goal is to create intimacy, it's not the case that I must offer vulnerable information that's going to put the other person in the position of taking care of me, but rather that I need to be present in the moment, not jumping to the stories I've created about my life. It's also about fine-tuning my understandings of social cues that may help me figure out how much is enough or too much. I'm learning to be patient and to build trust first, to brave the discomfort of getting to know people. I'm also listening to my gut to realize when I am not suited to be friends with someone.

I've come to recognize that I require a lot more depth in order to feel safe and connected than most people. It's more common for people to need to build a stronger foundation of trust before reaching that depth. It's a tricky situation: what I need for safety is precisely what makes many others feel unsafe. I'm learning now to watch for different intimacy styles, and to know that I need people who are less protected, not to chase people to make them more giving. We all have different personal boundaries and comfort levels, so what feels appropriate to one person might not to another. I like to dive straight into the deep stuff while other people may take a while to warm up before sharing more personal information. Neither of these approaches is better or worse than the other, but I get in trouble when I try to mold someone into being more like me or to make them adapt to my style of intimacy in place of their own. It's about accepting people for what they are giving me, and not pushing them to be someone different and go out of their comfort zone.

Related to this, I had a troubling relationship with an old friend where I always felt that I wasn't getting enough from her, and it didn't feel safe to have told her as much about myself as I did. Our pattern was that her holding back triggered me to offer more in hopes it would build intimacy, when in fact it did the opposite. I also resented that she didn't share more details about what she was going through, and it was particularly painful when I heard about things, like her partner's illness, from other people. I didn't notice what was going on until we got too entrenched in that uncomfortable pattern and it felt really crappy. Had I given credence to these feelings earlier on, I could have stepped back and realized we weren't right for one another before it got so painful. Pay attention to gut feelings; there's a lot to learn!

I've got some other tips for other oversharers out there. I've learned it's better for me to offer my stories when they're asked for than to offer them unsolicited. I have also learned to let others set the intimacy level first and then respond reciprocally.

To figure out where my boundaries are most comfortable, I pay more attention to my feelings in the moment. If I share this, what will I need to get back in response? What's the risk that I won't get it? Do I want to risk it? If the person is uncomfortable with what I share, I've crossed that line. I continue to make mistakes, but over time I'm getting better at being able to see where that line is and what works best for me. I pay attention to the past to help me learn.

I also know that there are certain things that I'm more likely to regret sharing with people, so I can protect those particular topics, at least until significant trust is built. Before I tell a secret, I imagine what it would be like to have that secret out.

EXPRESSING VULNERABILITY WILL HURT SOMETIMES

When I came up against writer's block with this book, I asked people in my community to come to an experimental event. My words flow when

I'm on stage before an audience, so I asked them to hear me out. My vision was to let loose a stream of consciousness on the material I was struggling with at the keyboard and record the results. I would be speaking off the cuff, I warned, so please come only if you can deal with things going very wrong.

I posted the invitation and then had a meltdown. I should cancel. How could I embarrass myself like this? Reveal my inadequacy? I'm a known public speaker. A published writer. I want a reputation for saying important, transformative stuff. This is part of what makes me feel valued. But my authentic self is hardly so articulate. Particularly when not rehearsed, I spill out things that are wrong or incomplete. I stumble or take too long to get to the point.

I was writing a book about belonging and yet I was afraid I would no longer belong, panicked at the idea of showing my authentic self.

The invitation was already out in the ether, so I forced myself to go through with my plan. During the event, I bounced back and forth between feeling great at times, and inadequate at others. Was I delivering? Afterwards I had one of those intense and painful vulnerability hangovers I described previously, feeling sure that everyone now knew I wasn't the person reflected in my public persona, that I was a sham. I still haven't entirely recovered, to be honest, and quail a little when I run into people who attended. Yet here you are, reading the book I needed to get out of me, so it was obviously a worthwhile gamble.

I need to remember that connection and belonging are irreducible needs of being human. Without them, I suffer. Having them requires opening myself up. If I'm unwilling to risk vulnerability, to risk getting hurt sometimes or showing my inadequacy, I am doomed to feel unfulfilled. If the risk is necessary, so is the need to learn to deal with it. If I need to let it all out on a dais to find the words for my book, I'm going to have to learn to accept that I may not always be as articulate as I'd like.

It comes down to cultivating a sense of worthiness. If I feel unworthy, I'm more likely to protect myself, to hunker down and avoid emotional risk. Alternatively, if I accept my imperfections—remembering that I'm worthy of love and belonging no matter how messed up I am—then I feel worthy, and therefore can dare to put myself out there, to trade vulnerability for the intimacy that will sustain me. That requires self-compassion, being kind to myself and recognizing that I've messed up at times, not because I am a bad person, but I was doing the best I could, trying to survive with the tools I had. It also requires that I recognize that I'm imperfect—and that that's okay.

I have to be willing to let go of not being who I think I'm supposed to be and just accept who I actually am. What makes me vulnerable is what makes me beautiful.

EXPRESSING VULNERABILITY
IS A PRIVILEGE

Conventional social attitudes cast vulnerability as weakness. Prominent thought leaders like Brené Brown have challenged that, instead viewing vulnerability as desirable and encouraging us to take off our armor and express who we are. Please know that it is vital to approach this kind of undertaking with nuance. Vulnerability is more safely accessible for privileged people whose traits are valued by our society. For those with marginalized identities, showing ourselves may not always be safe. If I had declared myself trans as a kid in suburban New Jersey, I would have risked social exclusion and bullying at the very least. Some trans kids—particularly those with other marginalized identities—risk far worse violence when their identities are known or suspected.

As another example, coming out as undocumented is an incredibly vulnerable act, and one that can end with functional incarceration (detention), deportation, and possibly physical violence or death. Or for Native people, the vulnerability of sharing their culture and resources led to genocide, as discussed earlier—this history has been wired into their bodies through historical trauma. It's no wonder that some descendants of Indigenous settlers self-protect.

Marginalized people need to learn skills for managing stigma and determining how to self-reveal so we can be seen while maintaining the degree of safety we need. (As we will discuss later on, some helpful skills for stigma management include reminding yourself that the problem is in the culture, not you, and finding community.) One way this self-protection can manifest is in the tendency to stay within a known community of people with similar experiences, which makes it more challenging for all of us to get to know people who don't share our identities.

WORK THE STEPS

How do we offer up our vulnerability? When is it valuable to armor up?

The first thing to remember is that fear of vulnerability is universal. It's just our human nervous system registering a natural protective reaction. We are not alone. Everyone has been wounded and feels a need to self-protect. If we allow our fears to rule us and keep ourselves hidden, however, we never have the opportunity to see that we can be loved.

Our defenses, while they make sense at some stages, become a habit and then aren't so useful. We have to keep reexamining them. Yes, we instinctively want to protect ourselves, but then we begin to see that being "defended"— building an emotional moat and walling ourselves up inside—also isn't safe. It's a "false refuge," as described by psychologist, author, and meditation instructor Tara Brach.[3] The moat gives us a temporary sense of safety but also keeps us from connection, which we need to feel fulfilled. By blocking out vulnerability, we also block out joy and happiness.

The key is to meet our vulnerability with kindness and compassion. We notice what is hard for us, we let it be there, and we offer kindness. Our inner experience exists, whether we like it or not, so we make room for it, with kindness and gentleness.

Start recognizing your habitual ways of moving away from vulnerability. Do you fall into depression? Blame? Anger? What are you accustomed to doing to get approval? What are the personas you put on, the ways you strive to be seen in the world?

As I mentioned earlier, I like to be seen as smart, and that puts pressure on me to perform. I feel the need to practice what I'm going to say so I always sound articulate. I do that because I don't want to embarrass myself and not look good. I'm afraid of other people seeing that I'm flawed and inadequate. That's my conditioning. The way around this is to make friends with my vulnerability, seeing it as the stuff that makes me human and connects me with others. Hiding what I perceive as my inadequacies is what will separate me from others and make me unrelatable. The tendency to want to hide it, on the other hand, is universal for humans and can bond me with others.

The more wounding we have, the stronger the armor. That armor helped us survive in the past. (For me, being "smart" bought parental approval.) When I bring gentleness and kindness to my wounding, I can soothe it. Hiding it, on the other hand, gives me no opportunity to be free.

We need to feel that others accept us and love us; indeed, to the extent that we don't, our survival is threatened. The more we feel we deviate from the standards of our culture, the more challenging this can be, so we need to make space for that. We live with this undercurrent in us that something's wrong with us, paired with the fear it will be discovered. If we accept our perceived "wrongness" and give ourselves love and compassion, then we no longer need to fear being "found out."

THE WORLD NEEDS YOU

Your genius is in your uniqueness. The injustice resides in the American Dream, which tells us that anyone can make it to the top, given enough determination, savvy, and grit, when in reality, we aren't all starting from the same place, the same "bottom," on our way up. Some of us have been pushed to the basement and have boulders placed in our way, so our inability to get ahead is translated as personal failure when it's really the fault of context. When we buy into that myth, we blame ourselves when we can't live our dreams. We feel shame and lock up those parts of ourselves that are denied value and respect in an effort to be less vulnerable.

But it's those very traits that are needed—your unique experience and culture, the stuff that makes you *you*.

I want you to know, you are the gift the world needs. You may not always—or ever—feel that's true. But try it on, because if you don't offer yourself up, we all lose out. We need what you have to contribute. That feeling of not-enoughness? That's not your failing. That's human! Feeling vulnerable, imperfect, and afraid is human. Naming it allows others to connect with you. We share our imperfectness. One of the most beautiful things we can offer to others is to hold space for these struggles that we all go through.

BRINGING IT HOME

Vulnerability is about allowing people to see us, as we are, in all our human messiness. It's the key to connection. We all deserve to know that our lives have value, that what we have to offer the world is useful, and that the people around us value and appreciate us beyond our surface. When we protect ourselves and don't show our vulnerability, we cut ourselves off from love, intimacy, and connection. They come to us through the same door.

While it is the key to connection, communion, and community, vulnerability heals only when there's a certain degree of safety. Some people may abuse it. We will get hurt sometimes. Relationship pain is an unavoidable aspect of being human. But when we can see this for what it is—perhaps the sign of a mismatch between two people—we can use our pain as a learning opportunity to help us make better choices in the future. The fear of rejection supports us in identifying the people who can best respect and appreciate us.

Providing safe space for someone else to be vulnerable is a tremendous gift to bestow, a gift from which the giver benefits greatly. It is a life-affirming experience to have someone offer you their vulnerability, to know that you have done enough for them to trust you with something so intimate. We should all be able to experience this.

When trust is building and vulnerability is being met and returned with a mutual gift of revelation and intimacy, that is where transformation, healing, and connection emerge. When the space between us is curious, brave, and safe, a new world is born. The key to healing—for ourselves and the world!—is the willingness to be (wisely, carefully) vulnerable and to connect with each other and create ways to make it safe for people to enter into that experience with us.

Embracing your own vulnerability is hard, but not nearly as hard as giving up on connection and belonging. Choose vulnerability—but choose it wisely. It is important to protect yourself without closing yourself off. Learning to navigate vulnerability carefully is paramount because vulnerability is the seed of connection. As you'll learn in the next chapter, connection can bolster us when we come up against hard times and oppression; it is the precursor and process by which we create a much better world.

Chapter 8

CONNECTION IS THE ANTIDOTE

My mom died young, in her sixties, in a car accident. Three months later, my father died as well, from internal bleeding related to his cardiovascular disease. Given the low severity of his disease, it seemed well before his time. But my siblings and I understood the real cause of death. My dad died of a broken heart. He just couldn't live without my mom. I don't think dying from a broken heart is just a metaphor. Without my mom, my father lost his primary source of belonging and connection.

Connection is that beautiful feeling I get when I see someone else, value them, and feel seen and valued by them.

We all want connection. We need it.

Social disconnection is bad for health and well-being. You didn't need me to tell you that, did you? Of course it is. It is well established that people with fewer and weaker social relationships die earlier on average than those who are more strongly connected.[1] Research findings indicate that the influence of social relationships on the risk of death is comparable with smoking and exceeds the influence of physical inactivity. Research indicates, too, that we feel less pain when we are with those we love, and that our feelings of self-worth are more dependent on our social connections than our financial status.

THE BIOLOGY OF DISCONNECTION

As discussed previously, our brains often respond to the world automatically and without our awareness. Sacrificing logic for speed helps us cut through the complexities and the immensity of information inundating us on a daily basis. We saw examples of how this attempt at efficiency can lead us astray, resulting in the faulty conclusions that can arise from negativity bias and confirmation bias.

There are many other biases that can distort our thinking, also arising from this adaptive purpose of allowing us to reach decisions quickly. Consider the so-called halo effect, which refers to the idea that our overall impression of a person influences how we feel and think about their character. This especially applies to physical attractiveness. Researchers have found that teachers perceived as attractive receive higher ratings in overall quality of teaching, clarity, and helpfulness than those perceived as less attractive.[2] Young kids perceived the teachers rated as attractive to be nicer and happier and believe they would learn the most from the attractive teachers.[3] This is yet another explanation for why people who don't fit the "mythic norm" are less likely to get or keep jobs. I know one fat university professor whose less-than-stellar reviews from her students—many of which suggested that she was a poor role model for applying the nutritional concepts she was teaching (a sign of the students' prejudice)—were cited when she was denied tenure and later fired.

Another bias, referred to as the "availability heuristic," has us placing greater value on information that comes to our mind quickly. If you can quickly think of multiple examples of something happening, you will believe what is more common. Research on television and "reality" programming suggests that Black men are more often depicted as criminals than men of other races (much higher, in fact, than actual statistics demonstrate).[4] Black suspects are also portrayed as more likely to pose threats of violence. With so much exposure to ideas like this, these images are in the forefront of our brains and we're more likely to grab onto the association and be less trusting of Black men.

Related to this, we're also programmed to put things—and other people—into categories, meaning that "othering" is biologically wired into us. Stereotypes serve a purpose because clustering people into groups with expected traits allows us to rely on information we already know about the person's group and quickly make decisions.

Since these categories, and the meanings ascribed to them, are reflections of social constructs, this shortcut comes with high costs. The beliefs about a group might not be accurate, and even if they may accurately describe some group members, they are unlikely to be true for every member. They also stop us from seeing the actual person in front of us. As members of society, we necessarily internalize the assumptions and meanings associated with these categories. Whether consciously or unconsciously, this affects our interactions and influences our decisions, such as whom to hire or whom to trust[5]—and whether our finger is quick on the gun trigger.

UNCONSCIOUS BIAS

Countless studies have confirmed the power of unconscious biases to shape everyday actions. Slap a white-sounding name on a resume and you're much more likely to get a callback than if you supply an identical resume with an African American–sounding name.[6] The same thing happens when racially dissimilar but otherwise matched pairs of trained testers apply for jobs in person.[7] It's hard to get good pain medication if you're not white—doctors have been found to recommend less pain medication for Black or Latinx patients than white patients with the same injury.[8] Even when facial expression is ambiguous, Black men are considered more hostile and threatening than white men.[9] Yet in all of these examples, the protagonists are unlikely to be conscious that their actions or thoughts are prejudicial.

I didn't think I held negative beliefs about People of Color, trans people, people with disabilities, fat people, or others in stigmatized groups. Taking the implicit association test (IAT)[10] was a mind-opener. The IAT is a measure of associative knowledge. It examines, for example, our reflexive response to seeing a Black face vs. seeing a white face by measuring how quickly test takers associate positive words with either image. Test takers are instructed to strike a certain computer key if a positive word like *wonderful* pops up on the screen, and are then told to hit the same key if a white face is shown. Next, the program asks them to press another key for positive words and Black faces. The test tracks how many errors occur and how quickly responses are made.

In every measure of bias that I examined—tests are available for age, weight, gender, religion, skin tone, race, disability, and more—I found that, like most test takers, I am biased toward people who resemble the mythic norm.

I've also guided many audiences through taking the IAT and have found that most people, like me, can "feel" their unconscious biases as they take this test. I noticed, for example, that I struggled to connect positive words with images of old people compared to my relative ease at doing so with images of young people. Check it out for yourself.

Many of the one-hundred-plus publications that have examined the IAT have found it to be a remarkably good predictor of behavior.[11] One experiment, for example, took a video of a white person who had taken the IAT talking with a Black person and looked for signs of discomfort, such as breaking eye contact or stumbling over one's words.[12] The IAT was a more accurate predictor of behavior than a person's own self-assessment of their attitudes about race.

I understand the desire to say "not me" if someone suggests you are prejudiced. Yet, bias resides inside all of us, whether we like it or not. Accepting the inevitability that you've absorbed some aspects of our toxic culture allows you to sit with your imperfection and sets the stage for cultural humility, curiosity, and openness. It's critical in this process not to blame oneself, but instead to extend acceptance and understanding toward our very human flaws and shortcomings. Accepting that you are not always who you want to be supports you in taking action and doing something about it. We may never be able to entirely avoid internalized prejudices, but we can certainly compensate for their effects.

STEREOTYPE THREAT

Stereotypes don't just influence how we perceive and interact with others; they also affect our thoughts about how others perceive us, which in turn impacts our behavior. A powerful example of this is a concept known as "stereotype threat," which describes a person's preoccupation about fulfilling a stereotype assigned to their social group. Three psychologists, Claude Steele, Joshua Aronson, and Steven Spencer, examined the effect of stereotype threat on different groups of students. Their studies in the 1990s, as well as numerous subsequent studies, demonstrated that even casual reminders that one belongs to a certain group significantly alters one's performance. For example, students who were subtly reminded that they belonged to a group that is stereotyped as academically inferior performed much worse on testing as a consequence of these reminders.[13]

Interestingly, even members of groups that are cast in positive ways suffered from similar referencing to their group's stereotype: Asian students, who were reminded of stereotypes about their excellent math skills, caved under this pressure and did poorly on testing.[14] The researchers concluded that preoccupations and worries about fulfilling a stereotype, whether positive or negative, can greatly impair one's ability to perform confidently and competently.

People in stigmatized groups aren't the only ones vulnerable to stereotype threat. White male math and engineering majors who scored high on the math portion of a standardized test, for example, did worse on a math test when told that the experiment was intended to investigate "why Asians appear to outperform other students on tests of math ability."[15] As another example, both male and female high school students did worse on a test of spatial skills when told that males are better at this type of problem-solving because of genetic differences.[16] Apparently, the girls were anxious they might confirm sexist assumptions, while the boys were anxious about living up to them (and no information was provided about non-binary individuals).

The mere threat of social exclusion gets in the way of thinking smart, as demonstrated in this interesting study: Participants were given an IQ test and then a personality inventory.[17] Some of the participants were then given false feedback from the personality inventory, told that they were "the sort of people who would end up alone in life." The participants then took another IQ test. Those who got the false feedback that they would be friendless in the future did significantly worse than on the earlier test.

A perceived threat to physical safety can also hamper thinking. In a study conducted in violence-prone neighborhoods in Chicago, for example, if a student's neighborhood had been the site of a homicide within the previous two weeks, they were much more likely to score lower on an IQ test.[18]

This research has profound implications for the way we educate our kids. We should put in place techniques to reduce stereotyping—and to help kids manage the very real harms that come from stereotypes. We can also set kids up for the lifelong practice of identifying and managing their unconscious bias. And of course, we should also ensure that the social climate at our schools is one of warmth and inclusion. There is so much more we can do to support families, communities, and the larger culture in providing opportunities for all kids to thrive.

Fortunately, even though we're predisposed to disconnection, we're also wired to connect. Let's explore that next.

THE BIOLOGY OF CONNECTION

We're born incapable of taking care of ourselves. You survived infancy because someone was motivated to take care of you, over and over again. Kids cry not just when they're hungry or sick or cold, but also when they are removed from their caregiver. Research shows that social separation actually causes pain in infants. It also shows that when an infant docs not receive consistent, attuned caretaking, the resulting stress leads to elevated levels of cortisol, contributing to a higher allostatic load in neglected children.[19]

Other studies confirm the need for social connection. A tragic example comes from the history of the treatment of children in orphanages. When infectious disease deaths climbed among the children, physicians attempted to keep the children isolated and minimize their handling by adults. Yet children kept dying at such alarming rates that for the sake of efficiency, doctors began completing their death certificates at intake. It wasn't until the children were held, rocked, and allowed to interact with one another that survival rates improved.[20]

Data on Romanian orphans from the 1980s, who languished, untended in their cribs, by the thousands, showed their development to be stunted by neglect.[21] Once adopted, developmental improvements were dramatic.

Research also demonstrates that epigenetic changes develop from cuddling a child. During one study,[22] parents of ninety-four babies were asked to keep diaries of themselves cuddling their babies beginning at five weeks after birth and log the infants' behaviors, like sleeping and crying. DNA swabs were taken four and a half years later. It was found that DNA methylation, which is an epigenetic change affecting gene expression, varied at specific sites between "high-contact" and "low-contact" children. One of these variations occurred within a gene related to the immune system and another in a gene related to the metabolic system. Consider the implications: disorders like fibromyalgia (an immune disorder) and diabetes (a metabolic disorder) and hundreds of other disorders and diseases later in life could be linked to less cuddling in infancy.

Social connection activates neurochemical processes. When you feel approval from others, even strangers, your brain releases opioids. These activate our brain's reward system by triggering release of dopamine, the neurotransmitter that regulates emotion and feelings of pleasure. When you help someone else, your body switches into tend-and-befriend mode, releasing another chemical, oxytocin. This motivates you to bond with others and to act in others' best interests. Oxytocin flows when a mother breastfeeds a child, when parents otherwise interact with their children, or when people physically touch in a caring way.

We're hardwired to connect. It's built into our biology. Social insults, viewed in brain scans, hit us the same way as a punch in the nose, lighting up the same structures and circuitry in our brain.[23] Staying socially connected is a need as critical as food and water.

When we are feeling unworthy and we protect ourselves from being seen, we are stuck in fight-or-flight or freeze mode. The primitive brain perceives separation, experiences mistrust, and then tries to control and defend, perhaps aggress. We have only weak activation of our prefrontal cortex, which is the brain area responsible for connection. We see ourselves as separate from one another.

From an evolutionary perspective, maybe we're in the midst of a paradigm shift. Our actions used to be dictated by our primitive brain, the one that initiates the fight-or-flight or freeze response, the one ruled by unconscious biases and toxic messages, the one that has been taught a fundamental unworthiness. Over the course of evolution, the human prefrontal cortex is growing and the interconnections are increasing so we have more control over the more primitive and reactive brain structures and are better able to move into the tend-and-befriend response, which fosters our need for connection and belonging. It can help us see past that separateness, feel empathy, experience our shared situation, and care and collaborate.

Consider the science. Neuroscientist Matthew Lieberman, director of UCLA's Social Cognitive Neuroscience lab, has spent decades studying how the brain responds to social interactions. Lieberman identified three neural networks in the brain that encourage social connection.[24] These networks have been mapped using functional magnetic resonance imaging (fMRI) and studied via psychological experiments. Blood flow increases in whatever part of the brain is active, and fMRI technology detects changes in blood flow, so the imaging allows us to see which parts of the brain are activated under different conditions.

The first network manages our ability to feel social pain and pleasure. When we experience social pain—a snub, teasing, rejection—the feeling is as real as hunger or other physical distress. In fact, the internal stress response to social pain is identical to that of physical pain.

This was hard for me to wrap my head around, so I dove into the research on social pain to learn more. In one enlightening experiment, researchers created an automated computer protocol that gradually excluded participants from taking part in a multiplayer game.[25] The brains of those who experienced this rejection showed increased blood flow to the anterior cingulate, which is the identical area that reacts to physical pain. So we're clear: social exclusion and discrimination literally cause pain—so much so that researchers found that Tylenol effectively reduces the anguish of social loss![26]

"Sticks and stones may break my bones, but words will never hurt me." That old childhood chant got it so wrong. I wouldn't want to repeat it to the parents of a kid who committed suicide because they were bullied. We need to take social pain more seriously. We need to recognize that social pain is hurtful, and that trauma can come from the banal, not just the extreme. We need to recognize, too, that it hurts if someone says it hurts. What hurts one person is influenced by their identity and history. It might not hurt someone else, but that doesn't mean it hurts less.

In the case of bullying, we know that when the victim receives social support, it lessens the harm.[27] When bystanders watch without intervening, on the other hand, their apparent indifference reinforces a victim's sense of alienation.[28] When we are told over and over that fat is bad, and no one stands up to counter the refrain, we come to agree that we are bad if we are fat. We need allies to step up. Had some adult showed compassion as I struggled at modeling school, my trauma might have been lessened. Instead, knowing my parents felt ashamed of me cemented my feelings of failure and inadequacy. I was too humiliated to reach out to my brother or friends, who might have been understanding and helped cushion the experience.

Research shows that suicide-related thoughts of those who have been victimized by bullying are very similar to those who are victims of chronic pain, again highlighting the link between social and physical pain.[29]

A second network, involving "mirror neurons" that are found through-out our brains, allow us to sense others' emotions and motivations, and represents the biological component of empathy. When you're having a connected conversation with someone, you are stimulating each other's mirror neuron system. You fall into a beautiful rhythmic dance, mirroring gestures and even matching heart rates.[30] You move your facial muscles to match each other's expressions, another of the many ways in which we deepen our understanding of what the other person is feeling. Studies have demonstrated that the same areas of the brain that correspond to different emotions, like happiness or shame, light up in both the speaker and the listener. This is a completely automatic response, hardwired in us to facilitate our ability to deeply connect with another's experience.

Other research indicates that our first impulse is to share, and that it takes more effort to be selfish.[31] To investigate this issue, David Rand, director of MIT's Human Cooperation Laboratory and the Applied Cooperation Team, and his colleagues performed ten studies using economic games. They found that research participants who reach their decisions more quickly are more cooperative. Furthermore, forcing them to decide quickly increases financial contributions, whereas instructing them to reflect before deciding decreases contributions.

Research also demonstrates that unfairness fires up pain centers in the brain.[32] In one experiment, strangers played an economic game while their brain responses were mapped.[33] You might expect that study subjects would experience pain when they lost money and satisfaction when they won. That proved true, but other players' behavior proved even more influential than personal gain. Reward centers were activated when fellow players treated them fairly—even if they won less money. The same brain areas are also involved when we see others experience social exclusion.[34]

Everyone wants to be liked, and receiving signs that others like us is central to our well-being.[35] Recent studies show how the brain responds to these signs. In one, researchers read letters from friends or significant others to research subjects as they lay in MRI scanners.[36] Each correspondent had written two letters: one full of affection ("I love you") and the other of facts ("You have brown hair"). Hearing the affectionate statements lit up the subjects' brain areas that recognize pleasure—the same area that reacts to eating sweets. The statements of fact had no such effect.

Think about the implications on workplaces. If positive social feedback is such a strong motivator, why don't we use it more? There's a lot of power in a kind word, which could further the connectedness of the folks in your workplace.

This is true for schools as well. Schools, which act as social institutions influencing the minds of kids, need to establish environments where all students feel that they belong. It is particularly important for this gesture of welcome and belonging to reach marginalized groups. One university began a program that targeted at-risk students with messages of welcome.[37] This simple extension of welcome had a huge impact, improving both academic performance as well as student health, demonstrated by a drop in health care visits.

Research has found that people react, at the neural level, more strongly to emotional signals from members of their own social groups than to those of "outgroup" members.[38] One study found that people were more accurate at mind-reading members of their own culture.[39] Another study found that our ability to empathize with another is also influenced by our perception of whether we belong to the same group. Researchers discovered, for example, that subjects' anterior cingulate cortex, which is the part of the brain that perceives emotions associated with pain, was more active when the subjects were of the same race.[40] If this means we are less attuned to people from other cultures, that may set the stage for misunderstanding and conflict. However, it does appear that this responsiveness is learned and that with exposure to other cultures, the brain can become more culturally attuned.[41]

The third neural network helps us to internalize cultural mores and values, enabling us to create vital connections with our social groups.[42] The technical term "harmonizing" describes the neural adjustments that cause us to be influenced by our groups' values and beliefs. The shame response is part of this; it reminds us if we are stepping beyond the boundaries of "acceptable" behaviors for our group and induces us to restrain our behaviors in order to be liked and accepted, making us more likely to conform to group norms.

In sum, we have a powerful innate ability to "feel," interpret, and respond to others' emotions and experiences. We are hardwired to attune to others, allowing us to establish deep resonance and connection.

CONNECTION IS OUR DEFAULT

Of all I've learned about the neuroscience of connection, what stands out most is that the social parts of our brain are most highly activated when other neural networks are dampened. This means that the social brain is the "default" network—that's actually the official scientific term—acting like a reflex so that we keep coming back to thinking about others' thoughts and feelings.[43]

CONNECTION AND SOCIAL CLASS

Social class, or socioeconomic status, refers to an individual's position vis-à-vis others in terms of wealth, education, and occupation. Prevailing narratives moralize social class, which fuels tremendous shame and judgment (by self and others) and gets in the way of connection.

Those raised in lower status environments have less agency and fewer opportunities to influence or make choices. They are forced to develop the resilience needed to cope with adversity. In contrast, those raised in more advantaged environments need to worry far less about making ends meet or managing persistent threats. Financial security, in particular, provides a general security that enables people to more confidently show up, expressing their individuality and personal preferences and developing and exploring their own interests. Less wealth, on the other hand, is less conducive to developing and asserting one's unique talents.

One of the strongest themes emerging from research examining social class and emotion is that lower-class individuals score more highly on measures of empathy. This plays out in how people treat others: In a series of four studies, for example, researchers found that lower-class individuals were more likely to help others than their higher-class counterparts.[44]

That lower-class people have been found to be more likely to help others suggests that greater resources may make higher-class people more selfish and therefore less likely to help others. This notion is supported by a series of studies by University of California, Berkeley psychology professor Paul Piff and colleagues,[45] who found that compared to lower-class individuals, "Higher-class people were more likely to show unethical decision-making tendencies, to take valued goods from others, to lie in a negotiation, to cheat to increase their chances of winning a prize and to endorse unethical behaviour at work."

Higher class individuals have also been shown to be less cognizant of others[46] and worse at identifying the emotions others feel.[47] Other research shows that higher-class individuals are less engaged during social interactions—for example, checking their cell phones or doodling—compared with their lower-class peers.[48]

Perhaps there is some acute advantage to membership in the "lower" class? I, for one, highly value the empathy that may be characteristic of the "lower" class! (If you are of higher socioeconomic standing or protective of others who are, you may be feeling defensive now. As a reminder, statistics help us make generalizations about groups, but they don't explain each individual's experience.)

CONNECTION AND ADDICTION

As we saw in chapter 4, we've got it all wrong when we frame addiction as a substance disorder. Instead, it can better be conceptualized as a social disorder, an inability to connect in healthy ways with other human beings. Cravings are a search for replacement sources of dopamine and other good-feeling chemical "shots" that we could, but for whatever reason aren't, getting from rewarding social ties.

Earlier, I noted that substances and behaviors trigger the release of dopamine and several other pleasure-related neurochemicals, making us feel good. Because we like to feel good, we go back for more. Nevertheless, it's not the substances or the behaviors that cause the addiction. Only a tiny percentage of people who engage in addictive substances or behaviors eventually become addicted. The rest of the people can walk away from those substances or behavior or only use them casually or recreationally.

The Rat Park scenario helps us understand what's really going on in addiction. Sure, the dopamine pleasure response plays a role. But with just a little bit of social stimulation and connection, addiction disappeared.

Even the rats who had been previously isolated and drinking the cocaine water left it alone when they were introduced to Rat Park.

Rats are routinely used in psychological experiments because they are social in ways similar to humans. Yet there's a vital social difference between humans and rats. Humans need to be able to trust and emotionally attach. Attachment theory, first conceptualized by British psychologist John Bowlby in the 1950s, is an important construct in psychology. The central concept of attachment theory proposes that when a child's needs are met by caregivers in a consistent, appropriate manner, this creates a feeling of security and safety in the child, allowing them to explore the world with confidence and ease. Children who don't experience secure attachment ("insecure attachment") are less able to trust and connect in healthy ways later in life.

Attachment theory elucidates the challenges faced by people on the margins. If we don't feel safe and secure and valued by those around us, it's very hard for us to connect with and trust others.

You've probably guessed that insecure attachment makes one more vulnerable to addiction. Insecure attachment—and the social disconnection that is associated with it—stimulates our brain's pain pathways and our stress responses, driving us to seek out other sources of dopamine, such as drugs.

The good news is that it is possible to learn to "securely attach," to rewire your brain to find pleasure in relationships and to seek human contact over substitutes. With practice, we teach our brain that the easiest way to find dopamine is to reach out to another safe human being.

That's much easier for a rat. Toss a rat into the Rat Park and they quickly assimilate. But people? It's less straightforward. We've also got to do the work of overcoming the lack of trust and the disconnection created in childhood and through a history of unbelonging. And importantly, we need to find safe people to connect with.

LOVE IS THE ANSWER

I know, it's a cliché. I'm not just getting new-agey on you. I'm talking science. Human connection can save us.

Picture this: You're walking down the street, in a good mood, and you see someone you know ahead. You wave, but instead of sending a friendly wave in return, they appear to look right through you. That sure didn't feel good. It's likely that your body responded automatically, by tensing. And if you're like me, "F you" probably popped into your mind, too. The next place my head goes is to thinking that person doesn't like me, which then riffs into "nobody likes me," and I'm lost in that old familiar shame sequence of thinking I'm unlovable.

What happened? It's likely I tapped into neural pathways that were embedded in my brain in childhood. All those times I needed mom and dad to be there for me and they were so immersed in their own lives that they couldn't respond taught me to withdraw.

To this day, I still have triggers that initiate that pathway. I'm healing, though. Even though my brain may take me there by default, the adult me has learned strategies so I'm less likely to go there, and when I do, I'm less likely to stay for as long.

What's key to soothing these triggers is the experience of feeling loved. I'm taking risks by entering relationships and letting people know when I'm feeling vulnerable and hurt and unloved. I'm letting them sit with me with the painful feelings. At times, I supplement my personal relationships with a therapist who provides an additional ear for my vulnerability. These experiences of love and acceptance help create new neural pathways in my brain and chip away at the strength of the old ones. Each new experience of love and acceptance modifies my synapses.

BRINGING IT HOME

If I were asked to predict someone's potential for happiness, I wouldn't ask about their race, gender, financial stability, or health, though these play a role. I'd want to know about their social network: about the strength of the bonds they have with their friends and family and about the degree to which they feel like they belong, both within their personal network and the larger culture.

Connection is vital to health, happiness, and well-being, and a fear of connection keeps us walled off and estranged from one another. When we recognize the systemic—and biological!—roots of our distance from others, we realize that others experience this, too. We're wired to both need and fear connection, but so are other people. We all share this, and we can bond over our shared need for connection.

We don't create connection. The connection is already there. Instead, we restore the connection that was interrupted by a culture of othering. Connection is inherently collective. We have to do it together. The more we say so, to each other, and see the same experience in others, the more we break out of self-blame. We're all experiencing woundedness—and that's where the light gets in. That's exactly how we come together. The woundedness you feel is not a flaw in you, it's your humanity. This human vulnerability—the need for belonging, for feeling valued and connected to others—and the distress we feel without it connects us to one another. Connection with others dissipates the shame of feeling that somehow you as an individual are defective.

The search for individual solutions is a trap that keeps us mired in injustice. Bonding together and supporting one another as we sit with our vulnerability and collectively resist systemic injustice creates a culture of belonging in the present as it also works to catalyze social, cultural, and institutional change.

This is what is needed from each of us, whether it is in our role as friends, health professionals, or members of a global community. It's in connection and shared struggle that beauty and tenderness lie. We have to learn it together and together create spaces for vulnerability, trust, and intimacy. This mission, and the skill-building that comes with it, is different from an interior, individualistic focus on self-love. It looks outward. Coping mechanisms like self-care and self-love are indeed important, but it's when we practice community care by organizing, supporting, and trusting each other, that we deepen the healing and paradigm-shifting.

Chapter 9

WHY SELF-HELP WON'T SAVE US

’m a sucker for a good motivational talk. I devour self-help books, have attended myriad "change your life" seminars, and subscribe to the email lists of many a personal growth guru. Many times I've fallen for the seduction of hope, the fantasy that this new practice or that radical idea will change my life, be it a diet, positive thinking, exercise, or a meditation technique.

I can't say they haven't given me my share of aha moments. But substantive lasting effect? Not so much, unless you count the lasting effect of blaming myself when the benefits of a new mindset waned or my enthusiasm for it diminished.

While it is true that my life has improved through adjustments of heart and mind, those changes resulted from more than my individual efforts alone. My individual efforts had to be supported by my environment to be effective. When I was being targeted for abuse at my job, no amount of affirmations or meditation practice could have helped me significantly if not bolstered by union action. I had the resources of a unionized workplace, with labor union staff and stewards to support me. Reinforcement like this is a great boon. If you are well resourced, you're going to do better, plain and simple, regardless of your grit or determination or other personal characteristics. Completely on our own, we may not have what it takes to get the life we want. Techniques like creating a budget and sticking to it can be helpful, but only if there's money in that budget.

This isn't to say that we should give up tugging on our own bootstraps or reaching for that next ladder rung. Rather, I'm pointing out how much easier it is to achieve when you have support networks. Our success depends more on our ability to leverage support and change our environment than it does on changing ourselves. Self-help methods that focus on the individual don't help much if they fail to account for the surrounding environment. If we discount the importance of environment, we end up blaming the individual for failing to succeed or to "be resilient." That's wrong. We need to update our definition of resilience to include its relational context. We need each other.

With the right mix of external resources, almost anyone can cope with most kinds of adversity. Those with supportive friends, savings accounts, a working spouse, and a retirement fund will be better able to roll with a layoff, for instance. Maybe they can even put resources into starting a new business, winding up in a better position than before. Unfortunately, optimistic scenarios like that make no sense for people without the same supports. If you're living paycheck to paycheck, getting laid off is a threat that could easily overwhelm your ability to manage.

Much research supports this notion of "differential impact," the theory that altering the environment changes individuals and that these changes depend in large part on the resources provided by the environment as opposed to individual motivation.[1] In the study cited in the previous chapter about the Romanian orphans, it was found that when these children were adopted by well-resourced families in Britain, years of delayed neurological and physical development were partially reversed.[2] Children who received greater opportunities for emotional attachment—with caregivers and with professionals like physical therapists and speech-language pathologists—showed greater developmental gains. An example like this challenges the notion that individual change relies on personal agency. Differences in access to resources is too often overlooked when we try to explain why people fail or succeed.

As another example, if you are relatively advantaged and your mom dies, you likely have a certain reservoir of resilience to draw on and a set of social circumstances that afford you some advantages. Maybe your employer will give you time off to take care of yourself. Perhaps you have money to cover burial costs and pay for supportive therapy. If you are less advantaged and your mom dies, the negative health impact instead may be magnified: perhaps funeral costs stress your already strained budget; perhaps she provided the free child care you depend on; maybe your already weakened immune system now finally gives out, making you more physically vulnerable to getting colds; or maybe the stress of dealing with grief on top of other problems exacerbates your diabetes.

"Unleash the power within," declares self-help guru Tony Robbins, promising that you can "break through any limit and create the quality of life you desire."[3] Yeah, right. Tell that to a trans kid of color whose parents just kicked him out of the house with only the clothes on his back and open wounds from his last beating. Those slogans just serve to make people feel terrible when they somehow can't "transform" their own lives. A positive attitude and a meditation practice are great, but don't be surprised if they aren't enough to save that kid. Nothing like that can (alone) bail them out so long as they're denied the safety and support we all need to survive and thrive. They'd be much better served if a guardian angel provided a loving home and supported their education.

Don't be suckered by stories of people who succeeded despite tremendous odds. Sure, they probably do have some remarkable qualities, like perseverance, intelligence, and grit. Consider Oprah Winfrey, a Black woman born into poverty and raised by a single teenage mom. The odds of her breaking out of poverty—let alone reaching the pinnacle of fame and material success—were certainly stacked against her. But Oprah didn't break free of poverty alone. She had the support of a loving grandmother and a church community. She found encouragement from teachers who believed in her. She received a full scholarship to attend college. Her admirable qualities allowed her to leverage these resources; she didn't do it alone.

Bettering our lives is a community endeavor, supported by individual effort.

My friend's doctor advised her to exercise as a means of treating her heart disease. Well, duh. She didn't need "expert" admonishment to know that exercise is valuable. She even had a treadmill in her house but was too stressed out from working two jobs and taking care of her kids to ever nail down an exercise routine. It was only after receiving a small inheritance from her uncle that she finally managed to start exercising regularly.

Am I suggesting that if you are overextended you should give up on exercise? Or pin your hopes on a surprise bequest? No! I am suggesting that you consider the conditions of your life first. Even if that seems pessimistic at first, it will help you conceptualize how and if that exercise routine is manageable. Your realism and understanding of your own situation may help you get it started, especially if it means you can avoid useless guilt for (understandably) not making exercise your top current priority.

RETHINKING DISADVANTAGE

I mentioned that Oprah was raised by a single teenage mom. What do the words *single teenage mom* conjure for you? On its own, the phrase is a setup that signals disadvantage. But if you toss aside our heteronormative "family values" bias, it's not hard to see that the risks for children raised by single teenage moms may have less to do with their parent's gender or relationship status or age than with financial instability, sexism, racism, ageism, and lack of social supports. Plenty of single mothers have the support they need to raise healthy, happy kids—even doing it better than many dual-parent families. Consider the many cultures where households consisting of multiple generations and extended family are the norm, providing a kind of small village to raise the kids. Remember to keep coming back to exploring systemic roots rather than making assumptions about individuals based on group status.

"LIFESTYLE" APPROACHES TO HEALTH IMPROVEMENT ARE INADEQUATE

If we pin everything on personal behavior change, whatever our concern—sickness, addiction, exhaustion—it's reasonable to think we're the problem. We imagine that what's at work is not systemic injustice but individual maladaptation, requiring an individual response. The message is that it's not society that's sick or "crazy" or messed up; it's you. There's a term for that: gaslighting. Stress has been pathologized and privatized, and individuals are assigned the burden for managing it.

Even the most personal stress takes place within a social context. If we don't address collective suffering and the systemic change that might alleviate it, wonderful techniques, like mindfulness as an example, lose their revolutionary potential and instead cause harm. The danger in a personal responsibility approach is not only personal, it also prevents us from considering a broader, more collective reaction to the crisis of inequity.

The "wellness" movement can feel like a religious cult. This may be easier to understand when you consider Karl Marx's description of religion as the "opiate of the masses." Though often misinterpreted, Marx was expressing collective responses to pain. Opium, at the time he was writing, was known not just as an addictive drug but as a painkiller, something that helps people tolerate unbearable conditions. Today's self-help movement is our modern-day opiate of the masses, helping us tolerate difficult lives without challenging the conditions that create it.

Our lives are difficult because of injustice and hard circumstances, not our inadequacy as individuals to be resilient. Anything that helps us cope with the conditions that cause our problems but doesn't engage with the root cause may only make things worse.

Resilience is conventionally defined as the ability to bounce back from difficult circumstances, but that definition falls short. Resilience also requires having the resources to support bouncing back. If resilience gets defined as an individual trait, individuals will get blamed for their inability to recover from adversity. Every challenge you experience personally, others have experienced too, another reason why resilience is not merely personal but relational, and why connection with others is essential to resiliency.

Consider, for example, how we interpret some of the maladies that trip us up. Did you ever have an asthma attack so severe you had to miss work? When resilience is considered an individual attribute, an inhaler may be prescribed. Yes, that may be helpful and allow you to get to work the next day, but it's even more helpful to also talk to your neighbor. When you learn that most residents in your apartment complex suffer from asthma, you may be able to organize a collective response that, say, drives your landlord to clean up the damp, dusty, moldy conditions so you (and your neighbors) no longer need inhalers.

Viewing resilience as an individual endeavor may have helped manage the disease, in other words (an opiate for the masses), but viewing it as political, we simultaneously address systemic and personal change for a more lasting solution.

"LIFESTYLE" APPROACHES TO HEALTH IMPROVEMENT RELY ON PRIVILEGE

I used to be a big believer in promoting the idea that good health is achieved by taking personal responsibility for habits like eating well and exercising regularly. That's much of the premise of my first book, *Health at Every Size*, often said to be the "bible" of the movement it's named for.

I appreciate that the book has been transformative for many. I'm proud to hear ongoing stories from readers who tell me the book saved their life or invigorated their professional practice, inspiring a much more rewarding path. Yet now I can also see the limits of the personal responsibility argument, how it leads readers astray, and how it reflected my unexamined privilege.

Valuable as it may be, it's also important to acknowledge that the ability to make personal behavior changes is a class privilege. By not naming this in my first book, I entrenched the problem. When not properly contextualized, a self-help book like the one I wrote takes responsibility off our culture's shoulders. The shame I carry now is that this individualized response to health and eating, which I promoted in my first book, is still strongly embedded in many people's conception of the Health at Every Size® movement. The ethos in my second book, *Body Respect*, coauthored with Lucy Aphramor, is different. It grounds the Health at Every Size concept in a social justice/systems-oriented frame. These newer ideas are supported and actively endorsed by the Association of Size Diversity and Health (ASDAH), the organization that has trademarked the HAES name, yet this approach does not have full traction in the HAES movement. I urge people who advocate for HAES to adopt this more updated understanding and to recognize the interplay between the personal and the political as we conceptualize healing. This requires a radical revisioning of health care and recognizing that it is not possible to define a health practice divorced of social context.

As Lucy Aphramor and I discuss in *Body Respect*, a focus on behavior change deflects attention from the more pernicious problem of systemic injustice, obscuring the reality that lifestyle factors account for less than a quarter of health outcomes. It puts the burden on the individual to assume personal responsibility for discomfort around food and weight and disease and adds a new stressor on one's health, because it lets people be blamed for not doing more to manage or improve their health issues.

Maintaining the primacy of individual lifestyle change is also problematic because it diverts efforts from the more important systems-level issues which might be addressed through collective action. Additionally, it gives the false impression that lifestyle components, like eating and activity habits, are in fact individual "choices," while ignoring the influence of social context and how it constrains or supports certain behaviors. Well-intended strategies like advising people to eat "a rainbow of foods" and prepare home-cooked meals are easier to follow if you have greater resources, like access to nearby grocery stores, money to spend in them, and time to cook up what you buy while it's still fresh.

It is well established, too, that lifestyle-oriented changes yield greater health improvement for people with greater privilege in their lives. Paradoxically, some of the "downstream" methods of tackling inequalities in health can widen the very inequity gap they target.

To be clear, behavior change is valuable, but it can't remove the stressors you face. No matter how you change your eating or activity habits, the factors that make up your lifeworld—challenges like stigma, job insecurity, poverty, and caregiver responsibilities—will remain unchanged. Naming inequity and systemically working toward a fairer world is important not just on a systemic level. On an individual level, naming and acknowledging the social roots of health inequities can help a person lighten up on the self-blame, realistically consider their life circumstances, and come up with solutions that best allow them to engage in self-care.

While health-promoting behaviors make sense for everyone, for individuals with hard lives, building a fairer society and helping them manage the challenges of poor treatment will matter far more to health outcomes than whether they eat their veggies. Focusing on systemic roots over individual-level paradigms helps not only marginalized people, but everyone, though the relative impact might be stronger for those who face more barriers.

THE SYSTEMIC APPROACH IN PRACTICE

If you'd asked me to write a chapter about behavioral practices for good health a couple of decades ago, I would have led with nutrition and exercise. It's the common expectation—and believing in it is probably why I made it my expertise. When obtaining my PhD in physiology, I specialized in nutrition, and I also have a master's degree in exercise science, in addition to a master's degree in psychotherapy. I even taught college courses in nutrition for fifteen years. But that's not how I'd do it today.

Examining our medical and social institutions' default focus on nutrition and exercise, and my own past orientation, provides a good way to understand both what's wrong with the old way of thinking about behavior change and how a systems-focused approach improves on the outdated models.

MYTH-BUSTING NUTRITION

First, nutrition. I've got a five-hundred-plus-page unpublished manuscript that I used as a textbook for students in my college nutrition courses languishing in my computer. It represents more than a decade of work. Yet it's still unpublished, because I no longer think it's right. I no longer believe in an emphasis on carbohydrates, protein, fat, vitamins, and minerals as the way to help people lead healthier, happier, more fulfilled lives. More rules and hang-ups about what to eat are precisely what we *don't* need. For one thing (and maybe you'll need to read this twice, it's so counterintuitive), data show that people who care less about nutrition quality tend to eat more nutritiously than people who focus on diet.[4] More than that, public health research into what affects our health finds that eating and exercise, combined, represent only about 10 percent of the overall impact of "modifiable determinants" (things we can change, as opposed to genetics).[5] It's also well established that health risks from the effects of stigma are far worse and make a much bigger difference than even the "unhealthiest" dietary habits.[6]

But, more important, I gave up this way of thinking because I've come to understand that most nutrition research conclusions are wrong. Hear me out. This topic has been well considered by many scientists who are busting the paradigm. Physician-scientist John Ioannidis's report "Why Most Published Research Findings Are False" is the most cited paper in *PLOS Medicine*. As he aptly puts it, "claimed research findings may often be simply accurate measures of the prevailing bias."[7] In an opinion piece published in the *Journal of the American Medical Association*, Dr. Ioannidis bluntly states that nutrition epidemiology is in need of "radical reform."[8] To perfectly capture the absurdity of the field, he writes about what would happen if you subscribe to popular conceptions about what's good and bad for you:

Eating 12 hazelnuts daily (1 oz) would prolong life by 12 years (i.e., 1 year per hazelnut), drinking 3 cups of coffee daily would achieve a similar gain of 12 extra years, and eating a single mandarin orange daily (80 g) would add 5 years of life. Conversely, consuming 1 egg daily would reduce life expectancy by 6 years, and eating 2 slices of bacon (30 g) daily would shorten life by a decade, an effect worse than smoking. Could these results possibly be true?

The answer to his rhetorical question is obviously no.

Ioannidis and his team—and others—have shown, again and again, and in many different ways, that much of what biomedical researchers conclude in published studies—conclusions that are used when we are advised to consume more antioxidants or less meat—is misleading, exaggerated, and often flat-out wrong. His work has been widely accepted by the medical community and published in the field's top journals.

Ioannidis blames two major factors for this dissonance: confounding and selective reporting. Confounding describes the misconception that A causes B when, in reality, some other factor, X, actually causes B. For instance, eating sausage may be associated with a shorter lifespan. So eating sausage makes you die young. Oops! Confounding! Maybe sausage eaters die early because the same people who eat sausage are also lower in socioeconomic status. Lower socioeconomic status is the confounding factor and actually drives the shorter lifespans of sausage eaters. Confounding comes up all the time in weight and weight-loss research, a topic I have explored in depth in my previous books. It is true that many diseases are more commonly found in heavier people, for example. But you'd be wrong to conclude from that that high weight causes disease.

If yellow teeth are common among people with lung cancer, do yellow teeth cause cancer? Of course not. Epidemiological studies show us relationships, but not causality. Studies show an association between high weight and cardiovascular disease, for instance, but not the fact that heavier people experience a stress response resulting from weight stigma and that stress is a major factor in cardiovascular disease. And common sense tells us that yellow teeth, like lung cancer, can result from smoking. Smoking—like stress—is the confounder.

Much confounding is residual, meaning we can't know if confounding is present unless we measure confounders. That doesn't often happen. For example, if we don't measure weight stigma, we'll never know about its possible role in anything associated with fat. As there is compelling evidence that weight stigma causes much of the disease we blame on fat, this huge oversight means that our prescriptions are causing the very problem they aim to solve.[9] To complicate matters, some confounders may not even be measurable, such as how a person's lifestyle might change over time, their genetic and epigenetic background, or the interactions of foods in their diet.

Ioannidis's second culprit, selective reporting, means that you're likely to read a lot of confounding studies. Studies that confirm certain established (or profitable!) points of view, he shows, are more likely to reach print and pixels. So, because people tend to believe the nutrition-causation link, a report showing a link between sausage and early death is more likely to be published than one that doesn't show that link. Research and conclusions that can be exploited by private industry are also more likely to be funded—and published—than research questioning those results. The food industry wields enormous influence over what questions even get asked, in addition to who asks them or how they are answered.

Speaking from my experience working in the field of weight science, academic careers depend on adhering to the status quo because research follows the money. Very little funding for "obesity" studies does *not* come from corporations who have a vested interest in the results. Even government funds are doled out by grant review committees composed of researchers with ties to private industry. In fact, I don't know of a single "obesity" researcher involved in government grant review committees, government policy panels, or major "obesity" research organizations who does *not* have some financial tie to a pharmaceutical or weight-loss company.

Distinctions have blurred among private industry, science, government, and medicine, and the line between promoting health and making a profit has grown less firm than you might imagine. Much of what is believed to be true about nutrition reflects the values of the food, diet, and wellness industries more than scientific fact. It's akin to letting the coal industry teach us about climate change.

Have you bought into the nutrition myths? Most of us have. It would be hard to exist in this culture without absorbing some of its mythology. Hint: if you've ever jumped on the bandwagon for a Paleo, gluten-free, low-carb, low-fat, low-salt, high-protein, or alkaline diet; or stocked up on a "superfood"; or avoided dairy or sugar, this includes you. Sure, some dietary restrictions make sense for individuals with specific diseases—forgoing gluten if you have celiac disease, for instance, or dairy if you're lactose intolerant—but no well-supported evidence proves that such "eliminations" can help any outside those minorities of sufferers.[10]

I write this knowing it will inflame some readers who are invested in their food hang-ups. Engaging in critical thought about our own buy-in to mythology can feel threatening. It is particularly insidious because our allegiance to those myths links so closely to our sense of self. When a nutrient or food is portrayed as offering an opportunity for long life, or to allow us to be seen as attractive and smart, or to get more done in the day, it plays on our insecurities. Adhering to nutrition beliefs can give us a sense of belonging and even a feeling of moral superiority—that we "know" what's best. Like religion. Also like religion, nutrition myths tend to tie us to myths of paradise past; indeed, the idea that we need to return to the diets of our ancestors seems to have a particular hold on people. It feeds off a sense that modernity is dangerous and unnatural, causing us ills from which only a get-back-to-nature diet can save us.

Our food fears get bolstered and legitimized by the claims of so-called lifestyle diets. Keto, Paleo, and gluten-free diets, for example, provide socially acceptable avenues for food fears and restrictions, veiled in health tones, which provide cover for the emerging diagnosis of orthorexia.* Avoiding sugar is seen as morally superior and wholesome, rather than recognized as a symptom of disordered or restrictive eating.

---

* Orthorexia refers to a disorder that includes symptoms of obsessive behavior in pursuit of a healthy diet. It is not currently an official diagnosis formally recognized in the *Diagnostic and Statistical Manual of Mental Disorder (DSM-5)*.

Experience shows me that asking people to challenge their belief system about particular foods or diets is akin to asking them to change their religion. It threatens their identity and a history of time, energy, and money invested in something that may not have been in their best interest. Their belief system not only nurtures their internal beliefs (if in a perverse way), it may buy them social currency or gain them acceptance and respect in their profession.

Assumptions about food and bodies are so deeply rooted and culturally supported that we may not even recognize them as ideas—opinions, really—to be analyzed and challenged. The difficulty some people may have in moving to an understanding that dieting, for example, is more likely to result in weight gain than weight loss, and that the pursuit of weight loss is damaging, not health promoting,* may be so overwhelming as to set up vehement—and sometimes unconscious—resistance. Particularly as this is tied to the fantasy of a better life, it may feel as if I'm taking someone's hope away.

Nutrition's role in good health is wildly exaggerated and misunderstood. Even in diseases where food choices play a more explicit role in management—as in celiac disease, lactose intolerance, or heartburn—a focus on putting what you know about how foods affect your disease into the context of your life is key to being able to implement any dietary changes. I'm not suggesting people ignore nutrition entirely—just that we put it into perspective. You need a critical mind to do that.

We build our lives and identities around powerful myths. We're fed fantasies that eating a certain way leads to easy weight loss, guaranteed health, or simple self-cures. It's easy to get suckered in. But I assure you, there is no magic in eating in a particular way.† The real secret to eating well depends on dumping food rules and mythical thinking.

---

* My previous books get you up to speed on these.

† I want to be clear: For people with certain disorders or diseases, dietary manipulation may be a medical necessity. But the benefits received by a person who has celiac disease when they avoid gluten aren't magical.

EATING THROUGH A SYSTEMS-INFORMED LENS

Consider this anecdote: A woman believes that she is too fat and wants to lose weight. By cutting back on her calories in recurrent bouts of restrictive eating (dieting), she's temporarily successful, losing a few pounds a few times. As a result of so-called "successful" dieting, she also finds herself uncontrollably binge-eating at times—something she'd never struggled with before. A "behavior change" (also known as "lifestyle change") approach would have the woman attempt to change her habits around food, by following a dietitian-prescribed diet, for instance, or trying to eat more intuitively.

A systems approach would have the woman take a step back and look at the systemic roots. While food habit change may be a part of the "solution," it leaves unchanged those social contexts that affect how she feels in her body and why she wants to lose weight. Looking to systems, we might work with the woman to explore how social determinants have a personal impact—for example, having the woman unpack the sexist advertisements that surround us and how she feels when she consumes this media. The idea is not that knowing that painful embodied experiences are rooted in systemic issues will somehow make a person immune to feeling the effects of these systems. Rather, it is acknowledging that these systems persist and that her body dissatisfaction and efforts to change take place within an unsupportive environment. By addressing the roots of why food is so conflicted for them, people are then empowered to make the individual changes that may be most helpful.

My first book encouraged "intuitive eating," an approach created and popularized by dietitians Evelyn Tribole and Elyse Resch in their 1995 book of that title.[11] Their model was subsequently validated by the research of Tracy Tylka and colleagues and continues to evolve.[12] As Tribole describes it, "Intuitive eating is a personal process of honoring health by listening and responding to the direct messages of the body in order to meet your physical and psychological needs."[13] I'm still on board with this concept. Applied in the right context, a transition from dieting to intuitive eating has been life-saving to many.

When context isn't considered, however, there are undeniably classist undertones to promoting intuitive eating. For those in privileged social positions, choosing foods and amounts that intuitively appeal might be a possible approach to eating, but for others, systemic conditions may not permit just following their bodies' cues. Consider a single mother who works full-time while also attending school. She struggles to find enough time and money to feed her kids, so eating necessarily takes on a pragmatic and functional role. She cannot simply decide to eat what she would most prefer at any given time. She may have to go beyond a comfortable level of fullness when food is available—for instance, if she has a free meal available at her restaurant job that she is not allowed to pack up and take home. Stopping at Burger King for Double Whoppers on the ride between school and daycare may be the most affordable and expedient choice for feeding the kids. Advising this woman to eat what she truly wants and stop when she is full is likely to only exacerbate the stress she may already feel by making her feel she is doing health "wrong." Her current strategies meet her conditions for time, money, convenience, and all the other values helpful in a decision of what's really going to be the most nourishing self-care.

Of course, spaces of belonging like class do not operate in isolation, either. Taking a systems approach also means considering how people relate to their bodies and their choices around food in relation to cultural stereotypes and tropes. Returning to our example, we might also consider how racism and sexism impact this woman's food choices (she is Latinx). She may face issues like unequal pay, further constraining her financially. Damaging ethnic tropes such as the stereotype that Latina women are pigeonholed as hypersexual may also lead to problematic beliefs about her body or her single mother status. These stereotypes may interact with each other and with classist assumptions to generate significant stress, which in turn may impact the way she experiences her body and makes choices around food.

Besides sexism, classism, and racism, a blanket prescription to listen to your body may fail in other ways. For example, it assumes that body signals are working appropriately, which may not be true for people with a history of trauma. A strong impulse toward body harm is not uncommon for trauma survivors and others. Body wisdom is not always to be trusted for other reasons as well. Remember our earlier discussion of how unconscious bias wires into us? We're predisposed to think in stereotypes and culturally accepted values. You've absorbed messages from diet culture that influence your food and eating preferences but may not be in your best interest.

Returning again to our example, I want to remind you, too, of the need to challenge conventional ideas about coping behaviors. Rather than being a sign of failure of will or character or a response to unmet emotional needs, for example, bingeing is often the body's attempt to restore health. The drive for calories that is at the root of a binge is likely a direct result of restrictive eating. In other words, the diet is the problem, and the binge the body's attempt at a solution. Help comes when we address the root problem—the diet. In this vein, we can show appreciation for the binge as a temporary solution when we don't have other skills—and focus on a more long-range solution to the problem of dieting consistent with ideas expressed in chapters 4 and 10.

Intuitive eating can be a tool to help people cope no matter what circumstances they're in, but it must be approached in a nuanced, trauma-informed, and social-justice-informed way. When we don't consider people's individual stories, we reinforce dominant narratives and cater to more privileged people by default.

Instead of first prescribing behaviors, we can help people examine the conditions of their lives that support and inhibit self-care. We can help them take stock of both challenges and resources in their lives to support them in moving away from self-blame and finding their power. Addressing the social determinants of health gives people the skills and control over their lives to improve self-care. Only then can practical discussions follow of appropriate, manageable, and compassionate self-care, whether it's being more thoughtful about hunger cues, stocking up on frozen veggies, or shoring up defenses to manage stigma and injustice. That helps us get at the crux of the matter.

Centralizing social justice means that you start from the perspective that our individual stories matter, looking at how we live our lives in relation to others and to power structures that open or constrain our options.* Without deliberately choosing this perspective, there is a tendency to default to the dominant narrative that renders invisible the struggles facing marginalized groups and how these barriers limit everyone's ability to be authentically and fully seen, to become aware of a fuller range of potential solutions, and to define what self-care means for them. Only after we have explored people's life circumstances can we consider what appropriate self-care looks like. Eating apples makes sense in some circumstances, while choosing French fries is far more valuable and health-promoting in others.

EXERCISE THROUGH A SYSTEMS-INFORMED LENS

To understand how a systems-informed lens can improve health behaviors, consider a different approach to self-care, one that's embedded in a social context. I'll use exercise as an example.

Few people would argue with the suggestion that exercise enhances health and well-being. Yet, this awareness rarely seems effective at motivating or sustaining active lifestyles. Nor does shaming people about their weight. Even if exercise helped people lose weight—and research shows it doesn't—the promise of weight loss hasn't proven to help people sustain a regular exercise habit.

On the other hand, a "systems approach" to increased exercise proves much more valuable. To see what that might look like, try the reflection exercise that follows. You can do it as a solo writing exercise, but it's best if you do this with a partner or a group so you'll be exposed to valuable ideas that you may not have thought of on your own.

---

* Hat tip to the Black Lives Matter movement for bringing attention to the fact that All Lives Don't Matter until Black Lives Matter.

I'm going to ask you to think back to different times in your life. If you think using different ages than I suggest will help you capture time periods in your life that were significantly different from one another, please adjust.

To help us see this more literally, I drew a picture representing a continuum of the amount of activity you get in a day.

Moderately Active

Not at all Active   Extremely Active

As you can see, I've asked you to view the bottom left of the horseshoe as representing no participation in activities, the middle as representing moderate levels of activity, and the right end representing participating in extreme amounts of activity.

Think back to when you were nine years old. Put a mark on the horseshoe that represents how active you were, with your age (9) next to it. Consider these questions:

- How active were you and what were you doing?
- What did you like about it?
- What helped you achieve that level of activity?
- What hindered your activity?

Try to make these observations nonjudgmentally. If you are doing this exercise with a partner or group, discuss your answers. If you are doing this solo, write them.

For ages sixteen, twenty-five, and your present age, also mark the horseshoe, write your age, and answer the questions above. (If you're younger, modify accordingly.) If there's another time period that seems significant to you, explore that, too.

Now it's time to analyze your data.

First, notice whether your activity levels changed over time. If they didn't, I promise you that at some point they will. If nothing else causes a change in habits, injury or aging will.

For most people, activity levels change over time. This is an important point because it helps us understand that the conditions of our lives help establish our activity habits and attitudes. For example, my parents would send me out as a nine-year-old kid to play. That was my job. There were a lot of kids in the neighborhood, and the cul-de-sac kept us safe and confined. Several families had pools in their yards, and we had plenty of green space. I was a good athlete, and playing sports got me attention and respect. I also remember it being fun. All of these factors contributed to my being regularly active.

At sixteen, likewise, I played on several high school and intramural sports teams, continued to enjoy sports, and continued to appreciate the attention for being a good athlete.

At twenty-five, my activity level had dropped off. I was working long hours and found it hard to find the time for sports. My activity level has been inconsistent through much of my adult life, slowing when I'm injured or overextended with work, increasing during warmer weather and family vacations.

Reflect on your exercise history and consider what conditions supported you in exercising regularly and what hindered you. For me, the supportive standouts would be whether an activity is fun and social. The biggest hindrance is lack of time.

Do this in a group and you will learn a lot more from others' experiences. This exercise helps me become aware that if I want to be more active, the key for me is to try to make it social, like getting on a team or participating in classes. When I'm overextended with work, I have to get more creative about making activity be part of what I do so it doesn't require extra time—like biking to appointments, having walking meetings with my colleagues or students, and so on.

Unlike me, you may discover that your hindrances stem from your attitude toward your body. When I was a kid, if your body served as a big target in grade school dodgeball, it was like kids had license to bully you. It makes sense that experiences like this color our current attitudes.

Whatever you discover from this activity, that's where the intervention lies. Approach this from a compassionate stance and consider how to maximize your resources and work through your challenges. What challenging conditions in your life are changeable? What are the activities that can be supported by the current conditions of your life? What resources can you grab onto?

Think critically, too, about your beliefs about exercise. For example, if you sometimes get on exercise kicks to lose weight, it may be helpful to know that's a myth. "What?" you might ask. "If I believe that, I might stop working out altogether!" In fact, though, the opposite is true. This awareness is important for many reasons, not the least of which is that when people exercise only for weight loss, they often give up on exercise when it doesn't have the desired result.

Research also shows that vigorous exercise is fun for some but not everyone, and that's supported by biochemistry. People vary in to what extent we secrete hormones (like endorphins) that lead to a "runner's high" feeling, making vigorous exercise more rewarding for some of us. Secrete a lot of endorphins and it may drive a strong desire for exercise and a feeling of dissatisfaction without it, fueling an exercise habit. Others may not get as much of a pleasure reward and likely won't be as athletic as their exercise-loving counterparts.

There is no "one size fits all" activity plan. As we all have different attitudes toward our bodies and movement and respond differently to activity, we need to address the meaning of activity in a person's life, and to get creative about how we can meet the need for movement.* A "just do it" attitude is not the answer.

---

* For some folks, like people with exercise compulsions or histories of disordered eating, sometimes the most self-caring thing you can do is *not* exercise. Trust that instinct (or your health care providers, if they're recommending stopping exercise) and know that eventually you can get to a place where movement is part of your life again.

WEALTH AND EMOTIONAL RECOVERY

As we've discussed, we can't separate the personal from the structural.

Many people are poor because of structural forces, like a labor market offering insufficient jobs at good wages, mass incarceration as the means for addressing drug problems, or lower pay for women compared to men and for People of Color compared to white people. According to US census data, on average, in 2017 women were paid 80 cents to every man's dollar. [14] It's significantly worse for Women of Color: Black women earned just 61 cents and Hispanic women earned just 53 cents for every dollar white men earned. [15]

And in case you buy into the myth that education is the great equalizer, let me dispel that, too, as it doesn't shield Women of Color from the pay gap. The pay gap actually widens for women at higher education levels and is largest for Black women who have bachelor's and advanced degrees. [16] Black women in particular trail behind in terms of income no matter how closely they follow the educational guidelines. Given the barriers Black women face at every step along the way—in being admitted to college, paying for college, and managing student loans—higher education is a massive undertaking without guarantees of financial payoff.

Transgender Americans also earn significantly less, experiencing poverty at double the rate of the general population, with transgender People of Color experiencing even higher rates. [17] The National Center for Transgender Equality has found that 43 percent of Latino, 41 percent of Native American, 40 percent of multiracial, and 38 percent of Black transgender respondents lived below the federal threshold for poverty in 2015. [18]

Disabled people suffer from income inequality too; research consistently finds they are less likely to be employed than non-disabled people, and when employed they receive, on average, lower pay. [19] Including workers of all occupations, those with a disability earn 66 cents for every dollar those with no disability earn. [20]

Most inequality analysis focuses on income rather than wealth. While income inequality is stark, it pales in comparison to wealth inequality. ("Wealth" refers to total assets minus debts, so it's a different measure than income, speaking to a larger history of money.) Women own only

32 cents on the dollar compared to men.[21] For Women of Color, the gap is a far worse: median wealth for single Black women is just pennies on the dollar compared to white men and white women.

Let me help put this into perspective by examining my own financial and educational background. You may have heard the expression "born with a silver spoon in their mouth." That phrase describes the life I was born into, almost literally. For those of us with a social justice lens, it's a derogatory trope, implying a sense of entitlement rather than recognition of the unearned advantages that led to the wealth. My parents didn't see it this way. They were so proud to be able to offer me opportunity that they actually bought a silver baby spoon and engraved it with my name and birth date to commemorate my birth.

My parents were proud of what our family had accomplished. Their parents came as penniless immigrants to this country, Jews escaping the pogroms of Poland, and only a generation later, my parents were thriving in the upper middle class.

We descended from people victimized by racial genocide overseas and continued to be victimized by anti-Semitism in this country. The narrative my parents imparted to me—and believed—was that anyone who tries hard enough could overcome adversity and succeed, that we had worked hard for and deserved our wealth and advantage. While the hard work was certainly true, this narrative invisibilizes the skin-color privileges that supported our success: from hiring advantages and GI Bill coverage for education and home ownership (which was often inaccessible to People of Color), to bank loans (often refused to People of Color), redlining (the practice of differentiating areas of a city by race, often leading to the denial of necessary goods and services to People of Color), police protection (not similarly granted to People of Color), and much, much more. Others who work just as hard but have fewer advantages don't get this outcome.

A deeper dive into family history reveals even more flaws in the notion that we live in a meritocracy. Consider my grandmother's story—she went from "rags to riches," seemingly embodying the American dream. Yet the backstory shows how illusory this is.

My grandmother came to America as a preteen, fleeing the Nazi occupation of Poland prior to World War II. The Nazis had occupied her home, stealing her family's food and belongings, terrorizing them, and relegating them to the floor while the police occupied their beds. Upon immigrating to the United States, she moved in with extended family in a tiny cramped tenement apartment on the Lower East Side of New York City. She spoke no English and got the only job available to girls in her situation, working long hours under unsafe conditions in a silk factory, where she was horribly exploited. Her family members worked similarly hard. All the family's earnings went toward survival; they struggled to make it, sometimes going hungry. Later, when they had greater income, the money was invested in my grandmother's brothers' education and denied to her.

Seeing no way out, my grandmother demonstrated extraordinary ingenuity: she stole a sewing machine and fabric and built a small business in the little time she had away from her factory job. She learned English and absorbed silk trade lore by listening to conversations among her bosses at work. The business she started, later called Bacon & Graham, thrived and was passed through my father to, at present, my brother. It's grown through the past eighty years, now employing over fifty people.

I asked my grandmother to tell me about Graham, presumably her business partner. The day she answered that question was the day I became a feminist.

My grandmother told me that nobody would do business with a woman, so she invented a fictitious male business partner. When people asked to speak to Mr. Graham, she would say, "Oh, Mr. Graham's not available right now, but he's asked me to help you."

So, let's review. How did my family fortune get started? Criminal activity (stealing) helped them overcome anti-Semitism and discrimination against immigrants, later bolstered by lying to combat sexism, and greatly supported by the racism that provided opportunities to white people while discriminating against People of Color.

Did my family work hard? Absolutely. But many people do. These stories are just a small snippet of the many unearned advantages I have had that paved the way for my financial success. As another example, it was easier for me to do well in college because it was paid for, along with my living expenses, by my parents, freeing me to focus on my studies.

My parents kept that engraved silver spoon in a safe deposit box, giving it to me on the day of my bat mitzvah. For them, it was an assertion of their commitment to providing advantages to support my success. For me, it's a reminder of injustice, that I didn't earn my financial advantages, and the responsibility that comes with that.

Incidentally, spoons are also an important metaphor in the disability community, yet with a very different meaning.[22] For people with disabilities, spoons represent the emotional resources a person has to draw from. Everything one needs to do throughout the day requires emotional resources, represented by a certain number of spoons. The spoons are replaced only when one rests and replenishes. If you run out of spoons, you are depleted and have nothing more to give to your day.

This metaphor conveys that for some, particularly people with disabilities, energy must be rationed, and it calls attention to what it takes for them to manage and accomplish tasks. Able-bodied people are less likely to consider energy expended on ordinary tasks like showering or getting dressed. Spoon theory explains the difference between those who don't seem to have energy limits and those who do.

It is not without irony that I note the contrast between the spoon metaphor in the two cultures. In my parents' culture the spoon is about unexamined privilege, signifying a celebration of wealth, a belief that it is deserved, and speaks to flagrant spending. People with disabilities don't have the luxury of not seeing their disadvantage; they need to remain aware that they have limited resources for survival so they can ration and conserve.

Something is wrong here. This is why our financial resources, health outcomes, personal care behaviors, and more need to be understood in a social context. Chalking health up to individual responsibility clearly misses the mark.

PRIVILEGE AND RESPONSIBILITY

The struggle to survive in an unjust society requires one to find wellness mechanisms to maintain a commitment to self, healing, nurturance, and community. It is the duty of all of us, but especially those with power and privilege, to dismantle the systems that harm us.

Having the tools to develop the intention and praxis of liberation requires doing the work on ourselves *and* actively dismantling systems we benefit from. Hunter Ashleigh Shackelford, a non-binary Black fat cultural producer, multidisciplinary artist, and community activist, shared with me some tangible ways in which non-Black people, especially white people, can show up and work to undo some of the damage that underlies our collective trauma and prevent it from going forward:

- **Make reparations**. We must be committed to giving property and financial resources to Black communities. Healing starts with acknowledging our legacy of contributing to and benefiting from the oppression of Black people globally.

  Here are some examples of worthwhile reparation efforts: donating to crowdfunding campaigns for individual Black people; amplifying Black people's work on social media; giving property; providing mental health services; offering vouchers for food, scholarships, and paid internships; donating time and labor to Black entrepreneurs; paying for child care for Black families; providing a platform for Black people to speak.

- **Decolonize**. It will take longer than our lifetimes to decolonize ourselves from systems of oppression that have existed for hundreds of years. But we can make a commitment to disrupt the historical trauma that gets carried from one generation to the next. This trauma consists of not just pain, but also the unconscious bias we pass on and the violence we inflict without knowing why we're doing it.

The work of decolonization requires learning (and relearning) how to humanize everyone, especially those across races and those descended from the African diaspora. Here are some steps to take to begin this project: Have difficult conversations with those who look and identify like you about how to unpack the internalizations of bias and violence toward those different from you. Be vulnerable enough to recognize that your privileges can lead you to make decisions or implement violence that you may not even realize, but that can deeply harm marginalized communities. Fight like hell for the world you want to live in and who you want to be within that world.

- **Repeat.** Audre Lorde said, "Sometimes we are blessed with being able to choose the time, and the arena, and the manner of our revolution, but more usually we must do battle where we are standing."[23] That is our call to action to develop ourselves when there's no one watching, when there's not a conflict to deescalate, when the goal is a freedom we cannot feel yet. We must be committed to moving tangible resources into Black communities and to the internal decolonization of the legacy of trauma we have inherited. Anything less represents complicity with the status quo.

Shackelford's excellent recommendations apply specifically to mitigating white supremacy and supporting Black liberation, but I hope they'll also help you to reflect on how you can support liberation from other sources of oppression.

BRINGING IT HOME

Self-help fails to deliver to the degree we've come to expect as it puts the responsibility on us as individuals and deflects attention from the inequitable access to resources and opportunity that support positive change. Leveraging resources will take you further than you can ever go alone.

Supportive families, employers, communities, and governments play a larger role in improving our lives than do our efforts at self-improvement. We can all play a role in providing opportunity for others to thrive and in advocating for systemic change. Now that you better understand this context and its importance, let's turn to resilience strategies and the practical information you need to heal.

Chapter 10

BUILDING RESILIENCE

and Other Personal Tools for Liberation

How do you bounce back when life knocks you down? What do you do with the urge to binge-eat or drown your sorrows with alcohol? That's what we're taking on in this chapter.

The term "resilience" refers to the process of adapting in the face of stress, adversity, and trauma. This chapter helps you rewire your brain so that your first instinct to manage stress and challenging emotions is thoughtful and caring, rather than a reactive behavior that may get you through the short term but doesn't serve you as well in the long term.

RESILIENCE IS *NOT* (JUST) AN INSIDE JOB

Our focus is on the inside job in this chapter, but I don't want you to lose sight of the bigger picture of resiliency—or the connections between personal and collective liberation. Though we may think we need to change ourselves when it comes to facing difficult times, research shows that resiliency has more to do with our ability to leverage resources in our environment and our circle of support—including things like health care, job opportunities, and social connections—than with our personal strengths. If you lose your job, for example, obtaining a scholarship is going to make attending college more feasible, helping you bounce back. Or perhaps you have family connections you can leverage to get a job interview. And hey, if the world was kinder to people who looked like you, your struggles would lessen. Resiliency is inherently social and political in nature and I'm going to remind you of that throughout.

Let's dive in by discussing some terms and ideas and then we'll put this info into practice.

ACCEPTANCE AND SELF-ACCEPTANCE

Accepting yourself is about believing you're good enough as is, that you deserve love and belonging. If you're not feeling good about yourself, why would you accept who you are? Self-acceptance might seem like giving up. It's not. It's facing reality. It's about sitting with the reality of being a flawed human and experiencing emotion, like humans do. It makes sense that we want to avoid pain, but the best way to do that, paradoxically, is to accept the pain, not run from it.

What helps me in a difficult moment is the awareness—born from experience—that avoiding pain typically causes more pain in the long run than just sitting with it in the short term. Think about rejection. It hurts when you get turned down for a date, but the greater damage will probably be that which you inflict on yourself. When we feel rejected, we often spiral into thinking that there's something wrong with us and that no one would want to befriend us. We may even feel unaccountably angry about how we were treated.

Acceptance means you surrender to the reality of what is in the moment, giving whatever you are experiencing permission to be, not fighting what is. It doesn't mean that you're giving up or that you don't wish that things had turned out differently or that you are flaw-free. Try to sit with this discomfort, without judging it and needing to make it go away. It allows you to have perspective. Yes, you may have gotten rejected. But that's all. It doesn't mean there is something wrong with you or that you are unlovable. Accepting what is gives you opportunity to learn from the experience and grow.

When you come up against traits you may not like about yourself, that's okay, too. We're all flawed; it connects us. When I first came clean about my eating disorder with a college friend, it opened the door to learning about her drug addiction—and for both of us to lighten our shame and isolation. Sharing your vulnerability can bond you with others; if people see you as perfect, they're unlikely to confide in you or invite your confidences.

Cultivate the skill of being with yourself with love and acceptance rather than judgment. If, instead, you focus on your unworthiness, you're going to want to hide from others. Please don't wait until you're perfect, however you define it, before you can accept yourself. Perfection will never come. Accepting that means that you recognize that you don't need to be "perfect" or anything other than who you are to be worthy of love.

Accepting ourselves is hard, but not nearly as difficult as spending our lives running from who we are and caught up in maladaptive behaviors.

COMPASSION AND SELF-COMPASSION

Compassion refers to having the awareness of someone else's suffering and wanting to alleviate it. Literally, it means "suffering with." It differs from pity because when you feel compassion for someone else, you realize that suffering and imperfection are part of the shared human experience. When you pity, on the other hand, you distance yourself and act more from a sense of duty. Pity isolates us while compassion connects us.

In self-compassion, you extend this same understanding to yourself. You recognize that you are human and that you suffer, and you offer yourself kindness. Self-compassion grows from acceptance. When I allow myself to feel my own suffering and accept that as an inevitable part of being human, I soothe that wounded person (myself) and soften. That makes it easier to examine my fears. I take back my power to handle the situation.

The power of self-compassion is not just an idea—it's real and physically manifests in our bodies, creating measurable improvements in our biochemistry. For example, cortisol, the fight-or-flight stress hormone, drops when we summon compassion. One study asked research participants to imagine receiving compassion from someone else and how it felt in their body.[1] Those told to picture receiving love and kindness had lower cortisol levels after the imagery than those in the control group. Other studies show that you also release the hormone oxytocin when you generate compassion.

How can you generate more self-compassion? That was a hard one for me, until I discovered this neat little trick. I excel at offering compassion to others. So I simply treat myself as I would someone else who's struggling. I ask myself, what would I say or do for someone else in my position? Then I try to put it in action on myself. It works! Sometimes when things are really tough, I write a letter to that hurting person (myself), as a compassionate and loving friend. I saved one of those sweet letters and bring it out when I'm down. It's always a tearjerker, but in a good way—what a good friend I can be!

PERSPECTIVE

Psychologist Tara Brach tells a story about Sherlock Holmes and Dr. Watson on a camping trip.* They fall asleep and wake up some hours

---

* Sherlock Holmes is a fictional private detective created by British author Sir Arthur Conan Doyle in the late 1800s. Dr. John Watson is his assistant and friend.

later. Holmes asks Watson to look up and tell him what he sees. Watson describes the millions of stars. Holmes then asks, "What does that tell you?" Watson spins off a story about galaxies and planets and God. Holmes is silent for a minute before he speaks. "Watson, you idiot, someone stole our tent!"

I tell this story to make the point that we all have distinctive ways of paying attention. While we all may see the same things, we project different meaning onto them. Our preoccupations tend to skew how we perceive things. (Maybe Watson was an amateur astronomer.) Sometimes they can blind us to what's important or narrow our view of what's possible.

Here's an example of how my own biases can cloud my ability to see the world as it is. Years ago, I met someone I had a great connection with. I spun out the fantasy that she could be my new best friend. Yet when I asked her to get together a second time, she said she wasn't available.

My traumatized brain—always on the alert to protect me from pain and keep me safe—concluded that more than a scheduling conflict was at work. She must not want to be friends with me. In keeping with the biologically wired confirmation bias discussed in chapter 5, I clung to my usual story that yet another person had found me flawed and uninteresting.

Fast-forward five years later. Out of the blue, I received an email from her saying that she was thinking of me and would love to reconnect. I was shocked. I had been so convinced she found me unlikable. Why did she want to connect now? Why didn't she call me years ago? Could I trust this?

We got together and, once again, made a marvelous connection. We had a great deal in common and it was very easy to talk. A more evolved person by then, I thought I'd try to keep an open mind and ask what had happened when we first met.

She reassured me that she legitimately had not been available at the time I had suggested. Meanwhile, she herself had misinterpreted something I said and felt too shy to speak up about it. *She* was scared of rejection. So she had left it to me to make a show of friendship and get us together, to prove I cared. Well, as you know, I'd talked myself out of that.

When I failed to propose rescheduling that early meeting, she decided that I must not want to be friends with her.

We both had wanted to connect, but our wounded brains led us both to self-protect and back away from the risk. This experience didn't just hurt in the moment—it reinforced our recurring inner narratives that we were unlovable.

We're all running scripts about ourselves and others that can blind us to what's really going on. Instead of seeing what's in front of us, we're streaming the archival footage in our head. We each get stuck in our particular pattern of thoughts—for most of us, it's beliefs that we're inadequate, that we're not enough, that we don't belong. In other words, our self-protectiveness itself fails to protect us. Avoiding pain causes pain. I try to remember that when I'm tempted toward avoidance.

So strong is my "I'm unlikable" narrative that I project it onto new relationships and turn it into a self-fulfilling prophesy. I created her rejection of me; it didn't come from her. Fear feeds this process. If I'm always scanning the world for evidence that I'm unlikable, that's what I'm going to see. Confirmation bias combined with a negativity bias sets us up for misery.

What I've learned is that I need to start by getting some perspective. I ask myself, *Why does it hurt?* For me, the pain often comes down to a lack of belief in my worthiness.

What's behind the stories that stream in your head? They're not entirely false or made up (I *did* experience rejection as a young person, leading to my unlikability fears), but clinging to them may keep us stuck in reliving them. Our inner narratives are current interpretations of past experiences. Investigate those tough questions about what's really going on, and whether your stories are true or whether they're a way to disengage and self-protect. What happens if you let go of the scripts—can you see anything else? Your addictions and avoidant behaviors perform a function and are meaningful. What are the roots? What are they protecting you from feeling?

The next step is recognizing that the distress you feel is a fact of being human. You are biologically wired to need connection. So of course, rejection is going to hurt. Your natural response might be self-criticism. Try not to go down that path. What I try to do is notice it, label it—"Oh, there's that same old story again"—and then let it go.

REAL BUT NOT TRUE

How do you gain the perspective to challenge the inner stories you tend to run with? You need to pause before you create your interpretations, then add a dose of compassion and kindness. This will allow you to come back to what's real instead of clinging to what you've created.

Tara Brach tells another story about a woman on a layover in an airport. Hungry and exhausted, she got some cookies, put them in her purse, and sat down at a table where a man was sitting and reading a newspaper. She, too, took out a newspaper and proceeded to read it.

She fished out a cookie as she read and ate it, and then the man reached into the bag and took a cookie for himself. She was weirded out but couldn't imagine what to say. She didn't want to make a scene. So, she stayed quiet and took another cookie and ate it, and then he did the same thing. Well, as this pattern continued, the woman, not surprisingly, got angrier and angrier. Eventually, just one cookie remained. To her astonishment, the man broke it in two and handed her half. Then his flight was called and he left. Only later did she reach into her purse and, finding her unopened bag of cookies, realize she had been eating his.

The stories we tell ourselves aren't always true! Yet we are so caught up in our interpretation of the world that we can't imagine any other version. We live our lives through storylines that keep us disconnected from our truths. We buy into belief systems about ourselves and others that keep us from truly seeing ourselves and each other.

Brach calls this pattern of storytelling "Real but Not True." This phrase reminds us that our experiences are not the same thing as our *thoughts* about our experiences. What happens to you is one thing, but it's different from the meaning you later attach to it in your thoughts. What we're thinking is a step removed, not the thing itself. The fact of the experience remains the same, but its meaning in your head may shift over time, and almost surely will differ from the thoughts and beliefs of others who shared the experience.

Because our thoughts and beliefs evolve, we constantly rewrite ourselves. We move from an authentic experience or feeling to an interpretation. We move from "I feel bad" to "I am bad, something's wrong with me." These beliefs are shaped by our culture and history. We get the message from the outside that we're not okay. That feeds the core belief that "something is wrong with me." Then we seek evidence to confirm our new belief. This "negativity bias," you may remember, wired into you as a means of protection, means that we glom onto whatever confirms our interpretation, our sense of unworthiness. So we believe something that is untrue, and it causes us pain.

"THEORIZING"

It is helpful to pinpoint what stressors trigger you. Some, like racism, may be unavoidable, so there's no way to adjust ourselves to solve the problem.

Consider the fact that mental illness is so prevalent in the Native American community, and that addiction, alcoholism, diabetes, and autoimmune disease afflict Native Americans more than other racial identity group. But as we discussed, this tendency doesn't come from their individual choices. It arises from social factors and intergenerational trauma that keeps them in vulnerable states and works against their immunity. In similar ways, this is what happens to people in all marginalized groups.

In a society that stresses people out, individualized solutions can't work. Given the existence of social injustice, suffering is going to happen disproportionately. While there is no individual solution to a cultural problem, we have to find ways to work with the hand we were dealt. Coming together in community helps us identify the common struggles and move away from self-blame and the burden of seeing yourself as a problem to be fixed. And so, we must "theorize."

bell hooks places "theorizing"—the work of naming one's experience and understanding how it connects to broader systems of oppression—at the center of survival. Theorizing is an interwoven process of understanding one's situation in terms of existing oppressive social norms, questioning those norms, and eventually opening your imagination to liberation from them.

Theorizing lets you take control of the narrative of your experiences in marginalization. When you theorize, you stop authorizing others to define your experience. This agency is important. If you think back to chapter

5, we saw that lack of agency allows stress to permeate and do its damage, explaining why stressed executives (who have high agency) are less prone to stress-induced disease and dysregulation than similarly stressed working-class (low-agency) folks. Theorizing is a way to develop your agency, and this can provide some insulation for those with marginalized identities. It's a way to reclaim ownership of your identity and take back power in an unjust world—even as the injustice itself persists.

Theorizing helps you realize that, for instance, it's not your fault you can't get a job. There are structural contributors (like racism, sexism, or ageism, or a crummy economy) that stand in your way. It is also, as hooks describes, a path to liberation.

When I was hurting badly from my eating disorder, I "saved" myself by going to school. My multiple graduate degrees were an attempt to think my way out—to learn everything I could about weight as a way to rise above my mess. (They were also a reach for "legitimacy" and worth in others' eyes.) What I came to see, by rethinking, was that my eating disorder, at root, was not about food or body insecurity; it was really an effort to banish pain.

Education was a liberating path for me because it led me to see the cultural roots of my discomfort with food and how I had absorbed toxic ideas that kept me from inhabiting my body comfortably. These ideas maintained a status quo that excluded me.

To heal, you've got to ask the hard questions about what's at the root and be willing to sit with the discomfort you find there. You may get to the insight that tells you that the world is unfair and stacked against you, or that the people who were supposed to protect you failed miserably and didn't teach you the life skills or provide the material or emotional support you needed. It may instead (or also) push you to understand that the world is unfair and you are benefiting from others' pain. Most likely, all of this is true at once.

"That's just a theory," people say, suggesting that it's not real. But hooks treats theory as an actual intervention. "Theorizing" enables you to make sense of what's happening and imagine your way forward to alternative futures and outcomes. That's why I undertook this book, to write myself out of pain and into a better future. As hooks explains, "When our lived experience of theorizing is fundamentally linked to processes of self-recovery, of collective liberation, no gap exists between theory and practice. Indeed, what such experience makes more evident is the bond between the two—that ultimately reciprocal process wherein one enables the other."[2]

CONNECTION

One of the most powerful healing strategies is connecting with others. Emotional isolation is a major risk factor for disease, addiction, illness, and even death. We need each other. We connect by sharing our vulnerability with others.

When I was still recovering from my eating disorder, I spoke in a support group about how ashamed I felt about a recent binge and how I hated losing control. I told them I felt I was too fat* and that my body revealed to others what a failure I was. The room was quiet for a little while, and then people started crying and talking about how well they knew those feelings and how much they hurt.

We didn't solve anything that day, but we drew connections among our assumptions. Why did we all suffer from these same self-judgments? Why were we all uncomfortable in our bodies? Of course, we all wanted to be thin. We saw how much better thinner people were treated. We wanted access to some of that love and appreciation. We wanted to be considered attractive. We sensed our only real value could come from thinness.

The thoughts were still painful, but there was magic in realizing that what I experienced was human, and that it was shared.

We came to recognize that our "body" problem wasn't actually in our bodies, but in a culture that didn't value those bodies. The shame belonged to our culture, not to us. By trying to control our bodies, we were doing what we could to survive. Knowing that let us see that what we needed was love

---

* In the context of this support group, it was valuable to name my fear of fat. However, in other contexts, it can hurt others who hear this, suggesting a judgment that thinness is better and fatter bodies are bad. Please be considerate of context when discussing these issues.

and kindness and understanding—not weight loss or food. And we recognized that we could offer solidarity to one another.

Note that social support is good wherever it comes from but particularly potent when it comes from someone you care about. If a stranger offers affirmation, you may not trust or accept it as readily. Which is not to say that strangers or anonymous hotlines can't be helpful. It's just not the same as finding support within your social network, if you can.

An interesting rat experiment reinforced the biological value of connection. Investigators gradually increased the temperature under the rodents' paws until they moved away. That was each rat's pain threshold, and they made note of it.

Next, they ran the experiment with two rats side by side and saw that when both rats were exposed to the heat, it could lower the pain threshold of the companion rat next to it, some of the time. When the neighboring rat was a stranger, there was no effect. But if the pair were cage mates together, there was an empathic increase in tolerance for pain. This holds up in human experience, too. If you hold someone's hand during a medical procedure, you'll feel less stress and recover more easily, especially if that hand belongs to a relative or friend. It's scientifically proven, as I'll discuss later.

SHORING YOURSELF UP

Now let's look at some ways you can shore up your own resilience in the face of pain and negative narratives.

FINDING YOUR OUTLETS

Outlets can release the tension (especially if it's a physical outlet), distract you, and help connect your mind and body while reminding you of what's important. All sorts of outlets work: various hobbies, working off the tension by pummeling a punching bag, screaming after a difficult meeting, dancing to your favorite music, talking with friends. Find what works for you. My favored childhood outlet was telling my problems to Tiggy, my trusted (stuffed) confidante. This (one-way) conversation helped me put language to my thoughts and feelings and better make sense of them. Whacking a tennis ball also gave me a satisfying way to release some of the energy behind these emotions.

USING HUMOR

As traumatic as it was then and for years after, I've managed to blunt the harshness of my modeling school experience by telling it as a funny story. I am far enough from that shamed and wounded kid now to see the humor in it. I enjoy it when others can chuckle with me, too. If I tell it right, it gets great laughs!

This is more than a few yuks—it's a tool for getting through and past intolerable situations. Humor reminds me that my community can identify with me and laugh with me at the world's wrongness. When I'm in difficult situations, I can sometimes get through them by thinking, *This will make for a great story.* I collect these accounts to bring back to my community, so they can tend to my wounds and break the oppressive spell with laughter and understanding.

EMBRACING IMPERMANENCE

When things are tough, it helps to remember that "this too shall pass." This is a catchphrase I often repeat, even for small things. When you see that it's true for passing annoyances—realizing that all it takes is one good night to get over feeling exhausted and depleted from sleep loss—you help scaffold an orientation toward acceptance of impermanency. If we believe in permanency, how can we see a way out of pain? The more we acknowledge impermanence—and treasure it—the more we can accept the flow of emotion and avoid getting stuck in our pain, including the pain that comes from clinging to happiness.

HANDLING REJECTION

Rejection is never easy. It's going to happen. It's going to hurt. And you can learn skills that will lessen the pain and will help you recover from it and move on with confidence.

You know that classically cliché rejection "It's not you, it's me."? Don't buy it. It's neither. It's more helpful to reframe rejection as something that happens because two people (or a person and an organization) just aren't a match. It's a relationship issue. Your skills are a mismatch for a particular job or your communication style doesn't match up with a potential new friend. The more you can reframe it, the less you will personalize rejection and get caught in a shame spiral.

Resilience involves recognizing that although one aspect of who you are may make you a mismatch in a particular relationship, it is not the totality of who you are. You have many other characteristics that make you kick-ass.

Rejection threatens our sense of belonging. To recover, we need to remind ourselves that we are appreciated and loved. If your work colleagues left you out of a lunch invite, get together with your dog-walking friends instead. If your kid was rejected by a schoolmate, make plans for them to meet a different friend. Or, when a first date doesn't return your texts, call your grandparents if it will help remind you that your voice brings joy to others.

FORGIVING YOURSELF

Please, in trying to heal, find a way to forgive yourself. Know that you are really doing the best you can in a world that doesn't adequately support you. This isn't about giving up, and it doesn't mean you can't do better, but you are trying as hard as you can right now to remove the stifling layer of shame and blame that befalls us all sometimes.

GRIEVING

Grieving is an essential part of the healing practice. This is especially important when we think of changing behaviors that have taken care of us and have made us feel good even when they were not always helping us.

To heal from my eating disorder, for example, I had to grieve the fantasy body—and subsequently, the person—that could have been. I believed at the time that thinness would eradicate the hips that telegraphed "woman." I had to grieve the loss of this fantasy, the story I told myself about the person I would become after losing the tell-tale weight.* I also had to grieve the time and energy I had lost to my eating disorder.

Fatter people, when they learn that repetitive dieting can cause weight gain, may also grieve their role in upregulating their body's maintenance weight. (This is the protective mechanism whereby your body increases its fat mass to protect you in the case of potential famine—a hangover from our prehistoric ancestors that explains why many dieters get heavier in the long run.)

The pain of this process can keep many people in denial. Who wants to accept the fact that they may have spent decades agonizing over their diets, and learn that their efforts had been doomed to failure and may actually have contributed to the weight gain they were trying to reverse? Particularly as this belief system is linked to hope for a better life, it can be hard to accept.

You may be angry at yourself for being victimized by diet culture. That's normal. Talking to others can help you transfer that rage to the culture, where it belongs.

You may also have to grieve the damages that resulted from your behaviors—like my friend who caused another driver's concussion by drunkenly rear-ending their car—and the many ways we can hurt others with our trauma responses.

---

* Reading that I, a slender person, considered myself too fat may provide valuable insight for some people. At the same time, it may cause harm to others. After all, you may be wondering, if Lindo thinks they're too fat, how are they judging bodies that are actually fat? I want to acknowledge the tension and offer this insight with the hope that readers can focus on the problem being in the internalized cultural idea, not my body or your body.

Grieving can be isolating. Our culture doesn't support staying with our pain, but rather fetishizes happiness. That you often can't really "do" anything about your pain also makes it difficult. You can apologize for bad behavior or offer restitution, for instance, but the results of your actions may still live on painfully.

Yet we are all grieving, whether it's about losing someone or something, about transition, or about facing our disappointment in ourselves or others. At this point in this book you may be grieving the pain of living amidst disconnection and inequity.

Ritualist, writer, and self-described "grief practitioner" Holly Truhlar eloquently writes,[3] "Grief opens us up to the fullness of our being, and we're not meant to go through it alone; we never were. We need to feel cared for, loved, and held, when we're grieving. We need a community—a village—to show up and see us, welcome us, thank us. We need to know the grief work we're doing is important. Because it is, especially in these transitional times." "[Grief] is absolutely what matters now, it's your soul calling: asking you to show up."

Don't run from your grief. Find its wisdom and healing power.

LEANING ON OTHERS

One of the best ways to heal a traumatized brain stems from connection with others. When you listen to others, actively and deeply, from a place of acceptance instead of judgment, mirror neurons see this compassionate relationship and internalize this behavior. If we do it over and over again, our brains actually rewire, biological proof that connection matters.

YOU'VE GOT THIS

Knowing that your brain is wired in ways that keep you mired in pain and that you have repeated these patterns for so long, it can be easy to think that you can't break out, or that you'll never change. But it is possible.

Recognize that your biology causes you to keep repeating these old patterns, and you can change that.

Let's turn our attention now to how you can rewire your brain in a way that shifts your habits of paying attention, so you can cultivate other ways of seeing things. One of the best ways to do this is through mindfulness, which is both an activity and a state of mind. In the next section, I'll be discussing mindfulness specifically as it applies to habit change.

MINDFULNESS

Meditation teacher, author, and researcher Jon Kabat-Zinn describes mindfulness as paying attention, in a particular way, on purpose, in the present moment, and nonjudgmentally.[4] It's about being aware, noticing and paying attention to thoughts, feelings, behavior, and everything else. It's about openness to turning toward negative experiences rather than trying to make unpleasant feelings just go away. Can you see how this might work to transform your coping behaviors? When we lighten up on judgment and accept the moment, it helps us to make more thoughtful choices rather than resort to damaging reactive behaviors. Mindfulness can be practiced at any time, whatever we are doing and whoever we are with, by showing up and being fully engaged in the here and now.

MEDITATION PRACTICE

Meditation is a way of practicing mindfulness. With a regular meditation practice, you can train your brain to better tolerate emotions and not be so vulnerable to needing to distract yourself or make them go away. It helped me stay with emotions that would previously have led to food binges or alcohol or drug abuse.

There are many forms of meditation, but the type I find most helpful as a regular practice is just sitting quietly and being mindful of my breath. Contrary to some popular conception, you don't have to join a cult, pay money, buy special clothes, or sit in lotus position. There's nothing fancy to it. There are three basic steps I recommend: sit or lie comfortably, breathe, and focus your attention on your breath. Focus on being in the moment and feeling the breath move through you. In this moment, there is no "other" and no judgment, just who you are. This is a moment to find your "ground." It gives you that little space to distance yourself from the story you may attach to whatever is going on.

Your mind will wander. You'll start thinking about the bills you need to pay and what you're going to eat for dinner. That's okay. Just notice these thoughts and gently bring your attention back to your breath. You will get distracted again and again—I like to just label it "thinking" and keep coming back to my breath.

This might sound too simple to affect behavior, but research tells us it works. A fascinating study on formerly incarcerated men who were substance-addicted exposed them to ten days of meditation training.[5] They were asked at the start and again ninety days later to report on their drug use. Those who practiced ninety days of meditation reported drinking 87 percent less alcohol and using 89 percent less marijuana. That was six times as effective as the conventional chemical dependency plan provided to a control group. This study is part of a mounting body of research that points to what I already know from experience: meditation practice makes a difference. Personally, I celebrate how it helps me sit with waves of emotion that would have previously had me driving down roads I don't want to go on. You can find mindfulness practices to try later in this chapter.

MEDITATION AND HABIT CHANGE

Thanks to neuroplasticity, we can change the habitual responses of our brain. For most of us, our brains are set to go into reactive mode and so we are less capable of staying with emotions. If you practice meditation, your brain grows more able to tolerate feelings. You can become a witness to your own experience and step out of the craving. The craving may seem to have the upper hand, but a meditation practice can weaken its hold by deconditioning you to its power. You won't necessarily banish the desire, but you are more able to acknowledge it as a part of being human and recognize its transience, making you less vulnerable to acting on it.

Let's review the trigger, behavior, reward process discussed in chapter 4 to understand how meditation can help you change problematic behavior. Say you're sensitive to social rejection. (That's called being human!) Your usual response is to reach for your vape. You draw in the smoke and savor the temporary feeling of pleasure and distraction, which further ingrains the biologic pathway so you are conditioned to keep choosing that response.

You can see some of the ways this is a problem. One of them is that the fix is temporary and you never really get satisfaction for the real need, which is feeling connected and accepted. Vaping soothed you briefly, but you still feel inadequate and unworthy. On top of the shame you felt from the rejection, you may have the added shame for vaping. Hating on yourself for vaping, or for whatever your habitual coping response is, just adds more fuel to your feelings of unworthiness and the drive to soothe yourself and get out of your pain. There's no way you can heal from addiction or move on from your coping strategies unless you address your shame. Just as you can't eat your way to happiness and stability, you can't shame or hate yourself into better behavior. The focus on inadequacy also takes you away from your present. You miss out on a lot of life.

So how does meditation practice help with addiction or addictive-like tendencies? Research shows more neural density, cortical thickness, and overall activity in the prefrontal cortexes of regular meditators. Their "thinking brains" more readily come online, leaving them less susceptible to cravings. Meditation allows you to witness your impulses, giving you the opportunity to make choices.

Meditation also stimulates endorphin release. Endorphins make you happy and stimulate dopamine release, another excursion down the pleasure pathway.

Several research studies scanning the brains of experienced meditators may have identified another mechanism by which meditation tamps cravings.[6] The meditators' brains have relatively reduced activity in the part of the brain called the "default mode" network, a brain network involved in self-related thinking and mind wandering. Part of this network, called the posterior cingulate cortex, is activated not necessarily by craving itself but when we get caught up in it. This same brain region quiets down when we let go—when we step out of the process by exercising curious awareness of what's happening In other words, a regular meditation practice may be teaching the brain not to get sucked into a craving. This is quite different from typical addiction recovery: rather than teaching you to "just say no," a regular meditation practice may lessen your desire for the addictive substance or behavior.

MINDFULNESS IN A SOCIAL CONTEXT

When I was studying for my master's degree in contemplative psychotherapy at a school with Buddhist roots, I asked about the relationship between the mindfulness techniques we were taught and larger social change. How could mindfulness better the world? I got the same facile response from every teacher: "Meditate on it." As if meditating alone was enough to transform society. Meditation was presented as an individual, personal practice, meant not to address a flawed world but to mute my personal reaction to it.

Well, that's not Buddhism. Buddhism, from which mindfulness was derived, seeks to address systems of oppression that cause human suffering. Its teachings are grounded in notions of interdependence, recognizing that we can't separate our personal healing and transformation from that of our larger culture. When all we do is focus on self-awareness, without a simultaneous emphasis on social consciousness and taking action, we are disconnected from our environment. Mindfulness aimed exclusively at improving the lives of individuals misses the whole point. There's a term for that, "cultural appropriation," that refers to a dominant group borrowing a cultural practice from a marginalized group and changing it for its own benefit, ultimately erasing its origins and meaning.

Other traditions do honor the culture surrounding Buddhism. Engaged Buddhism, for example, a term credited to Vietnamese Zen master Thich Nhat Hanh, draws the connection between personal and collective liberation. During the Vietnam War, Nhat Hanh and his community of monks and nuns had to decide how to react to the bombing of villages surrounding their monastery. Should they stay put and continue to meditate (for the greater good of humankind) or should they go out into the streets to help the wounded? They decided to do both, to practice mindfulness while helping people.

BREATHE IN SOCIAL JUSTICE

I have a hiatal hernia. (Yes, slender people get them too. My doctor probably missed early diagnosis because of fatphobia; had a larger person presented my symptoms it might have been more readily seen. This example is but one of many that demonstrates that medical reliance on BMI is harmful to people of all sizes.[7])

On those rare occasions when I experience symptoms from my hernia, it can be terrifying. I feel like I can't get air and I'm going to pass out and die.* This visceral awareness of breath as essential to life helps me understand that I can't take breathing for granted. It helps fuel a meditation practice where I focus on being conscious of my breath—and knowing that nothing is more important in that moment than that breath.

Watching the heart-wrenching video that captured Eric Garner's murder, turning his death into a national discussion about racism and police brutality (less discussed was the fatphobia), evoked deep emotion for me. Eric was an asthmatic, and as he struggled for breath, he repeated the words, "I can't breathe," eleven times. *Eleven times*. I was stunned watching the video, as it seemed so clear to me that I was watching a murder. How could this happen? I discussed his death and my reaction with a Black friend, who was not surprised by the video. "Welcome to my world," she said. "Me and other Black people live our lives with the awareness this could happen at any time to any of us."

---

* The choking sensation that I experience is a less typical hernia symptom. More common is to experience heartburn.

Whoa. This was years ago and I'm still processing that. White privilege underlies my surprise that Eric Garner could be murdered by a police officer, someone with a job mandate to protect people. Not everyone can afford that kind of naivete, as my friend so eloquently pointed out. For some people, the simple act of breathing requires a constant vigilance well beyond my experience.

Meditation is much more than you alone on a cushion. The practice is strengthened when we integrate the awareness that some people are struggling to breathe because systems like white supremacy, patriarchy, and other forms of oppression have us in a chokehold. We're all trying to breathe in a world that isn't set up for us all to breathe. We can use our meditation practice to engage with it, rather than retreat from our collective reality into individualism.

The nonjudgmental acceptance of what is enables us to make sense of our experiences and allows us to learn to meet ourselves with compassion. Meditation can't make the oppression go away, but it can help heal the wounds of oppression. By cultivating our ability to sit with our experiences, it can also teach us to extend that compassion to others, allowing for greater empathy and countering the othering that upholds oppressive systems.

MEDITATION AND TRAUMA

Meditation isn't for everyone. It can lead to dark places. Someone vulnerable to PTSD, for example, may need to avoid paying such close, sustained attention to their internal experience. Forms of meditation other than the formal, sitting-with-eyes-closed style can be helpful starting points, such as walking meditation or yoga. Be thoughtful about whether it feels right for you. If you are coping with trauma, you may want to seek out guided help from a trauma-informed and trained professional.

TRANSFORMING CRAVINGS
AND ADDICTIVE BEHAVIORS

When we get curious about our cravings, we notice that our urges are made up of bodily sensations—we may sense tightness, for instance, or restlessness—and that these sensations come and go. These are transient pieces of experience that we can manage from moment to moment rather than getting sucked into an overwhelming craving that we feel we have to react to.

If you smoke or stress-eat or check email compulsively, if you can't resist responding to texts when you're driving, see if you can tap into your natural capacity to bring your attention to the here and now and to your immediate sensations. Try to just be curiously aware of what's happening in your body and mind in that moment. This is an opportunity to either perpetuate a painful habit loop or step out of it.

Suppose, for example, you feel that urge to check your email, though you know it's a distraction from your work and may prevent you from meeting a pending deadline. Pause and take a few minutes to reflect on what you're feeling. Consider whether your inbox will provide what you're looking for. Intellectually, of course, this reflection may be easy. You know you're looking for distraction and your inbox can provide that. But you know, too, that taking the time to check that inbox is going to increase the mounting pressure you're feeling at your job.

In the past, you may have tried the "just say no" approach, trying to control your behavior cognitively. That requires action from your prefrontal cortex, which, as you'll remember, goes offline when you're stressed. So it's not going to work very well in this moment when you need it. Rationally you may know that an email check won't solve social anxiety, but your rational mind isn't in a position to help right now.

See what happens if instead you go *toward* your feelings, rather than resisting them and trying to make them go away. Curiosity about our feelings can take us away from fear-based reactivity and into being. When we discover that our cravings are made up of body experiences, we can follow them.

Ask yourself: *What am I feeling in my body?* Our cravings and our emotions are not just "feelings" or mental states, but include physical changes in our bodies. The more you can see that these are just body sensations, the more you can learn to ride them out. You may notice a restlessness, or tension, or speediness. If you just sit with that experience, you'll also see that bodily experiences come and go. Try to let your feelings percolate without trying to fix them. It's okay if judgment comes up—it's natural—but try not to follow it. For me, it helps to label it. I say to myself, "I am feeling judgment," and then refocus on my breath.

Cravings take on different forms over time. Mindfulness helps you not get sucked into your cravings. That practice alone—and, particularly, in the beginning—is probably not going to stop you from your habitual behaviors. But what it will do is help you get more in tune with your body and slowly help reduce your cravings and develop more nourishing ways of managing those cravings.

It's important to show yourself some compassion during this process. I remind myself that whatever I'm going through is just human, that we all experience emotion, and that we all have difficulty staying in the present moment. It also helps to maintain my sense of humor: "There goes my monkey brain again, but now I can come back to breathing."

WHEN YOUR CRAVING IS FOR FOOD

If you call yourself an "emotional eater," have you considered the possibility that your out-of-control drive to eat, even (or especially) when dieting, is actually a biological response to restriction itself? That far from some perverse mind game, it's part of a hormonal cascade generated to get your body more of the calories it craves?

If that's true, the unexpected reality is that the only way to reduce your cravings is to dump the restrictive regime you've set in place and start responding to your bodily cues. Then you will be less vulnerable to your environment.

Diet culture teaches us to restrict our calories and to view certain foods or styles of eating as "bad" and to be avoided. The result is that most of us know guilt and restriction. Is that true for you? If so, dietitian and author Christy Harrison describes how to turn around that way of thinking:

> The "I want ice cream" thought isn't the problem, and the act of bingeing on ice cream is a completely understandable way that your body is trying to get its needs met. In the absence of guilt, restriction, and deprivation, those urges and behaviors tend to dissipate on their own, without us having to mentally think ourselves out of them. The real solution isn't to use mindfulness to overcome your food cravings, it's to honor them and give yourself full permission to eat *enough* food, and a wide enough variety of foods, so that the cravings don't have such a hold on you anymore.[8]

Food isn't an addictive substance. It's food deprivation that makes food feel addictive.[9] Steering away from the foods you love doesn't work to reduce calorie intake.

Therapist, author, and speaker Judith Matz explains that "when you give yourself permission to eat all types of foods, formerly forbidden foods stop glittering. Now, you're in a much stronger position to consider emotional overeating. Keep in mind that everyone eats for emotional reasons at times, but if it's the primary way that you soothe yourself when you feel distress, it's worth taking a deeper look." Matz suggests that you start with self-compassion: "Yelling at yourself for overeating only fuels the binge! Instead, gently tell yourself that you are experiencing distress and food is a way, for now, to take care of yourself. Remind yourself the day will come when you no longer rely on food in this way. You've spent years engaged in dieting and overeating. Of course it will take time to undo these behaviors."[10]

More advice on eating can be found in books by Harrison, Matz, coauthors Tribole and Resch—oh, and me, both alone and with coauthor Lucy Aphramor.[11]

THE MINDFULNESS MOVEMENT

The mindfulness movement tells us to work on ourselves by being more mindful, nonjudgmental, and accepting of circumstances. That said, the emphasis on "nonjudgmental awareness" and acceptance can disable critical thought, which can be a trap. By deflecting attention from unjust social structures and material conditions, mindfulness is easily coopted as a tool supporting the status quo. It's also much more popular among more privileged people, who benefit from the status quo and may be less invested in changing it. For those reasons, I recommend supplementing what is typically understood as mindfulness with this next step: reflection and theorizing.

Lean into what's going on and consider what's fueling your feelings. You may not fully understand, but use this as opportunity to explore ideas as they come up. As Brené Brown advises, "rumble" with the stories you're telling—that is, embrace the vulnerability and stay curious. Consider what happens when you try to separate events from your interpretations of events. Are there other possible interpretations?

This is the time, too, to make those connections between your story and its structural contributors. You are a human who was set up for this particular response, and others experience this too. What are the roots? Once you have a better handle on what's going on, you can make an informed decision about how best to handle it and take care of yourself.

SELF-CARE

When considering self-care, it's helpful to recognize a continuum of options. We can't always be completely present in our lives—that would be exhausting—and sometimes harm reduction is all the self-care we need or can manage. Here are three options to consider when you're having a hard time.

1. **Lean in.** Sitting with our uncomfortable feelings lets us make use of the feelings, rather than be simply bowled over by them. I look

for safe ways to lean into my discomfort: strategies like creating a safe space, which can be as simple as brewing a cup of tea (the ritual of making it and cradling the warm mug helps as much as drinking it). It can mean going for a walk outside, finding nature or even a patch of grass, riding my bike, playing with my dog, or talking to a friend.

2. **Distract.** Sometimes embracing the discomfort is more than we can handle. That's okay. Give yourself permission to be distracted—maybe read a novel or watch a movie. It will not erase your pain, but it can give you some breathing room.

3. **Avoid**. You're human. Sometimes avoiding your stressor will be all you can manage in the moment. When that's the case, there's nothing wrong with soothers like comfort eating. Some avoidance strategies—like drugs or alcohol—may not be viable options for everyone, but for some of us they can be useful tools for occasional downtime and social connection and can allow us to better manage our moods.

Try not to judge yourself for which option you choose. Instead, reflect and notice how it works for you. As you develop your felt sense, it will affect your future choices. For example, as you notice that you can tolerate sitting with your discomfort more than you feared, and as you find it more effective than your usual avoidance behaviors, you'll more likely turn to it in the future.

Now we'll look at some other helpful practices. Remember that everyone is different, so you might have to try several approaches to find the best fit for you at any given time.

IMAGERY

One of my favorite tricks for managing stressors is "priming my brain" through imagery. When I'm in a hard circumstance, I try to imagine what a compassionate person would say to me in this moment, and how they would they take care of me. For some people, conjuring a specific image of a person (or being) is helpful. I tried this once, in a desperate circumstance, imagining Yoda* in the room with me, giving me advice. He had sage wisdom! Many times, I've thought about the people who love me, and I imagine being wrapped in a hug or kind words. Controlled research studies prove that imagery is effective at stimulating hormones that soothe you.

TOUCH

I don't think it will surprise you to learn that touch can be healing. Much research documents that physical touch stimulates the release of oxytocin and reduces our release of cortisol. Oxytocin sends signals to the prefrontal cortex, which in turn sends signals that calm the amygdala, which is the fear center. It's like a fire extinguisher.

One study examined three conditions during which women received a shock to their ankles while an MRI scanner detected brain changes.[12] The research subjects also answered questions about their subjective experience of pain. In one group, the individuals were alone in their scanners. In another group, individuals were holding the hand of the lab technician, and individuals in the third group were holding hands with their spouses. The response was predictable, confirmed by subjective report and the activated brain pathways. Those who were alone felt pain, those with the lab techs felt the shock but less pain, and those with their spouses felt the shock but no pain.

The Touch Research Institute has conducted more than a hundred studies on the effects of massage therapy on many functions and medical conditions.[13] Their research identified many benefits, including reduced pain

---

* Yoda is a character in the Star Wars movies, known for his sage wisdom. Parenthetically, Yoda was also my nickname in college. I never asked why it was bestowed on me, scared I might learn it had more to do with my small stature or looks than anything else. (He was a funny-looking little green creature, about 3 feet tall.) Nonetheless, I'm a huge fan of Yoda and gladly answered to the name. My favorite Yoda quote, which inspired me in managing the stigma put on my short stature: "Size matters not. Look at me. Judge me by my size, do you? Hmm? Hmm. And well you should not. For my ally is the Force, and a powerful ally it is."

(e.g., from fibromyalgia), decreased autoimmune problems (e.g., increased pulmonary function in asthma and decreased glucose levels in diabetes), enhanced immune function (e.g., increased natural killer cells in HIV and cancer), and enhanced alertness and performance (e.g., EEG pattern of alertness and better performance on math computations).

GRATITUDE

Research documents the value of a gratitude practice—that is, intentionally thinking about the things you feel grateful for—in rewiring your brain. It's also one of our best defenses to counteract the brain's negativity bias. Consciously tapping into what we feel grateful for allows us to acknowledge the goodness in our individual lives and in the world. In the process, I always recognize that the source of that goodness lies at least partially outside me, helping me connect to something larger than myself as an individual—usually other people or nature. Gratitude helps people feel more positive emotions, become more capable of handling challenges, appreciate good experiences, improve health, deal with adversity, and strengthen relationships, among many other benefits.

One study looked at what happens when people wrote letters of gratitude to other people, compared to a second group writing thoughts and feelings about negative experiences and a third group without a writing activity.[14] Those who wrote gratitude letters reported significantly better mental health than other participants at both four and twelve weeks following the exercise.

Almost a quarter of the gratitude writers sent their letters to their intended recipient in the end, which was optional. The act of writing the letter resulted in improved mental health, regardless of whether the letter was sent. This suggests that you don't have to actually communicate your appreciation to someone else in order to benefit from feeling your gratitude.

In the same study, three months after the letter writing began, fMRI scans revealed more activity in the letter writers' prefrontal cortexes than the other groups. Merely expressing gratitude may have lasting effects on the "thinking" part of the brain, thus helping you make better decisions and better manage your emotions.

GROUNDING EXERCISES

Humans have a tendency to get lost in our heads. Have you ever found yourself arriving at a destination and not remembering the process of getting there? Grounding exercises can help us reconnect with our body and restore our connection to the world. We all have very different experiences of what grounds us. It could be the feeling of your feet solidly on the floor or your back against a chair. My friend feels most grounded when floating on her back while swimming—she describes the feeling of weightlessness as a welcome relief from the body dissatisfaction that dogs her. For someone else, it may be eating a raisin, and the awareness of how that raisin connects them to the earth and to the many people who tended it.

It's valuable to learn what grounds you and to practice grounding yourself when you're feeling uneasy or emotionally triggered. The following are simple and practical exercises and practices you can use to help ground and soothe yourself. If you practice these when you're not triggered in the moment, you can actually create "muscle memory" so they are more likely to be automatic behaviors when you need them.

Hand on Heart

Place your right hand over your heart so that the heel of your hand is at your heart and your fingertips are at your collarbone. You can also put your left hand on top of your right to apply more pressure. When you do this, you are applying pressure to your polyvagal nerve, which activates the parasympathetic nervous system, producing a calm and relaxed feeling in the body.

Butterfly Tap

Cross your arms at your chest so that your hands are resting on your shoulders. Alternately tap one hand and then the other against your shoulder. This exercise stimulates the brain cross-laterally, which means it makes each half of the brain talk to the other. Getting them in conversation this way activates our prefrontal cortex and allows it to soothe the amygdala, your so-called fear center.

Breathe

It's simple. Just pay attention to your breathing.

Body Scan

This exercise may be triggering for people with body image concerns, so do be thoughtful about whether it's right for you.

Sit or lie comfortably and let your breathing slow. Bring your awareness to your body and notice what you're feeling. Do you feel tightness in your shoulders, back, neck, or anywhere else? Do you feel pain or discomfort? Do you have a feeling of concentrated "energy" or pulsing around a certain area? Start at your head and systematically focus on each area of your body on your way down—scalp, ears, nose, mouth, neck, shoulders, chest, and so on—and really notice what sensations you have in each area.

Eating Meditation

This exercise helps us jump into the experience of eating and appreciate it. All we're going to do is eat a raisin, paying attention as you do it.

For many people, eating is fraught with anxiety. This exercise could be triggering to some people, particularly if you have an eating disorder or a history of chronic dieting. It's very normal for people who've had trauma around food (dieting, other forms of disordered eating, food insecurity, etc.) to feel panicked when asked to slow down and eat mindfully, and that's a direct result of the trauma. It doesn't mean they're "bad at eating mindfully," it just means that their bodies are in survival mode and trying to make sure they're not deprived again. Use your discretion as to whether the exercise is right for you.

Start by just feeling the raisin in your hand. Roll it around, maybe toss it from hand to hand. How does it feel? Sticky? Wrinkly?

Now hold the raisin up to your nose, close your eyes, and take a good sniff. What does it smell like to you?

Now look at the raisin. Notice its color, shape, texture. Look at its folds, the darker hollows.

Have you gotten distracted during this process? Maybe your mind started wandering off to thinking about what you're going to eat for lunch. Or maybe you were thinking this is a silly exercise, not sure of the point. That's normal. Just notice that you're distracted and come back to the raisin.

Now, think about eating the raisin. Can you imagine what it will taste like? Do you want to eat it or not? Does anything happen in your mouth or stomach when you think about eating the raisin?

The time has finally arrived to put the raisin in your mouth, but don't bite into it yet! Just let it roll around in your mouth. Let your tongue feel its texture and wrinkly surface. Can you taste the raisin already by just sucking on it in your mouth?

Okay, you've been waiting for this moment. Bite into your raisin! Notice what happens when you do this. Can you feel the flavor burst out with each bite? Do you enjoy the taste or not?

When you are ready, swallow your raisin. Imagine it making its way down to your stomach, offering up its nutrients and flavors to give you energy and pleasure.

What was that like? Did the raisin taste different than you expected?

Think about the long journey the raisin took to get here, how it began as a juicy grape on a vine, how it drew nutrients from the soil and the sun and the air around it, how it was cared for and ultimately picked by someone's hands. Think about the grape being dried out until it attained raisinhood. Take a moment to give thanks for all the things in nature and for all the people who helped create that little raisin. Did those considerations affect your appreciation for that raisin?

Many people find that when they take the time to be fully present with eating, they become better attuned to sensations of hunger and fullness. They also find that food tastes very different than they imagine, and that the amount of pleasure they get out of eating is linked to the degree of their hunger. They are better able to discern what tastes good to them—and find greater pleasure in eating.

What was it like to do that for you? Did you notice anything new or different? It's amazing how something as simple as paying attention to eating can pull us out of our autopilot mode and change our perception. Try being mindful the next time you eat, using this model. See what you learn from it.

Mindful eating is not a diet, and it's not about helping you control or restrict what you eat. It's about experiencing food more intensely. You can eat ice cream mindfully, if you wish. You might enjoy it a lot more if you slow down and allow yourself to fully experience the sensations. Or, you might discover that the idea of ice cream was better than the actual eating of it. You might decide, partway through, that your body has had enough—and that finishing everything on your plate is no longer appealing. Mindful eating can help us see whether the food we're eating is really meeting the need behind the craving. It can also help us get more in touch with our hunger and fullness, which supports us in eating nourishing amounts.

CONNECTION MATTERS

Self-reliance doesn't always work when the deck is stacked against you. That's why I want to come back to where we started in this chapter, and remind you that resilience isn't wholly an inside job. Finding opportunities in your environment—for instance, maybe some kind people will fund your Kickstarter campaign to get the gender-affirming surgery you need?—can go a long way to offsetting the limiting possibilities of personal change in an unjust world.

Or maybe you can help fund someone else's Kickstarter campaign. Let's not lose sight of how important it is to be responsible with the privilege of having money and to keep advocating for a more just and empathetic world, one that supports all of us in thriving.

SOCIAL SAFETY NETS INCREASE RESILIENCY FOR INDIVIDUALS

In countries where the government provides a social safety net such as free universal health care, paid sick leave, and subsidized child care, people have been found to be happier[15] and healthier,[16] which makes it easier for them to overcome adversity. People suffer psychologically without these supports.[17] As recently reported by the World Bank, social support networks are particularly pivotal for impoverished and/or marginalized communities.[18]

It's not too hard to understand why social safety nets are valuable: imagine if you contracted the coronavirus and you lived in a place that provided free (and adequate!) health care and sick leave. Paid sick leave allows you to take time off without the fear of being fired, and universal health care means you will get treated for your illness. Because you are supported in staying home, these also reduce the risk that you will infect others, which is just one of the many ways that social safety nets benefit people across the economic spectrum.

Social safety nets can also help prevent hard times; one study,[19] for example, documented that throughout a person's lifetime, resiliency is associated with less frequency of adverse events in one's life. Several studies have shown that states with strong social welfare policies—for example, those providing tax credits and better health care—had fewer citizens reporting disabilities than states that didn't embrace these policies.[20]

WHEN YOU ARE REALLY STRUGGLING*

There have been days when I've felt broken and stuck. I didn't want to go to work, to answer phone calls. I didn't even want to get out of bed. I want

---

* This section was inspired by reading materials by Faith Harper, an author, licensed professional counselor, and sexologist who provides excellent guidance for managing trauma, its associated maladies, and more.

to write something for you in case that is what you are going through—or so you have something to turn to when you need it. I'm living evidence that things can shift over time.

It's okay if you don't believe in yourself today, if you don't think that you have the strength to keep going or that you will ever see the change you want for yourself. So many of us have these lapses where we stop believing in ourselves, even consider suicide. You are not alone.

I want you to know that I believe in you. Just hear that and take it in. Please keep going. I am holding space for you until you get back on track.

I don't need to know you personally to know that you, as a human being, have value. The world needs each one of us and our uniqueness. You are not failing; we, as a culture, are failing you. If you turn your back on everything, we can't come to understand why we failed you and how we can do better. Giving your community that opportunity allows us to be better, not just for you, but for the many others in similar circumstances. The world needs to adapt to make space for you and others like you. We need you. I need you. So keep going, okay?

I won't promise that tomorrow will be better. But somewhere, somehow, I know that you can find a reason to keep going. I know that eventually the pain you are feeling now—and whatever you are going to learn from it—will help make the world a better place. I believe in you.

BRINGING IT HOME

The next time you're jonesing for the ice cream that looked oh-so-good on that TV commercial or tempted by the "Buy Now/Pay Later" fantasy of owning the vacuum cleaner of your dreams, it's helpful to become more aware of your sudden turn to autopilot. Then pause. That's all. Just break the automatic reactivity. I gave you some tools, such as mindfulness techniques and grounding exercises, to make it easier.

Eventually you'll be able to laugh at the impulse, see that your brain has been hijacked, and make a more thoughtful choice. I know it's not as easy as it sounds. You won't see the effect of the pause immediately, but research shows that having individual experiences of breaking impulsivity is additive in its own right and contributes to breaking habitual responses over the long run.

Know, too, th.. sometimes ice cream—or a new vacuum cleaner—constitutes the best choice!

Contemplative practices like those described in this book don't just help us sit with difficult emotions and change our behaviors. These practices can also reveal the narratives we've internalized to understand the world, help us develop more empathy for others, and help us become more intentional in how we respond to others and engage in the world. They can be the bedrock for social change.

Also, remember that your resiliency is bound up in others and in social institutions. Recognizing that there are external contributors to resilience helps us lessen the self-blame that may arise when we struggle. When you're going through a hard time, try turning to the people around you and looking for outside resources that can bolster you. Recognizing that our resiliency isn't just about being strong and pulling ourselves up by our bootstraps can also highlight the need to help people build their support systems—and to provide the structural support that allows individuals and communities to thrive.

Now that you've got some of the practical tools to explore your inner world and bounce back when life throws you curve balls, let's turn our attention to the self-love movement. Can it help get us out of this mess?

Chapter 11

BEYOND SELF-LOVE

oving yourself as is. Loving yourself just because you're enough. Loving your body because it's your home. Self-love is a feeling, not an idea. It's your birthright.

Self-love isn't conditional. We don't love ourselves because we've lost a few pounds. If that were part of the deal, we'd have to withdraw our love when we regain the weight. Instead, self-love is appreciation for the underlying you that persists through the changes. It is unconditionally valuing yourself.

It's about showing compassion for yourself when you get rejected and devalued—and knowing you're okay, just right actually, anyway. It's about showing compassion for yourself when you come up against parts of yourself that you don't like. It's about forgiving yourself for the things you've done to survive and how that may have wired into habits that don't serve you as well today.

Self-love is also about allowing ourselves to feel rage at the people and culture that have hurt us, grieving for the loss of a loving relationship with our bodies, and opening to the possibility of connection and belonging.

NOT A MAGIC BULLET

There's a myth in the body positivity movement that teaches us that when you're feeling unwelcome in the world because of your body, self-love is the magic bullet. Unfortunately, there are limits to the self-love prescription—its effectiveness drops off where your self meets others in a society that dehumanizes you in your body. If you feel bad in your body, it's because our culture has targeted your body for abuse. Self-love alone cannot fix that.

The body positivity movement's narrow focus means its tools can't work as predicted—or at all. Yes, we all need self-love to cope with body shaming and to resist internalizing it, yet self-love is not the cure but the response. All the self-love in the world won't prevent discrimination or systemic oppression. It can't help others see you for who you are. For marginalized people, and writ large collectively, a self-love focus is the spoonful of sugar that makes the oppression go down.

Consider an incident in my life—a story about the damage body shame can do. Sure, self-love can help me recover from it, but how would self-love have prevented it?

The glass bowl I was washing in the sink slipped from my hands and shattered, sending a shard of glass through the flesh of my ring finger. I knew it was more than a cut. I suspected I'd severed the tendon. Dutifully, I took myself to the hospital emergency room. Nope, the doctor told me, the tendon was intact and the nerve would heal on its own over time. My primary care physician later said the same thing. I wasn't convinced. I'm a scientist and physiologist, so the structure and function of the body is literally my business. I knew enough to know that my symptoms suggested a torn tendon and that delaying treatment could result in permanent damage, so I asked over and over again to see a specialist, urgently, now.

This is not the story of a doctor examining my sliced-up finger and prescribing weight loss, which is something that happens to fat folks all the time. That experience and others like it—of being profiled and dismissed, based on what status or lack-of-status signals your body is transmitting—is body injustice, and it's a central focus of the Health at Every Size and body positivity movements. I'm a slim person, however, so that particular example of body injustice is not part of my experience—but if we track my story all the way through the health system and almost to the courtroom, we will indeed see body injustice rear its ugly head.

At some point, I caved and gave up on self-advocacy. If my health care providers are convinced I am wrong, maybe I am. After all, they're the experts, right?

When I was finally allowed an appointment with a hand specialist, my fear was confirmed. My tendon was torn, and because too much time had passed, it was no longer repairable. As a result, I now suffer persistent pins-and-needles sensation in that finger and can't bend it, which makes typing a challenge—a not insignificant problem, given that I work as a writer. These were avoidable outcomes with proper diagnosis and timely treatment—both of which I'd rallied for.

I went into mediation with the insurance company to hold them accountable, and it's in this place, the aftermath of the injury, that the body injustice of our health system and our wider culture presented itself.

It seemed like a straightforward judgment. My concerns and their responses were all expressed in writing, including their own specialist's determination that a full recovery could have been expected if I had received the timely care that was repeatedly requested and denied to me. But during my deposition, the attorney representing the insurance company asked me about my pending top surgery. If you're thinking, but wait, there's no connection between a finger injury and top surgery, you're right. There's not.

I live in the San Francisco Bay Area, a politically progressive place where I've been "living" my gender identity confidently for decades. I have supportive, progressive-minded friends and colleagues and a workplace where I'm valued, and I am well educated on gender identity. Body acceptance has been my life's work. I'm considered a leader in the body positivity field. I teach practices that help you relearn the skill of self-acceptance, and in both my previous books I share tools to help you advocate for yourself in institutional and medical settings. Yet I was completely unnerved by this question—and that was its intent. The lawyer cannily invoked the stigma associated with my body and gender identity specifically to undermine my confidence and show the arbitrator that I was "less than." It was a reminder: You're trans. Know your place. The intent was to shock me, and thereby shift the power dynamic between us in a case he knew he couldn't win, and hopefully turn me into a bad witness for myself. The intent, too, was to evoke the assumed prejudice of the arbitrator.

Sadly, it worked to destabilize me. We didn't even get past the deposition to the arbitration stage. Eliciting my own internalized oppression was enough. A lifetime of stigma and discrimination plus internalized shame and pain flooded me. Angry and unhinged, I started stumbling over my words. My hesitation and sudden inability to explain myself in the deposition made me look like I was confused about the basic facts of my case. Hearing myself speak was like hearing a stranger. I speak from stages for a living and had long considered myself articulate, but suddenly I was having trouble finding words and even focusing. (This is a classic trauma response.)

The settlement the insurance company came back with was far less than I'd anticipated or deserved. It was also far less than my attorney anticipated prior to the deposition.

What does it tell us when a person who has spent decades practicing and teaching people to find their power can be so threatened as to lose the ability to communicate and advocate for themselves? It tells us that shame reinforces inequity. That it can be deployed against us, as both cause and result of social exclusion. It shows us shame's political and economic effects—which is why the current conversation on body positivity doesn't quite do it justice or give us the tools for navigating it.

My attorney advised me to take the inadequate settlement. I'd performed so poorly in the deposition, he said, that we had no hope of securing what the case was really worth. And if I refused the offer and proceeded with further legal action, he would not represent me. Anxious just to end the ordeal, I agreed.

Transphobia was winning.

But when I learned that the settlement would come with a nondisclosure (confidentiality) agreement, my response was visceral. I know from my work and personal experience how important testimony is to our ability to heal from stigma and discrimination, and how harmful it can be to keep our abusers' secrets. Silence allows the shame to grow and the oppression to persist. I knew I needed to be free to tell this story, not just for my own recovery and well-being, but to support others in recognizing the challenges transgender people face. I couldn't sign off on that.

I went rogue, working outside the mediation system and around the transphobic attorneys. I contacted the hospital's complaint department to call them out on their transphobia, and we came to a workable compromise. While putting nothing in writing, the hospital increased the settlement offer after I pledged to use the additional money for education on trans issues.

My attorney waived his commission on the additional amount. That was the right thing to do, of course, as he had done nothing to earn the extra dollars, but he doesn't get a pass. He offered no apology or acknowledgment that he had sold me out in the face of transphobic tactics.

In retrospect, I see that shame had initially immobilized me, which was why the insurance company's lawyer used it. He weaponized my marginalized status for an economic end. Only once I could curb my shame and recognize that the system was the problem, not me, could I take back my power.

Do stories like this always end in triumph? Absolutely not. Privilege paved the way for me. The insurance company's fear that I would use my considerable platform for public exposure threatened the system itself. Someone more marginalized, with less social support and confidence and fewer public communication skills or resources, would likely have been stuck.

My challenging the system required resources many don't have. Privilege supports us in standing up for our values. As another example, I once was asked to keynote a body image conference at a large university. The details were in place and I was just about to sign the contract when the organizer dropped, "By the way, I understand you're a lesbian. We have a policy of not endorsing gay or lesbian lifestyles, so I need to know that you're not going to mention that in your talk." Whoa! Deal breaker. I don't know if the topic would have come up, but I do know that I come as a full person and couldn't agree to those terms. I ripped up the contract, abandoning an otherwise lucrative and valuable opportunity.

Had I been less established in my career or less financially secure, I might have swallowed my principles and chosen differently. Poverty and other disadvantage sometimes push people to compromise their values.

This helps us understand that self-love can support us personally but cannot eradicate systemic oppression or the cultural norms that accompany it. It will not help people decode those signals and see other people accurately. I can love myself thoroughly and radically and I will still be misgendered in the world, othered, and disempowered. Self-love doesn't change the circumstances creating the pain and harm. This means that a focus on self-love, especially for people with dominant identities (like the cisgender white woman privileged by mainstream body positivity) becomes a personal way to cope with systemic oppression *without challenging the oppression*. In other words, a focus on self-love helps people with otherwise dominant identities individually cope with and maintain the status quo that otherwise benefits them. It doesn't help all of us band together to change that harmful status quo.

One would think that body positivity proponents, with their keen understanding that fatphobia is a source of injustice, should understand as much as anyone that the body is the site for injustice. Queer bodies. Racialized bodies. Trans bodies. Disabled bodies. Old bodies. All marginalized bodies and identities are a site for injustice.

Body positivity is necessarily about combating oppression and figuring out how to thrive despite it. That's why I want to see body positivity ideology shift from a dominant story to include all our stories and identities, and why I want us to develop the skills of body autonomy and belonging, to help us heal personally and collectively from systemic discrimination while challenging and dismantling it. Our bodies will remain our bodies; they're going to continue sending signals about who we are. What needs changing is not our bodies, and it's more than changing how we feel about them. What needs to change is how the rest of the world receives and interprets those signals they're sending. Instead of being signals that indicate someone's status or lack of status and therefore whether a person will be welcomed into belonging and safety, let's create a context in which all of us belong—with our body autonomy intact, valued, and seen for who we are.

Right now, for the most part, in our body positivity courses, platforms, and communities, we rely on self-love to cope with the injuries that come from being excluded from belonging in our families, workplaces, communities, and nations. Shouldn't it be our body positivity project, personally and collectively, to create the conditions in which belonging is possible for all bodies?

There's no room in our social justice movements for only one identity and only one story. We need to hear all the stories and all the solutions in order to heal. We need to see other people who look like us in order to be welcome, and we need to learn skills for creating belonging in order to be able to cope with and change a culture that's currently hostile to us and to create the alliances necessary to be the best we can be.

That's why, if we move beyond the dominant narrative in the body positivity community, we're also going to have to move beyond its primary tool of self-love. Yes, self-love *is* an important self-reclamation and self-preservation tool. Yes, it has space-making cultural consequences for trans, fat, disabled, and other marginalized bodies. I argue, however, that the need for practicing and reclaiming self-love is a testimony to how far-reaching and all-consuming oppression and body-based injustice truly is. That we need to constantly affirm and reaffirm and strive to love ourselves is itself a reaction to and symptom of systemic rejection. I don't want us simply to cope with body-based oppression on an individual basis. I want us to eliminate it. To eradicate the rejection, we've got to change our social conditioning and the culture around us.

RADICAL BELONGING

A focus on self-love means that we individualize a collective problem. Predictably, that erases many experiences of body oppression and ends up reinscribing body-based oppression and exclusion in the very community and movement that could be functioning as a model for radical belonging.

We all know by now that individualism doesn't solve collective problems. This book, though it recognizes the value of self-love, doesn't stop there. The project of this book—and in our lives—is to move beyond self-love into radical belonging. Individual self-love cannot change the world, but finding ways to belong to one another and offer one another refuge can. It can help shift the ground we stand on until, one day, more bodies are valued and all of us belong.

All the self-love in the world doesn't prevent other people from othering or trans-shaming or fat-shaming you. And when all you hear is a dominant narrative that doesn't represent you, the self-love edict can push you even further from finding your soul.

When I was suffering with an eating disorder, my investment in the dominant "healing" narrative only served to further my entrenchment. The commonplace understanding of eating disorders is rooted in the mainstream cis narrative that women want to be thinner because they are taught it's beautiful and they see that beauty is a woman's main (or only) path to cultural power. To gain acceptance, therefore, and avoid marginalization, women restrict their food, exercise excessively, take laxatives, or throw up.

But what if the dominant story isn't your story? What if you have an eating disorder and you're not a cis woman? What is your eating disorder narrative? And how do you treat it? What if the roots of your story emerge from the realities of race or poverty, disability or age? Why do we only see images of young cis white women when we discuss eating disorders?

As you know, I'm genderqueer. The roots of my eating disorder stemmed from feeling like my body—and how people treated me—did not match my felt sense of gender. My dieting wasn't about trying to gain currency by achieving the female beauty ideal. What I wanted was a masculinized body that would match who I felt I was. I wanted to do away with the breasts and broad hips that led people to treat me as a woman and stopped me from wearing the clothes I liked. I wanted to look down and see a body that looked like how I imagined myself.

Because the story of where eating disorders come from didn't align with my experience, neither did the solutions. Based on that misunderstanding, my route to healing was more circuitous, painful, and prolonged than it should have been. Only later in life, when I could better construct my own narrative, did I start to understand the challenges and complexities that blocked my path to embodiment.

I've heard a similar story from Gloria Lucas, a community organizer and founder of Nalgona Positivity Pride, a Xicana-Indigenous* body-positive organization that provides intersectional eating disorders education and community-based support. Lucas identifies as a Brown woman. The mainstream eating disorder resources and body positivity movements failed her by ignoring the role of colonization, assimilation, systemic oppression, and racism. Her eating disorder played out amid potent messages that People of Color receive about their bodies, that they're inferior, dirty, and unattractive. Mainstream eating disorder thought failed to recognize this.

"We have been left with no other option but to create our own opportunities of representation and healing," Lucas writes, explaining her motivation for founding Nalgona Positivity Pride.

Young, straight, cis, white women are not the only ones who experience eating disorders. They're not the only ones who suffer from fatphobia and discrimination. Their experiences are not the only experiences in our community. When only one story runs down the center lane, we crowd out nonmainstream narratives and close the route to healing and belonging for the rest of us. Those whose lives do align with the mainstream narrative are also harmed when we limit ourselves to a menu of healing opportunities based on a narrow, tired interpretation of our lives.

BRINGING IT HOME

All the self-love and self-help in the world will not erase exclusion. It will not prevent other people's socially conditioned reactions to our bodies and the fact that we're going to find it everywhere we go. Practicing self-love, internally, will not counteract external biases, prejudices, and even outright bigotry. In other words, loving yourself isn't an inoculation that prevents

---

* Whereas *Chicana* describes a Mexican American woman, *Xicana* transcends that definition, connecting the person to a recognition of their indigenous identity that is often overlooked by many Mexicans.

discrimination against you or others who look like you. Self-love doesn't address social conditioning or challenge and change the systems it is borne out of.

Prescribing self-love to an Indigenous woman doesn't reduce the number of murdered or missing Indigenous women. Practicing self-love doesn't mean that employers are going to hire a trans person (or that a lawyer won't trans-shame to get an advantage in a court case about a severed tendon!). Feeling good and lavishing care upon herself doesn't prevent a fat woman from getting slurs screamed at her in a parking lot. Loving her hair doesn't prevent a Black student from getting sent home from school for wearing braids or locs.

We're all navigating other people's biases against our bodies, and personal self-love, no matter how robust, doesn't prevent that. It simply helps us recover from the pain of those inevitable experiences.

This is why we need to liberate our bodies. Body liberation is about claiming ownership over our bodies. It doesn't just release you from having to meet someone else's ideal of beauty; it's about trashing the concept of beauty as currency altogether. It's about stretching beyond the limiting stories that are usually told and dumping the cultural ideas about what makes a body valuable. Sometimes that means allowing our bodies to just be as they are, wearing fatkinis and flaunting our stretch marks. Sometimes, as in the case of some trans people, reclaiming requires changing our bodies, perhaps through surgery and/or hormones, to transition to a body that feels like home, that represents who we are.

The culture may not rise up to celebrate your body and your choices. You don't personally have the power to make that happen alone or immediately, but collectively, we can build movements that bend the arc of justice in the long term. Your power lies in being able to make choices about how you express yourself regardless of what those choices mean for others.

I make choices about the cultural signifiers of gender that are under my control, like haircuts and clothes and body modification. I accept that others may not see me for who I am and that I can't control that. It's my body to inhabit regardless of what it may telegraph to others or how it may influence how I am treated. It's my challenge to build my resilience so that I can manage misgendering or transphobia, or any of the other ways the cultural construction of my identities can make me a target for stigma, discrimination, marginalization, and invisibility. A large part of that resilience comes from connection and from my participation in the collective struggle for belonging.

Self-love is not enough, but the individual and collective pursuit of body liberation can help us heal and help us grow a new world, where we all belong.

Chapter 12

COMING HOME

We're in a kayak, paddling between banks of mangrove trees. Our guide is telling me about how he studied in Canada before coming home so he could preserve, share, and teach his Mayan culture to visitors from within Mexico as well as tourists, like me, from other countries. Throughout the day we slow down or speed up to rejoin my partner and son, together in another kayak. There's no one else in sight this entire day, as we slowly paddle through the canal, listening to stories about Mayan traders from a thousand years past, their boats loaded with salt, honey, cacao, and dreams of wealth.

The four of us stop to eat lunch, to swim in an open lagoon, or to explore areas our guide is keen to show us. He points out tree leaves and plants, describing their healing and culinary properties. He identifies the leaf his grandmother makes into a compress to reduce the sting from bug bites. He breaks off pieces for us to taste, enthusiastically sharing family recipes featuring individual plants.

Back in our little kayak together, talking about our lives, he asks about who Anne and Isaac and I are to one another. He hasn't understood that we're a family. I can feel him trying to figure us out—especially me. He asks questions and I don't mind. We're engaging with each other in an open-hearted, curious way.

His questions continue, and we get to talking about my name. My body, my gender, and my family might be confusing and warrant sincere questions, but my name he understands. In Spanish, which he speaks fluently, *Linda* means beautiful. The "a" at the end marks it as feminine—exactly why my parents chose it for me. Exactly why I struggle with it. I've had top surgery, I dress in masculine clothing, and I wear my hair short. Although I don't take hormones, when I look in the mirror I don't read myself as woman. My friends and the people close to me tell me the same. That when they see me, I read as genderqueer, not female. One person told me it was only the name on my books that indicated "woman" to her, not my physical presentation. All of which explains why my new friend might be curious about me, about my family, about my name. That "a" on the end doesn't line up with the person in the boat with him. The connotation of feminine beauty just doesn't resonate. I explain as best I can and then he has an aha moment. "You're Lindo!" he exclaims, masculinizing the noun in Spanish.

He's right.

When he explains that meaning takes on nuance with the masculinized ending, reflecting more of a beautiful essence rather than physical beauty, it seems even more right.* I like the way it messes with constructions of beauty *and* gender.

Lindo. Yes, I am Lindo. There's continuity there, a specificity I recognize. I can still be the beautiful human my parents dreamed of. I can still be my history, me. Just not the feminized version, because I was never a girl. I was never Linda, not really. But Lindo? Lindo, I recognize. This new name—that's not new at all, just slightly, rightly different—feels like home to me.

The process of arriving at this place—at home in your own skin, welcome in the world—isn't a solo journey, no matter what we may hear about self-help or self-love. Sure, a lot of the work, including some of the practical tools I've shared in this book, is internal and personal. But even when each of us takes on these tasks, all the self-love in the world doesn't prevent

---

* Other Spanish speakers inform me this isn't a universally understood definition; nonetheless, his declaration had profound impact for me.

other people from othering, body-shaming, dehumanizing, or oppressing you, nor does it change how your central nervous system responds to this threat. We can't do this on our own. We need to create spaces where we can meet each other and validate each other. No human body is born alone. None of us can survive alone, and certainly none of us can thrive alone. What makes everything better—including the world!—is when we welcome each other and are welcomed in return.

In the previous chapter, I debunked that myth that when our surroundings feel hostile, self-love is the answer, and I traced the limits of that self-love prescription. We looked at how it can boost you to face the world in the short term, but the concept's efficacy ends at the point where your self meets others in a society that dehumanizes and privileges some bodies over others. If your self-image takes a dive in those moments and leaves you scrambling to recover, it's not because you failed to love yourself enough. It's because the world is still hostile to people who look like you. Self-love can't fix the world that causes the self-loathing in the first place.

To understand and confront the stigma, discrimination, and even violence we encounter—in our schools, workplaces, public spaces, and even homes—we need to widen the lens, pulling back from our individual psyches to take in the structural oppression around us. The game is rigged, and those of us with marginalized identities (and any identity, but especially communities of people who are most oppressed) must continually, intuitively, and consciously manage other people's impressions of us. Everywhere we go, our bodies precede us and announce the social taxonomy associated with our particular kind of body. That, in turn, triggers reactions from other people that are rooted in unconscious biases or conscious prejudices.

For thirty years, I worked on and studied diet culture, weight bias, fatphobia, and eating disorders, but I've come to see these as just one site of body-based oppression. The past several years have given me a new understanding of my own experience of disordered eating and substance abuse. I hadn't been wrong to blame diet culture and my internalized fatphobia for my perfect storm of addictions, but I hadn't gone far enough. My discomfort in my body stemmed from the dehumanizing gender binary that made me feel not entirely human (everyone else was *boy* or *girl*—what was I?!). That pervasive sense of body-wrongness imposed on me by our culture isolated me from other people and the community we all need to make life worth living. Gendered oppression—that narrow understanding of gender as either male or female and nothing else—had isolated me from family, friends, lovers, and colleagues. It separated me from career opportunities and financial rewards I deserved. It had pushed me to a place in my life where dangerous diets and drugs seemed safer company than other people.

Expanding beyond body positivity to see this gender and social oppression revealed that my fatphobia, my eating disorder, and the substance abuse that followed arose from being misgendered for so much of my life.

The effects of oppression are visceral and damaging, and none of us should have to endure it. That these experiences inhabit every corner of our daily lives and can burrow into each of us is tragic. It must change. To heal injuries inflicted by a hostile world and survive in it, we've got to stop the harm necessitating all that recovery in the first place. We've got to start by identifying the oppression that's creating all these injuries and eliminating it everywhere we find it. That requires understanding how oppression works systemically. Hierarchy, inequity, and exclusion aren't accidents or unfortunate incidents. They're designed into our workplaces, governments, and social norms.

This work also requires identifying and correcting for the ways we are complicit in the oppression on a social level—that is, examining how our conditioning has produced (and continues to produce) conscious and unconscious biases and reactions in us. This is hard and requires life-long self-reflection. It also requires commitment to learning about and being respectful of cultural identities of diverse groups. This learning needs to be approached with humility, requiring that we step outside of ourselves and be open to other people's identities in a way that acknowledges their authority over their own experiences. Recognizing that each person brings something different to the proverbial table of life helps us see the value of each person. An individual's lived experience is rich and more complicated than can ever be explained by our ideas about them.

We must locate ourselves in systems of oppression, grapple with the ways in which we are privileged, and use our agency to advocate for social change. We have to build our social analyses and implement collective practices so that we can create a culture of belonging in which every body is welcome, everywhere. We need to develop more robust skills and practices in being together and creating refuge for each other. This is how we teach each other how to see each other for who we really are and how we create space for all bodies to matter and for each of us to belong—in our skin, and to each other.

The pain that comes from exclusion is social, spiritual, emotional, psychological, and acutely physical. We should strive, as individuals and as a community, not to inflict this kind of lasting damage on each other. When we do experience this kind of pain, we should attend to it and feel it, because truly making contact with it and feeling it, ourselves, can motivate us to stop harming each other and instead take care of each other and ourselves. We need to see our social anxieties and the symptoms of disconnect not as psychological problems or flawed, weak, bad parts of ourselves, but as opportunities. Only by recognizing that we fear rejection can we see how essential it is to our well-being that we connect, which can be exactly the thing that propels us toward each other. We all have fears around social connection. That's called being human. We'd do better to bond and support each other around those fragilities and with our common desires to be liked and appreciated. Fear of rejection and exclusion can be the thing that motivates us to be kinder to each other so we can live together.

Instead of trying of make the woundedness go away, let's create a safe place to be ourselves, to trust each other and come together in our woundedness. I want us to belong to each other. The fragility that each of us carries around connection is one of the things that makes us beautiful.

That is what happened for me in a kayak on a Mexican river with a Mayan man curious enough to ask who I really am—and willing to believe me when I told him. His openness to truly seeing me helped me see myself. This day-long conversation, this new name, this recognition of me for who I am, arose from curiosity. It came from a willingness to be vulnerable and admit confusion and ask questions. It came from a willingness to revise assumptions and biases to accommodate the lived reality—and body!—of the very real, precious person in front of him. It came from cultural humility, the recognition that we don't know what contexts and traditions have shaped us. It came from trust; my identity wasn't being used against me, so

I knew I could safely answer questions and reveal myself. And it came from a recognition that we can be different and still know one another and offer welcome. I think if he and I were more similar, our conversations might have been more constrained and we wouldn't have learned so much from and about each other—or ourselves. Our difference allowed us to find a place where we could humble ourselves and invite each other in.

When I returned home from that trip, I extended the invitation to myself. I invited myself, once again, to be more of myself. I tried out the new name, *Lindo*, in my own mouth. Slowly, across the months and years, I tried it out with my partner, friends, and trusted colleagues. By inviting them to call me Lindo, I invited them to recognize me for who I am. I invited them to truly know me.

To be known, accepted, and loved for who we truly are is what we all want. We all want to be seen, named, and welcomed as is—in a kayak, around the kitchen table, at our jobs, on the streets, in our families, and everywhere else in the world. The world doesn't have to be perfect for us to do this and experience this right now. Though the wider world is unsafe, we can create tiny worlds within it. We can grow our resilience and eventually widen those safe harbors until we make a world in which everyone matters and everyone is welcome. We won't see the full results of our efforts in our own lifetimes. Yet we still have to strive to develop the personal resilience and public collectives that will let us live beautifully in the world right now, as it is, as freely as humanly possible. The solution is not found in the end point. It's in coming together in the collective struggle.

We don't do it to win. We do it because it's right. We do it to embrace our common humanity. We strive, unapologetically, if imperfectly, to do the right thing, and over time that right thing will become normal and the world will become more welcoming for more of us—maybe even all of us. In the meantime, we create intentional, welcoming communities of love and radical belonging. Let's make it so.

You belong in your body, you belong in this world, and we belong together.

EDUCATIONAL TOOLS

CONTENTS

These tools are freely distributable and downloadable at lindobacon.com.

MANIFESTO FOR BODY LIBERATION

- For trans people, body liberation means access to surgery and hormones and other respectful health care. It also includes the right to choose an appropriate bathroom.
- For everyone on the LGBTQIA+ spectrum, it includes the right to marry and to adopt and raise kids. It also means the right to housing and employment that cannot legally discriminate against sexual orientation and gender identity and the ability to donate blood to those in need.
- For intersex people, it means the right to exist as they were born and the right to make their own choices about body manipulation.
- For women, body liberation includes reproductive rights, freedom from rape culture and body commentary, and the right to dress any way they want.
- For fat people, body liberation includes access to quality health care. It means ending governmental and employer policies aiming to create incentives for losing weight or defining parental neglect standards that are related to children's weight. It also means repealing laws mandating that schools weigh students on a regular basis and send reports to their parents along with dietary and exercise recommendations.
- For disabled people, body liberation includes opposition to institutionalization, forced sterilization, involuntary surgery, and lack of accommodations.
- For the neurodivergent, it means access to quality health care that covers the full cost of their medical needs. It also means decriminalizing mental illnesses and removing police from psychiatric facilities.
- For sex workers, it includes decriminalizing sex and asserting the right to use our bodies in ways we choose. It means showing compassion for people who feel forced to sell rights

to their bodies for survival and providing options that make this unnecessary.

- For Black people, Indigenous people, and other People of Color, it includes protecting the sanctity of their bodies and eliminating police violence, extra surveillance, and racial profiling.
- For religious people, it includes the right to wear—or not wear—clothes of their choice and openly practice their faith without fear of retribution.
- For impoverished people, it means providing opportunity to earn money and safety nets for survival and well-being.
- For all of us, it means:
  - the right to define our own rules for relationships (beyond heteronormative marriage) and the right to participate in varied forms of consensual sex (however uncomfortable others may find it)
  - abolishing the criminal "justice" system and replacing it with transformative justice practices
  - securing rights to survival needs, like universal access to nutritious food, safe housing, medical care, clean air, and water

For all of us, body liberation means the right to inhabit our bodies with dignity and respect.

Body liberation can help us be ourselves, belong in our bodies, and belong across difference.

CRITICAL AWARENESS EXERCISE

ASSESSING THE CULTURAL IMPACT ON QUALITY OF LIFE

Part 1: Identifying the Impact of Social Identity Categories

Each of the social identity categories in the following chart regulates and shapes the course of our lives in some way. In the first column on the left, rate the impact these factors have on you personally on a scale from –5 to +5.

Negative numbers mean that how you are treated based on this aspect of yourself has a negative impact on your life, while positive numbers indicate that you feel culturally advantaged based on that aspect. In other words, if racism has a negative impact on your life, you would choose a negative number for race. Choosing a negative number about race doesn't indicate lack of pride or suggest that you have any negative feelings about your race, just that racism exerts a negative influence on you.

–5 means a social identity category affects your life for the worse, to a very strong degree.

0 means a social identity category has no discernible effect on your life.

+5 means a social identity category makes your life a lot easier and more comfortable.

After you have finished rating all the categories in the first column, proceed to the columns on the right, putting as many or as few check marks in the appropriate categories.

Try to complete this quickly, choosing a "gut" response. Later, you can return and adjust your responses.

Rate the impact (−5 to +5)	Social Identity Category	Matters in how you perceive yourself (✓)	Matters in how others perceive you (✓)
	Race/Ethnicity		
	Age		
	Socioeconomic status		
	Religion/Spiritual Orientation/Faith		
	Sexual Orientation		
	Gender		
	Dis/Ability		
	Education		
	Mental Health		
	Family/Reproductive status		
	Language (including what languages you speak as well as fluency, accent, diction, etc.)		
	Habitat (where you live)		
	Citizenship		
	Other appearance traits (examples: height, weight, tattoos, birthmarks)		
	Other:		

Part 2: Reflection Questions

Use your discretion in pondering these questions. Some may be emotionally triggering, particularly if you have a history of trauma. Consider self-care strategies that will help you as you engage. Consider, too, delving into the questions with a group, a friend, or professional help.

1. What does this exercise tell you about your relative power in the world?
2. What does this exercise have to do with health?
3. What does this exercise have to do with body dissatisfaction and eating disorders?
4. Which identities do you think people first notice about you?
5. Which identities do you notice first in other people?
6. Which identities matter most in your self-perception?

7. Which identities matter least in your self-perception?

8. Which identities do you think matter most in others' perception of you?

9. Which identities do you think about most often?

10. Which identities do you think about least often?

11. Which identities are visible to others, and which invisible? Which do you have a choice about visibility? What do you consider in making that choice?

12. Which identities are you most comfortable sharing with others?

13. Which identities are you most proud of?

14. Which identities are you least comfortable sharing with others?

15. Which identities are you ashamed of?

16. Which identities did you struggle the most with growing up?

17. Which identities do you face oppression for most often?

18. Which identities do you receive advantages for most often?

19. Which of these identities have shifted over time? Which do you anticipate shifting in the future?

20. Reflect on the stories that support why you chose the numbers in the first column. Include the larger events and consider, too, the smaller microaggressions or advantages that pile up. Also consider the "nagging feelings" that aren't as easily "provable."

21. Share your stories with others. Ask their stories. Imagine the experiences of people in different identity groups.

22. Reflect on the challenges in your life today that may have developed as a result of your negative experience. How can you move forward in situating the systemic roots of these challenges, and lightening up on the self-blame, shame, or other effects?

23. Reflect on any positive aspects of who you are today that may have developed as a result of your negative experience.

24. What can you do to find and strengthen your power and resilience?

25. Consider identities that make you feel relatively advantaged. What are some concrete ways you could use your privilege (unearned advantage) responsibly?

26. How are these questions valuable and applicable in clinical practice?

Part 3: Reflection Exercises

Choose a category for which you had a high negative number, if any. **Think about an experience** that illustrates why you chose this number. Yours may be a dramatic incident, or it may be smaller microaggressions that cumulatively led to this number.

Journal about that experience. Consider writing in a stream of consciousness: Don't worry about writing in complete sentences. Don't worry about spelling, grammar, or even making sense. Jot down any and all words, images, and ideas that come to mind.

For some people, your thoughts may immediately go to an experience of trauma. That's not unusual. Make a choice about how to take care of yourself. If you can, use this as an opportunity to explore it. Or, you may want to temporarily protect yourself and try to chase it out of your mind by writing on another topic. As an example, my go-to journaling when I need to feel uplifted is to write about something I feel grateful for. If I write in a fast stream of consciousness, I can usually chase bad thoughts away and move into a sense of love and appreciation.

Share with a partner. The listener's role is to listen and communicate to the speaker that you hear them. No judgment. It's okay to sit together in silence and just share space together. Try to lighten the performance pressure. The goal is just to be with your partner as they share their experience.

Afterward, the listener asks questions intended to help deepen their understanding of the other person's experience. Again, try to avoid judgment or commentary and to keep the focus on learning.

Role Switch. Trade roles and do this exercise again.

Part 4: Journal Reflection

Reflect on any positive aspects of who you are that may have developed from or be related to the negative experience you chose in Part 3. This time let your journaling be more thoughtful as opposed to stream of consciousness.

- For example, did the pain of your experience contribute to your sensitivity to others' pain today, perhaps making you more empathetic and caring?
- As another example, many people find that having a foreign accent contributes to social discrimination. However, are there positive attributes that come with the ability to speak more than one language?

Learning Objectives:

- Offers an opportunity to reflect on privilege/disadvantage.
- Provides the potential to experience connection—both feeling "seen" and seeing someone else.
- Helps us find our power by recasting our experiences of disadvantage through our story of resilience, recognizing that we are better people because of—not in spite of—how we got here.

Were the learning objectives achieved? For some people, the second and third objectives may have backfired, resulting in feelings of increased alienation, disconnection, and victimization. If so, please don't stop here. Can you explore this more? Is there a safe person you can find with whom you can discuss this and experience connection? Can you get professional help?

Process the reflection with your partner.

CRITICAL REVIEW

The objective of helping people understand privilege and disadvantage may be more valuable for privileged people who are less likely to see the ways they are advantaged. Disadvantage, for those who experience it, is more well known, not something someone who is disadvantaged needs to be reminded of. This exercise, therefore, can be criticized for centering on whiteness and other forms of power, using marginalized people as props to help advantaged people see how privileged they are. Privileged people need to see, somehow, the privilege they live in. Still, by refocusing on advantage, we end up reproducing privilege within the context of the exercise.

For disadvantaged people, the primary value may be in the reinforcement that there are systemic contributions to their challenges, which could help them to lighten up on self-blame for their circumstances.

SEX, GENDER, AND SEXUAL ORIENTATION: A PRIMER AND GLOSSARY

Sex categorizes people as *male*, *female*, or *intersex*. It considers characteristics such as sex chromosomes, gonads, internal reproductive organs, and external genitalia. *Intersex* is a term used to refer to people born with biological characteristics that don't fit the conventional definitions of female or male. *Transsexual* is an older term used to identify people who have changed or want to change their body through surgeries, hormones, and/or other body modifications to have physical characteristics of their desired sex. It is no longer commonly used and best chosen only if individuals choose to self-identify as such. Sex, like gender, is socially constructed, meaning that the boundaries of the categories reflect cultural values. The older view of sex as solely biological has been discarded by physical and social scientists alike. The phrases "assigned male at birth" (AMAB) or "assigned female at birth" (AFAB) replace the old concept of biological sex, acknowledging that someone, often a doctor, is making a decision for someone else. That assignment may or may not align with a person's gender.

Gender refers to the socially constructed roles and behavior associated with sex—in other words, the symbolism of masculinity and femininity connected to being a *man* or *woman*. The term *cisgender* is used for someone who identifies as the gender conventionally associated with the sex they were assigned at birth, and the term *transgender* is used for someone who identifies with a gender that differs from that conventionally associated with the sex they were assigned at birth. Cisgender people are said to be "gender-conforming," while transgender people are described as "gender-nonconforming." The terms *genderqueer* and *non-binary* are used for people who don't fit into the male/female binary. *Trans* is an inclusive term that encompasses people who are "queering" (deviating from norms) gender, including those who identify as transgender, non-binary, gender-queer, etc.

Sexual orientation describes people based on who they are emotionally, romantically, and/or physically attracted to or not. Vocabulary is changing, and the definitions of some terms currently in usage reflect an outdated, binary understanding of sex and gender. *Gay* and *lesbian* people are attracted to others of the same sex. The term *homosexual* is outdated and considered offensive by many. Some lesbian and gay people refer to themselves as *queer* as a means of reclaiming the word and acknowledging its cultural deviance. Others use it to include identities that don't neatly fit into the typically binary categories. *Heterosexual* people are attracted to people of a different sex, on the binary. *Bisexual* people are men and women who are attracted to both men and women. *Asexual* people feel little or no sexual attraction for others. *Pansexual* people are generally attracted to other people irrespective of their gender identity. *Demisexual* people don't experience sexual attraction unless they form a strong emotional connection with someone. The term *sexual preference* is discouraged as it has been historically used to suggest that who we are attracted to is a choice and therefore can and should be "cured."

LGBTQIA+ is an acronym for "lesbian, gay, bisexual, transgender, queer, intersex, and asexual/aromantic." Sometimes the Q is instead intended to reflect "questioning," for someone who is not sure which category or categories they might fit into. The "A" can also refer to Agender or an Ally. The plus sign is an acknowledgement of the complexity of identity and intended to include others who identify with this community. Sometimes the acronym LGBTQ2S is used, with the "2S" referring to two-spirit people who have both masculine and feminine spirits, a cultural identity that originated with Indigenous people.

ADDITIONAL TERMINOLOGY ASSOCIATED WITH GENDER PRIVILEGE AND OPPRESSION

Sexism refers to both discrimination based on sex and the attitudes and stereotypes that promote that discrimination. The term *sexism* is applied to discrimination towards women and people of other genders, and not to prejudice against men, as men as a class hold institutional power denied to others. Men are undoubtedly affected by sexism, but because of their privilege they don't experience it in the same way that people of other genders do.

Heterosexism is the belief that heterosexuals are inherently superior to people of other sexual orientations.

Homophobia refers to negative attitudes and feelings toward people who are identified or perceived as being lesbian, gay, or bisexual.

Heteronormativity is the belief that people fall into distinct and complementary genders (man and woman) with natural roles. It's a system that works to normalize behaviors and societal expectations that are tied to the presumption of heterosexuality and an adherence to a gender binary.

Cissexism is the belief that cisgender people are inherently superior to those who don't gender conform.

Transphobia refers to negative attitudes and feelings toward people whose gender identities, appearances, or behaviors deviate from social norms.

Privilege refers to the unearned advantages conferred by social identity, backed by institutional power, such as male privilege, heterosexual privilege, cisgender privilege, and able-bodied privilege.

Entitlement refers to believing oneself to be inherently deserving of certain privileges or special treatment. Because of privilege, entitlement is often not conscious to the beholder, who may not see and understand the ways they act with entitlement. *Gender entitlement* refers to a person privileging their own perceptions, interpretations, and evaluations of other people's genders over the way those people understand themselves.

THE GENDER MANIFESTO

It is important to emphasize that these conceptual frameworks—sex, gender, and sexual orientation—can be viewed as a continuum, with socially constructed definitions of categories, as opposed to having an objective basis. Conventional ideas about these categories support a hierarchical system that confers power on some as it disempowers others. Expecting people to conform to binary categories denies the reality of human diversity and limits our full expression. Few of us fully fit the socially sanctioned binary categories in all ways and at all times, and all of us pay a price for internalizing or policing them.

It's okay to be a man or a woman, if that's what you choose. It's okay to be masculine or feminine or to choose categories that defy the binaries. It's okay to choose fluidity across the categories. Where we go wrong is when we allow our culture, our history, or even our biology to define us. We all get to make choices for ourselves about how we identify as well as how we express ourselves. We get to change our minds, make up new categories that describe our particular identity, and change our bodies, too, if we so choose.

TOOLS TO SMASH THE GENDER BINARY

Two easy ways you can help smash the gender binary and support trans folks is through proper pronoun usage and making bathrooms accessible. A special call-out to cisgender people: use your privilege to advocate for others.

PRONOUNS

Why is it valuable to ask for and respect people's personal gender pronouns?

- You can't always know someone's personal gender pronouns by looking at them.
- Asking and correctly using someone's pronoun(s) is one of the most basic ways to show your respect for their gender identity.

Some people may consider this practice silly or oversensitive, or perhaps too "politically correct" for their taste. If so, this is an opportunity to reflect on privilege.

Odds are you are accustomed to being seen for your gender identity and aren't concerned that someone will wrongly project their ideas about gender onto you. It's common for people with privilege to believe that their experiences are universal and not be aware that others have very different experiences.

Not everyone has the luxury of being "seen" or acknowledged accurately. This contributes to a feeling that we don't belong and a sense of alienation and "wrongness."

Rather than being a meaningless exercise in identity politics, asking for and respecting others' pronouns is an acknowledgment of a person's innermost identity, conferring respect and dignity. It is your opportunity to help others to feel seen, to know that who they are matters, and to widen the circle of belonging. It also helps remind all of us that gender is a social construct, which can help lighten the pressure we all feel to gender conform and measure up to gendered ideals like beauty standards.

The benefit is far greater than merely showing kindness and respect. Your world will be much richer for it.

Consider, too, that while the practice of asking or announcing one's gender pronouns is well accepted as valuable in progressive and trans-friendly communities, it is not without controversy. The practice has backfired for me and many other trans people, forcing us to either lie or out ourselves when it may not be safe. A therapist friend, for example, participated in a recent conference where they were asked to provide their pronouns. This put them in an uncomfortable position. While they use they/them pronouns personally, they were choosing not to in professional settings, knowing that they would lose clients and potential referrals if this were more generally known.

Please respect the choices that individuals make about whether to reveal their identities. Make choices about whether to ask someone's pronouns with respect and care. When you do ask, try to provide opportunity for someone to opt out in a comfortable way that doesn't disclose what the question might mean for them.

It's becoming increasingly common for cisgender people to declare their pronouns, intended as an acknowledgement that you can't always know someone's pronouns and as a sign of solidarity and support for trans people. Please be thoughtful about this practice and examine your intention. Is it because you sincerely want to include everyone? Or is it about virtue-signaling (demonstrating your wokeness)? If you are cisgender, declaring your pronouns is rarely an act of vulnerability though it may be to a transgender person. Do be thoughtful about respectful practice. Have these conversations with one another.

BATHROOMS

Providing safe, gender-inclusive bathrooms goes a long way toward expanding spaces of belonging—and to educating people that gender flows beyond the binary. You can help make change by advocating. Practically, you can encourage businesses to change their bathroom signs to a more apt symbol of a toilet/sink, or perhaps something a bit more playful like the sign I once saw in a coffee shop, "WHATEVER. Just wash your hands."

Some of the previous information is repeated on the sample handouts that follow. Consider sharing them with others.

Guidelines for Setting an All-Gender Inclusive Tone at Meetings and Events

- Use inclusive language. For example, you can refer to "people" instead of "men and women," or "staffing" instead of "manpower." Or, if you really want to emphasize inclusivity, you can refer to "people of all genders."
- Get in the habit of using the singular "they" when a specific gendered pronoun is unnecessary.
- Consider asking people to introduce themselves with their names and their pronouns, if they'd like to share them. For example, "Hi, I'm Lindo, and I use the pronouns they and them. Please share the name you like to be called. Feel free to also share your pronouns, if you're so inclined." This sends the message that you are not making assumptions about anyone's gender. The addition of "if you're so inclined" may lessen the dynamic of putting people on the spot. However, if you feel this practice will have the effect of singling out someone in the room, avoid it.
- Add pronouns to name tags.
- When in a group, avoid identifying people with gendered language. Instead of the "woman in the front," for example, you can refer to the "person in the red shirt."
- If bathrooms in the meeting space are not already all-gender, consider putting an all-gender sign on them.

Nametags That Incorporate
Respectful Pronoun Practices

Consider including your name and personal gender pronouns when nametags are used.

LINDO BACON

THEY/THEM/THEIRS

Why is it important to ask for and respect people's personal gender pronouns?

- You can't always know someone's personal gender pronouns by looking at them.
- Asking and correctly using someone's pronoun(s) is one of the most basic ways to show your respect for their gender identity.

Some people may consider this practice silly or oversensitive, perhaps too "politically correct" for their taste. If so, this is an opportunity to reflect on privilege.

Odds are you are accustomed to being seen for your gender identity and don't have the concern that someone will wrongly project their ideas about gender onto you. It's common for people with privilege to believe that their experiences are universal and not be aware that others have very different experiences.

Not everyone has the luxury of being "seen" or acknowledged accurately. This contributes to a feeling that we don't belong and a sense of alienation and "wrongness."

Rather than being a meaningless exercise in identity politics, this is an acknowledgment of a person's innermost identity, conferring respect and dignity. It is your opportunity to help others feel seen, to know that who they are matters, and to widen the circle of belonging. It also helps remind all of us that gender is a social construct, which can help lighten the pressure we all feel to gender conform and measure up to gendered ideals like beauty standards.

The benefit is far greater than merely showing kindness and respect. Your world will be much richer for it.

Restrooms for All

I want to support businesses that are welcoming and inclusive and that cultivate a sense of warmth and belonging for everyone. Bathrooms that are open to people of any gender are an important way to provide this warmth and inclusion. They also make a statement, helpful for everyone, that gender is not a binary category.

To make your space more inclusive and respectful, please change your restroom signs to acknowledge that gender is not limited to men and women and to include those who don't fit into those categories.

If you have a single occupancy restroom, it's particularly easy. Just replace your gendered sign with one that says "All-gender" or simply "Restroom."

If you only have two multi-stall bathrooms and aren't in a position to build a third, please consider steps you can take to make your existing bathrooms more inclusive. Perhaps you can replace your signs with a simple "All-gender" sign with an explanation: "This is a gender-inclusive restroom with multiple stalls. It is open to users of any gender identity or expression." Or, perhaps you can add gender-affirming signage to segregated bathrooms that states: "You are welcome to use the restroom that best aligns with your gender identity."

The culture will shift as we recognize that we don't need those distinctions and can share spaces. Can you label your bathrooms so that people feel empowered to use a bathroom that is most comfortable for them and can trust they won't be harassed inside?

NOTES

Introduction

1   Russell B. Toomey, Amy K. Syvertsen, and Maura Shramko, "Transgender Adolescent Suicide Behavior," *Pediatrics* 142, no. 4 (October 2018): e20174218, https://doi.org/10.1542/peds.2017-4218.

Chapter 1

1   Audre Lorde, *Sister Outsider: Essays and Speeches* (Berkeley, CA: Crossing Press, 2007).

2   Carlos Maza and Like Brinker, "15 Experts Debunk Right-Wing Transgender Bathroom Myth," *Media Matters*, March 19, 2014, https://www.mediamatters.org/sexual-harassment-sexual-assault/15-experts-debunk-right-wing-transgender-bathroom-myth.

3   A. Hasenbush, A. R. Flores, and J. L. Herman, "Gender Identity Nondiscrimination Laws in Public Accommodations: A Review of Evidence Regarding Safety and Privacy in Public Restrooms, Locker Rooms, and Changing Rooms," *Sexuality Research and Social Policy* 16, 70–83 (2019). https://doi.org/10.1007/s13178-018-0335-z.

Chapter 2

1   Sarah L. Szanton et al., "Allostatic Load: A Mechanism of Socioeconomic Health Disparities?," *Biological Research for Nursing* 7, no. 1 (July 2005): 7–15, https://doi.org/10.1177/1099800405278216.

2   bell hooks, *Feminist Theory: From Margin to Center* (Boston: South End Press, 1984).

3   N. J. Justice, "The Relationship Between Stress and Alzheimer's Disease," *Neurobiology of Stress* 8 (April 2018): 127-133. https://doi.org/10.1016/j.ynstr.2018.04.002.

4   Jay Smooth, "How I Learned to Stop Worrying and Love Discussing Race." Filmed

November 15, 2011, at Hampshire College. TEDx video, 11:56, https://www.youtube
.com/watch?v=MbdxeFcQtaU.

5   A. Tomiyama, D. Carr, E. Granberg, et al., "How and Why Weight Stigma Drives the
      Obesity 'Epidemic' and Harms Health," *BMC Medicine* 16, no. 123 (August 2018).
      https://doi.org/10.1186/s12916-018-1116-5.

6   M. R. Lowe, S. D. Doshi, S. N. Katterman, and E. H. Feig, "Dieting and Restrained Eat-
      ing as Prospective Predictors of Weight Gain." *Frontiers in Psychology* 4 (September
      2013): 577. https://doi.org/10.3389/fpsyg.2013.00577.

7   P. S. Maclean, A. Bergouignan, M. A. Cornier, and M. R. Jackman, "Biology's Response
      to Dieting: The Impetus for Weight Regain," *American Journal of Physiology: Regula-
      tory, Integrative, and Comparative Physiology* 301, no. 3 (September 2011): R581–R600;
      P. Sumithran, L. A. Prendergast, E. Delbridge, et al., "Long-Term Persistence of
      Hormonal Adaptations to Weight Loss," *New England Journal of Medicine* 365, no. 17
      (October 2011): 597–604.

8   E. Fothergill, J. Guo, L. Howard, et al., "Persistent Metabolic Adaptation 6 Years After
      'The Biggest Loser' Competition." *Obesity* 24 (8) (May 2016): 1612–1619. https://doi
      .org/10.1002/oby.21538.

Chapter 3

1   Fancy Feast, "The Gym Isn't Usually a Safe Space for Fat Women, but It's Become My
      Sanctuary," *Buzzfeed News*, January 19, 2019, https://www.buzzfeednews.com/article
      /fancyfeast/weight-lifting-fat-woman-gym-strength-fitness-gender.

2   V. J. Felitti, R. F. Anda, D. Nordenberg, et al., "Relationship of Childhood Abuse and
      Household Dysfunction to Many of the Leading Causes of Death in Adults: The
      Adverse Childhood Experiences (ACE) Study," *American Journal of Preventive Medicine*
      14, no. 4 (May 1998): 245–58.

3   R. E. Norman, M. Byambaa, R. De, et al., "The Long-Term Health Consequences of
      Child Physical Abuse, Emotional Abuse, and Neglect: A Systematic Review and Me-
      ta-Analysis," *PLOS Medicine* 9, no. 11 (November 2012): e1001349.

4   M. A. Bellis, H. Lowey, N. Leckenby, et al., "Adverse Childhood Experiences: Retro-
      spective Study to Determine Their Impact on Adult Health Behaviours and Health
      Outcomes in a UK Population," *Journal of Public Health* 36, no. 1 (March 2014): 81–91.

5   Ragen Chastain, "The Inconvenient Truth About Weight Loss Surgery," *Ravishly*,
      March 14, 2017, https://ravishly.com/2017/03/14/inconvenient-truth-about-weight-loss
      -surgery.

6   Reproduced from Linda Bacon, *Health at Every Size: The Surprising Truth about Your
      Weight*, 2d ed. (Dallas: BenBella, 2010).

7   P. C. Patel and S. Devaraj, "Height-Income Association in Developing Countries: Evi-
      dence from 14 Countries," *American Journal of Human Biology* 30, no. 3 (2018). https://
      doi.org/10.1002/ajhb.23093.

8   W. E. Frankenhuis, and M. Del Giudice, "When Do Adaptive Developmental Mecha-
      nisms Yield Maladaptive Outcomes?," *Developmental Psychology* 48, no. 3 (May 2012):
      628–42.

9   A. S. Alberga, I. Y. Edache, M. Forhan, and S. Russell-Mayhew, "Weight Bias and
      Health Care Utilization: A Scoping Review," *Primary Health Care Research & Develop-
      ment* 20 (2019): e116. https://doi.org/10.1017/S1463423619000227.

10   Ibid.

11   Saidiya Hartman, *Lose Your Mother: A Journey along the Atlantic Slave Route* (New York: Farrar, Straus, and Giroux, 2007).

Chapter 4

1   Robert Sapolsky, "Are Humans Just Another Primate?," lecture, California Academy of Sciences, February 15, 2011, San Francisco, YouTube video, 1:16:08, https://www.youtube.com/watch?v=YWZAL64E0DI.

2   B. Knutson, S. Rick, G. E. Wimmer, et al., "Neural Predictors of Purchases," *Neuron* 53, no. 1 (Jan. 2007): 147–56.

3   Malissa A. Clark, Jesse S. Michel, Ludmila Zhdanova, et al., "All Work and No Play? A Meta-Analytic Examination of the Correlates and Outcomes of Workaholism," *Journal of Management* 42. no. 7 (Feb. 2014): 1836–73.

4   Katherine A. DeCelles and Michael I. Norton, "Physical and Situational Inequality on Airplanes Predicts Air Rage," *Proceedings of the National Academy of Sciences* 113, no. 20 (May 2016): 5588–91, https://doi.org/10.1073/pnas.1521727113.

5   Bruce Alexander, *The Globalization of Addiction: A Study in Poverty of the Spirit* (Oxford: Oxford University Press, 2010).

6   L. N. Robins, D. H. Davis, and D. N. Nurco, "How Permanent Was Vietnam Drug Addiction?," *American Journal of Public Health* 64, suppl. 12 (Dec. 1974): 38–43.

7   S. S. Luthar, P. J. Small, and L. Ciciolla, "Adolescents from Upper Middle Class Communities: Substance Misuse and Addiction across Early Adulthood," *Development and Psychopathology* 30, no. 1 (Feb. 2018): 315–35.

8   Johann Hari, "Everything You Think You Know about Addiction Is Wrong." June 2015. TEDGlobalLondon video, 14:43, https://www.ted.com/talks/johann_hari_everything_you_think_you_know_about_addiction_is_wrong.

9   M. Milyavskaya and M. Inzlicht, "What's So Great about Self-Control? Examining the Importance of Effortful Self-Control and Temptation in Predicting Real-Life Depletion and Goal Attainment," *Journal of Social Psychological and Personality Science* 8, no. 6 (Jan. 2017), 603–611, https://doi.org/10.1177/1948550616679237; W. Hofmann, R. F. Baumeister, G. Förster, and K. D. Vohs. "Everyday Temptations: An Experience Sampling Study of Desire, Conflict, and Self-Control," *Journal of Personal Social Psychology* 102, no. 6 (June 2012):1318–35, https://doi.org/10.1037/a0026545.

10   ACLU Foundation. "The War on Marijuana in Black and White," 2013, https://www.aclu.org/sites/default/files/field_document/1114413-mj-report-rfs-rel1.pdf.

11   Centers for Disease Control and Prevention, "Social Determinants of Health," https://www.cdc.gov/nchhstp/socialdeterminants/faq.html, accessed July 23, 2019, citing: A. R. Tarlov, "Public Policy Frameworks for Improving Population Health," *Annals of the New York Academy of Sciences* 896 (1999): 281–93.

12   A. R. Tarlov, "Public Policy Frameworks for Improving Population Health."

13   P. M. Lantz, J. S. House, J. M. Lepkowski, D. R. Williams, R. P. Mero, and J. Chen, "Socioeconomic Factors, Health Behaviors, and Mortality: Results from a Nationally Representative Prospective Study of US Adults," *JAMA* 21, no. 279 (1998): 1703–1708. https://doi.org/10.1001/jama.279.21.1703.

14   Jacqueline Hill et al., "Understanding the Social Factors That Contribute to Diabetes: A Means to Informing Health Care and Social Policies for the Chronically Ill." *Permanente Journal* 17, no. 2 (2013): 67–72, https://doi.org/10.7812/TPP/12-099.

15   W. C. Knowler, P. H. Bennett, R. F. Hamman, and M. Miller, "Diabetes Incidence and Prevalence in Pima Indians: A 19-Fold Greater Incidence than in Rochester, Minnesota," *American Journal of Epidemiology* 108, no 6 (December 1978): 497–505.

16   Centers for Disease Control and Prevention. National Diabetes Statistics Report, 2020.Atlanta, GA: Centers for Disease Control and Prevention, U.S. Dept of Health and HumanServices; 2020. https://www.cdc.gov/diabetes/pdfs/data/statistics/national-diabetesstatistics-report.pdf.

17   American Diabetes Association, "Standards of Medical Care in Diabetes—2019 Abridged for Primary Care Providers," *Clinical Diabetes* 37, no. 1 (Jan. 2019): 11–34, https://doi.org/10.2337/cd18-0105; Leslie J. Baier and Robert L. Hanson, "Genetic Studies of the Etiology of Type 2 Diabetes in Pima Indians," *Diabetes* 5, no 53 (May 2004):1181–1186. https://doi.org/10.2337/diabetes.53.5.1181.

18   National Institute of Diabetes and Digestive and Kidney Disorders, "Diabetes Prevention Program (DPP)," https://www.niddk.nih.gov/about-niddk/research-areas/diabetes/diabetes-prevention-program-dpp, accessed November 7, 2019.

19   Diabetes Prevention Program Research Group, W. C. Knowler, S. E. Fowler, R. F. Hamman, C. A. Christophi, H. J. Hoffman, A. T. Brenneman, J. O. Brown-Friday, R. Goldberg, E. Venditti, and D. M. Nathan, "10-year follow-up of Diabetes Incidence and Weight Loss in the Diabetes Prevention Program Outcomes Study," *Lancet* 374, no. 9702 (2009): 1677–1686. https://doi.org/10.1016/S0140-6736(09)61457-4.

20   Tracey Tylka, Rachel Annunziato, Deb Burgard, Sigrun Danielsdottir, Ellen Shuman, Chad Davis, and Rachel Calogero, "The Weight-Inclusive Versus Weight-Normative Approach to Health: Evaluating the Evidence for Prioritizing Well-Being Over Weight Loss," Journal of Obesity (2014). https://doi.org/10.1155/2014/983495.

21   L. Bacon, J. Stern, M. Van Loan, and N. Keim, "Size Acceptance and Intuitive Eating Improve Health for Obese, Female Chronic Dieters," *Journal of the American Dietetic Assocation* 105 (2005): 929-936. https://doi.org/10.1016/j.jada.2005.03.011.

22   A. J. Tomiyama, B. Ahlstrom, and T. Mann, "Long-Term Effects of Dieting: Is Weight Loss Related to Health?," *Social and Personality Psychology Compass* 7, no. 12 (2013): 861–877.

23   Look AHEAD Research Group, "Eight-Year Weight Losses with an Intensive Lifestyle Intervention: The Look AHEAD Study," *Obesity* 22, no. 1 (Jan. 2014): 5–13.

24   Look AHEAD Research Group, "Cardiovascular Effects of Intensive Lifestyle Intervention in Type 2 Diabetes," *New England Journal of Medicine* 369, no. 2 (July 2013): 145–54, https://doi.org/10.1056/NEJMoa1212914.

25   T. Mann, A. J. Tomiyama, E. Westling, et al., "Medicare's Search for Effective Obesity Treatments: Diets Are Not the Answer," *American Psychologist* 62, no. 3 (April 2007): 220–33.

26   P. S. Maclean, A. Bergouignan, M. A. Cornier, and M. R. Jackman, "Biology's Response to Dieting: The Impetus for Weight Regain," *American Journal of Physiology: Regulatory, Integrative, and Comparative Physiology* 301, no. 3 (2011): R581–R600. Also: P. Sumithran, L. A. Prendergast, E. Delbridge, et al., "Long-Term Persistence of Hormonal

Adaptations to Weight Loss," *New England Journal of Medicine* 365, no. 17 (2011): 597–604.

27   Tracy L. Tylka, Rachel A. Annunziato, Deb Burgard, et al., "The Weight-Inclusive versus Weight-Normative Approach to Health: Evaluating the Evidence for Prioritizing Well-Being over Weight Loss," *Journal of Obesity* 2014, article 983495 (2014), https://doi.org/10.1155/2014/983495.

28   Olga T. Hardy et al., "What Causes the Insulin Resistance Underlying Obesity?," *Current Opinion in Endocrinology, Diabetes, and Obesity* 19, no. 2 (2012): 81–87, https://doi.org/10.1097/MED.0b013e3283514e13.

29   J. Ludwig, L. Sanbonmatsu, L. Gennetian, et al., "Neighborhoods, Obesity, and Diabetes--A Randomized Social Experiment," *The New England Journal of Medicine,* 365, no. 16 (2011): 1509–1519, https://doi.org/10.1056/NEJMsa1103216.

30   J. M. Hunger, J P. Smith, A. J. Tomiyama, "An Evidence-Based Rationale for Adopting Weight-Inclusive Health Policy," *Social Issues and Policy Review*, 14, no. 1, (2020): 73-107, https://doi.org/10.1111/sipr.12062.

Chapter 5

1   Drew Westen, Pavel Blagov, Keith Harenski, Clint Kilts, and Stephan Hamann, "Neural Bases of Motivated Reasoning: An fMRI Study of Emotional Constraints on Partisan Political Judgment in the 2004 U.S. Presidential Election," *Journal of Cognitive Neuroscience* 18 (2006):1947-58. https://doi.org/10.1162/jocn.2006.18.11.1947.

2   J. E. LeDoux, "Emotion Circuits in the Brain," *Annual Review of Neuroscience* 23 (March 2000): 155–84.

3   Arash Javanbakht and Linda Saab, "What Happens in the Brain When We Feel Fear: And why some of us just can't get enough of it" *Smithsonian Magazine*, October 27, 2017, https://www.smithsonianmag.com/science-nature/what-happens-brain-feel-fear-180966992/.

4   M. E. Lachman and S. L. Weaver, "The Sense of Control as a Moderator of Social Class Differences in Health and Well-Being," *Journal of Personality and Social Psychology* 74, no. 3 (1998): 763-73. https://doi.org/10.1037/0022-3514.74.3.763.

5   Gary D. Sherman, J. J. Lee, A. J. C. Cuddy, et al., "Leadership Is Associated with Lower Levels of Stress," *Proceedings of the National Academy of Sciences* 109, no. 44 (October 2012): 17903–7.

6   M. G. Marmot, G. D. Smith, S. Stansfeld, C. Patel, F. North, J. Head, I. White, E. Brunner, and A. Feeney, "Health Inequalities Among British Civil Servants: The Whitehall II Study," *Lancet* 337, no. 8754 (June 1991):1387–93.

7   Your Fat Friend (an anonymous writer), "On 'Tough Love' and Your Fat Friend's Health," *Healthcare in America*, April 17, 2016, https://healthcareinamerica.us/on-tough-love-and-your-fat-friend-s-health-bec20b13af78. Be sure to track down her book, currently in press.

Chapter 6

1   Ben Fell and Miles Hewstone, "Psychological Perspectives on Poverty," Joseph Rowntree Foundation, June 4, 2015, https://www.jrf.org.uk/report/psychological-perspectives-poverty.

2   Da'Shaun Harrison, "When Marginalized Folk Take Our Lives, It's Because the State Already Has," *Wear Your Voice*, September 12, 2019, https://wearyourvoicemag.com /news-politics/to-the-left/capitalism-suicide-racism.

3   Mary O'Hara, *The Shame Game: Overturning the Toxic Poverty Narrative*, (Chicago: Policy Press, 2020), page 66.

4   Daniel Hamermesh, *Beauty Pays: Why Attractive People Are More Successful* (Princeton: Princeton University Press: 2011).

5   Rod Hollier, "Physical Attractiveness Bias in the Legal System," *The Law Project*, March 2017, https://www.thelawproject.com.au/insights/anchoring-bias-in-the -courtroom. American Society of Plastic Surgeons, "2018 National Plastic Surgery Statistics," 2019.

6   American Society of Plastic Surgeons, "2018 National Plastic Surgery Statistics," 2019, https://www.plasticsurgery.org/documents/News/Statistics/2018/plastic-surgery -statistics-report-2018.pdf.

7   Christine Ma-Kellams, Margaret C. Wang, and Hannah Cardiel, "Attractiveness and Relationship Longevity: Beauty Is Not What It Is Cracked Up to Be," *Personal Relationships* 24 (2017): 146–161.

8   Caleb Luna, "Treating My Friends Like Lovers: The Politics of Desirability," *The Body Is Not an Apology*, March 17, 2018, https://thebodyisnotanapology.com/magazine/how -to-be-fat-caleb-luna-sub/.

9   Mia Mingus, "Moving Toward the Ugly: A Politic Beyond Desirability," Femmes of Color Symposium Keynote Speech, Oakland, CA (August 21, 2011), https://leavingevidence.wordpress.com/2011/08/22/moving-toward-the-ugly-a -politic-beyond-desirability/.

10 Audre Lorde, *Sister Outsider: Essays and Speeches* (Berkeley, CA: Crossing Press, 2007).

11 Diana Goetsch, *This Body I Wore* (New York: Farrar, Straus and Giroux, forthcoming).

12 Human Rights Campaign, "Violence Against the Transgender Community in 2018," accessed December 30, 2019, https://www.hrc.org/resources/violence-against-the -transgender-community-in-2018.

13 Andrew Pollack, "A.M.A. Recognizes Obesity as a Disease," *New York Times*, June 18, 2013, https://www.nytimes.com/2013/06/19/business/ama-recognizes-obesity-as-a -disease.html; Harriet Brown, "How Obesity Became a Disease," Atlantic, March 24, 2015, https://www.theatlantic.com/health/archive/2015/03/how-obesity-became-a -disease/388300/.

Chapter 7

1   Kimberlé Crenshaw, "Demarginalizing the Intersection of Race and Sex: A Black Feminist Critique of Antidiscrimination Doctrine, Feminist Theory, and Antiracist Politics," *University of Chicago Legal Forum* 1989, article 8 (1989): 139–67.

2   Brené Brown, *Daring Greatly: How the Courage to Be Vulnerable Transforms the Way We Live, Love, Parent, and Lead* (New York: Avery, 2012).

3   Tara Brach, *True Refuge: Finding Peace and Freedom in Your Own Awakened Heart* (New York: Bantam, 2013).

Chapter 8

1   J. Holt-Lunstad, T. B. Smith, and J. B. Layton, "Social Relationships and Mortality Risk: A Meta-analytic Review," *PLoS Med* 7 (2010): e1000316. https://doi.org/10.1371/journal.pmed.1000316.

2   Jennifer Bonds-Raacke and John D. Raacke, "The Relationship between Physical Attractiveness of Professors and Students' Ratings of Professor Quality," *Journal of Psychiatry, Psychology, and Mental Health* 1, no. 2 (Jan. 2007).

3   B. Hunsberger and B. Cavanagh, "Physical Attractiveness and Children's Expectations of Potential Teachers," *Psychology in the Schools* 25, no. 1 (1988): 70–74.

4   Mary Beth Oliver, "African American Men as 'Criminal and Dangerous': Implications of Media Portrayals of Crime on the 'Criminalization' of African American Men," *Journal of African American Studies* 7, no. 2 (2003): 3–18. www.jstor.org/stable/41819017.

5   Linda Hamilton Krieger, "The Content of Our Categories: A Cognitive Bias Approach to Discrimination and Equal Employment Opportunity," *Stanford Law Review* 47, no. 6 (July 1995), https://doi.org/10.2307/1229191.

6   M. Bertrand and S. Mullainathan, "Are Emily and Greg More Employable than Lakisha and Jamal? A Field Experiment on Labor Market Discrimination," *American Economic Review* 94, no. 4 (Sept. 2004): 991–1013.

7   D. Pager, B. Western, and B. Bonikowski, "Discrimination in a Low-Wage Labor Market: A Field Experiment," *American Sociological Review* 74, no. 5 (Oct. 2009): 777–99.

8   S. H. Meghani, E. Byun, and R. M. Gallagher, "Time to Take Stock: A Meta Analysis and Systematic Review of Analgesic Treatment Disparities for Pain in the United States," *Pain Medicine* 13, no. 2 (Feb. 2012): 150–174, https://doi.org/10.1111/j.1526-4637.2011.01310.x.

9   K. Hugenberg and G. V. Bodenhausen, "Facing Prejudice: Implicit Prejudice and the Perception of Facial Threat," *Psychological Science* 14, no. 6 (2003): 640–643, https://doi.org/10.1046/j.0956-7976.2003.psci_1478.x.

10   A. G. Greenwald, D. E. McGhee, and J. L. K. Schwartz, "Measuring Individual Differences in Implicit Cognition: The Implicit Association Test," *Journal of Personality and Social Psychology* 74, no. 6 (June 1998): 1464–80.

11   Tony Greenwald, "The Implicit Association Test," interview by Mahzarin Banaji, *Edge*, February 12, 2008, https://www.edge.org/conversation/the-implicit-association-test. One review is found here: I. W. Maina, T. D. Belton, S. Ginzberg, et al., "A Decade of Studying Implicit Racial/Ethnic Bias in Healthcare Providers Using the Implicit Association Test," *Social Science and Medicine* 199 (Feb. 2018):219–29, https://doi.org/10.1016/j.socscimed.2017.05.009.

12   Allen McConnell and Jill Leibold, "Relations between the Implicit Association Test, Explicit Racial Attitudes, and Discriminatory Behaviour," *Journal of Experimental Social Psychology* 37. no. 5 (Sept. 2001): 435–42, https://doi.org/10.1006/jesp.2000.1470.

13   C. M. Steele and J. Aronson, "Stereotype Threat and the Intellectual Test-Performance of African-Americans," *Journal of Personality and Social Psychology* 69, no. 5 (Nov. 1995): 797–811.

14   Sapna Cheryan and Galen V. Bodenhausen, "When Positive Stereotypes Threaten Intellectual Performance: The Psychological Hazards of 'Model Minority' Status,"

Psychological Science 11, no. 5 (Sept. 2000): 399–402, https://doi.org/10.1111/1467 -9280.00277.

15 J. Aronson, M. J. Lustina, C. Good, K. Keough, C. M. Steele, and J. Brown, "When White Men Can't Do Math: Necessary and Sufficient Factors in Stereotype Threat," *Journal of Experimental and Social Psychology* 35 (1999): 29–46. https://doi.org/10.1006 /jesp.1998.1371.

16 Angelica Moè, "Gender Difference Does Not Mean Genetic Difference: Externalizing Improves Performance in Mental Rotation," *Learning and Individual Differences* 22, no. 1 (2012): 2024, https://doi.org/10.1016/j.lindif.2011.11.001.

17 R. F. Baumeister, J. M. Twenge, and C. K. Nuss, "Effects of Social Exclusion on Cognitive Processes: Anticipated Aloneness Reduces Intelligent Thought," *Journal of Personality and Social Psychology* 83, no. 4 (Oct. 2002): 817–27.

18 Patrick Sharkey, "The Acute Effect of Local Homicides on Children's Cognitive Performance," *Proceedings of the National Academy of Sciences* 107, no. 26 (June 2010): 11733–38, https://doi.org/10.1073/pnas.1000690107.

19 National Scientific Council on the Developing Child, "The Science of Neglect: The Persistent Absence of Responsive Care Disrupts the Developing Brain," https:// developingchild.harvard.edu/wp-content/uploads/2012/05/The-Science-of-Neglect -The-Persistent-Absence-of-Responsive-Care-Disrupts-the-Developing-Brain.pdf.

20 Deborah Blum, *Love at Goon Park*, (New York: Basic Books, 2002), cited in Louis Co-zolino, *The Neuroscience of Human Relationships: Attachment and the Developing Social Brain*, 2nd ed. (New York: Norton, 2014): 4.

21 C. Beckett, B. Maughan, M. Rutter, et al., "Do the Effects of Early Severe Deprivation on Cognition Persist into Early Adolescence? Findings from the English and Roma-nian Adoptees Study," Child Development 77, no. 3 (May–June 2006): 696–711.

22 S. Moore, L. McEwen, J. Quirt, et al., "Epigenetic Correlates of Neonatal Contact in Humans," *Development and Psychopathology* 29, no. 5 (2017): 1517–38, https://doi .org/10.1017/S0954579417001213.

23 Matthew D. Lieberman and Naomi I. Eisenberger, "Pains and Pleasures of Social Life," *Science* 323, no. 5916 (Feb. 2009): 890–91.

24 Matthew D. Lieberman, *Social: Why Our Brains Are Wired to Connect* (New York: Crown, 2013).

25 N. I. Eisenberger, M. D. Lieberman, and K. D. Williams, "Does Rejection Hurt? An FMRI Study of Social Exclusion," *Science* 302, no. 5643 (Oct. 2003): 290–2.

26 G. R. Durso, A. Luttrell, and B. M. Way, "Over-the-Counter Relief from Pains and Pleasures Alike: Acetaminophen Blunts Evaluation Sensitivity to Both Negative and Positive Stimuli," *Psychological Science* 26, no. 6 (June 2015): 750–8.

27 J. Duong and C. Bradshaw, "Associations between Bullying and Engaging in Aggres-sive and Suicidal Behaviors among Sexual Minority Youth: The Moderating Role of Connectedness," *Journal of School Health* 84, no. 10 (Oct. 2014): 636–45, https://doi .org/10.1111/josh.12196.

28 D. Espalage, T. Pigott, and J. Polanin, "A Meta-Analysis of School-Based Bullying Prevention Programs' Effects on Bystander Intervention Behavior," *School Psychology Review* 41, no. 1 (2012): 47–65.

29 M. T. Smith, R. R. Edwards, R. C. Robinson, and R. H. Dworkin, "Suicidal Ideation, Plans, and Attempts in Chronic Pain Patients," *Pain* 111, no. 1–2 (Sept. 2004): 201–8.

30   R. Feldman, "The Neurobiology of Human Attachments," *Trends in Cognitive Sciences* 21, no. 2 (Feb. 2017): 80–99, https://doi.org/10.1016/j.tics.2016.11.007.

31   D. Rand, J. Greene, and M. Nowak, "Spontaneous Giving and Calculated Greed, *Nature* 489 (Sept. 2012), 427–30, https://doi.org/10.1038/nature11467.

32   Alan G. Sanfey et al. "The Neural Basis of Economic Decision-Making in the Ultimatum Game," *Science* 300, no. 5626 (June 2003): 1755–58, https://doi.org/10.1126/science.1082976.

33   G. Tabibnia and M. D. Lieberman, "Fairness and Cooperation Are Rewarding: Evidence from Social Cognitive Neuroscience," *Annals of the New York Academy of Sciences* 1118 (2007): 90–101.

34   Giovanni Novembre, Marco Zanon, and Giorgia Silani, "Empathy for Social Exclusion Involves the Sensory-Discriminative Component of Pain: A Within-Subject fMRI Study," *Social Cognitive and Affective Neuroscience* 10, no. 2 (Feb. 2015): 153–64, https://doi.org/10.1093/scan/nsu038.

35   R. F. Baumeister and M. R. Leary, "The Need to Belong: Desire for Interpersonal Attachments as a Fundamental Human Motivation," *Psychological Bulletin* 117, no. 3 (May 1995): 497–529.

36   T. K. Inagaki and N. I. Eisenberger, "Shared Neural Mechanisms Underlying Social Warmth and Physical Warmth," *Psychological Science* 24, no. 11 (Nov. 2013): 2272–80, https://doi.org/ 10.1177/0956797613492773.

37   Paul Tough, "Who Gets to Graduate?" *New York Times*, October 27, 2014, http://www.nytimes.com/2014/05/18/magazine/who-gets-to-graduate.html?_r=0.

38   R. J. Sisk, "Team-Based Learning: Systematic Research Review," *Journal of Nursing Education* 50, no. 12 (Dec. 2011): 665–69, https://doi.org/10.3928/01484834-20111017-01.

39   J. Y. Chiao, et al., "Cultural Specificity in Amygdala Response to Fear Faces," *Journal of Cognitive Neuroscience* 20, no. 12 (Dec. 2008): 2167-74. https://doi.org/10.1162/jocn.2008.20151.

40   Reginald B. Adams Jr., Nicholas O. Rule, Robert G. Franklin Jr., et al., "Cross-Cultural Reading the Mind in the Eyes: An fMRI Investigation," *Journal of Cognitive Neuroscience* 22, no. 1 (2010): 97–108.

41   Maia Szalavitz and Bruce D Perry, *Born for Love: Why Empathy Is Essential—and Endangered* (New York: HarperCollins, 2011).

42   Nalini Ambady, "The Mind in the World: Culture and the Brain," *Observer* (May/June 2011), https://www.psychologicalscience.org/observer/the-mind-in-the-world-culture-and-the-brain.

43   Matthew D. Lieberman, *Social: Why Our Brains Are Wired to Connect* (New York: Crown, 2013).

44   W. Li, X. Mai, and C. Liu, "The Default Mode Network and Social Understanding of Others: What Do Brain Connectivity Studies Tell Us," *Frontiers in Human Neuroscience* 24, no. 8 (Feb. 2014): 74, https://doi.org/10.3389/fnhum.2014.00074.

45   P. K. Piff, M. W. Kraus, S. Côté, et al., "Having Less, Giving More: The Influence of Social Class on Prosocial Behavior," *Journal of Personality and Social Psychology* 99 (2010): 771–784, https://doi.org/10.1037/a0020092.

46   Paul K. Piff, Daniel M. Stancato, Stéphane Côté, et al., "Higher Social Class Predicts Increased Unethical Behavior," *Proceedings of the National Academy of Sciences* 109, no. 11 (March 2012) 4086–91, https://doi.org/10.1073/pnas.1118373109.

47 M. W. Kraus, P. K. Piff, and D. Keltner, "Social Class, Sense of Control, and Social Explanation," *Journal of Personality and Social Psychology* 97 (2009): 992–1004.

48 M. W. Kraus, S. Côté, and D. Keltner, "Social Class, Contextualism, and Empathic Accuracy," *Psychological Science* 21 (2010): 1716–23.

Chapter 9

1 M. Ungar, "Practitioner Review: Diagnosing Childhood Resilience: A Systemic Approach to the Diagnosis of Adaptation in Adverse Social Ecologies," *Journal of Child Psychology and Psychiatry* 56, no. 1 (2015): 4–17.

2 C. Beckett, B. Maughan, M. Rutter, et al., "Do the Effects of Early Severe Deprivation on Cognition Persist into Early Adolescence? Findings from the English and Romanian Adoptees Study," *Child Development* 77, no. 3 (2006): 696–711.

3 Tony Robbins, *Unleash the Power Within*, https://www.tonyrobbins.com/events /unleash-the-power-within/, accessed July 18, 2019.

4 M. S. Himmelstein, A. C. Incollingo Belsky, and A. J. Tomiyama, "The Weight of Stigma: Cortisol Reactivity to Manipulated Weight Stigma," *Obesity* 23, no. 2 (Feb. 2015): 368–74, https://doi.org/10.1002/oby.20959.

5 H. Park, A. M. Roubal, A. Jovaag, et al., "Contributions of a Set of Health Factors to Selected Health Outcomes," *American Journal of Preventive Medicine* 49, no. 6 (Dec. 2015): 961–69, https://doi.org/10.1016/j.amepre.2015.07.016; C. M. Hood, K. P. Gennuso, G. R. Swain, and B. B. Catlin, "County Health Rankings: Relationships Between Determinant Factors and Health Outcomes," *American Journal of Preventive Medicine* 50, no. 2, (Feb. 2016): 129–35, https://doi.org/10.1016/j.amepre.2015.08.024.

6 M. Vadiveloo and J. Mattei, "Perceived Weight Discrimination and 10-Year Risk of Allostatic Load Among US Adults," *Annals of Behavioral Medicine* 51, no. 1 (Feb. 2017): 94–105, https://doi.org/10.1007/s12160-016-9831-7.

7 J. P. A. Ioannidis, "Why Most Published Research Findings Are False," *PLOS Medicine* 2, no. 8 (2005): e124.

8 J. P. A. Ioannidis, "The Challenge of Reforming Nutritional Epidemiologic Research," *JAMA* 320, no. 10 (2018): 969–970, https://doi.org/10.1001/jama.2018.11025.

9 L. Bacon and A. Severson, "Fat Is Not the Problem—Fat Stigma Is." *Scientific American*, July 8, 2019. https://blogs.scientificamerican.com/observations/fat-is-not-the -problem-fat-stigma-is/.

10 Alan Levinovitz, *The Gluten Lie: And Other Myths about What You Eat* (New York: Regan, 2015), provides good debunking. But do read critically as the book reproduces many myths about weight.

11 Evelyn Tribole and Elyse Resch, *Intuitive Eating: A Revolutionary Program That Works*, 4th ed. (New York: St. Martin's, 2020). The original book came out in 1995; this latest edition contains a more updated understanding.

12 T. Tylka, "Development and Psychometric Evaluation of a Measure of Intuitive Eating," *Journal of Counseling Psychology* 53 (2006): 226–40; T. Tylka and A. Kroon Van Diest. "The Intuitive Eating Scale–2: Item Refinement and Psychometric Evaluation with College Women and Men," *Journal of Counseling Psychology* 60, no. 1 (2013):137–53.

13 Evelyn Tribole, "What Is Intuitive Eating?," September 12, 2018, https://www .intuitiveeating.org/what-is-intuitive-eating-tribole/.

14   Institute for Women's Policy Research, "Fact Sheet: The Gender Wage Gap: 2017," https://iwpr.org/wp-content/uploads/2018/09/C473.pdf.

15   Ibid.

16   AAUW, "The Simple Truth About the Pay Gap: Fall 2018 Edition," https://www.aauw .org/files/2018/10/AAUW-2018-SimpleTruth-nsa.pdf.

17   Sandy E. James, Jody L. Herman, Susan Rankin, Mara Keisling, Lisa Mottet, and Ma'ayan Anafi, "The Report of the 2015 Transgender Survey," National Center for Transgender Equality, https://transequality.org/sites/default/files/docs/usts/USTS -Full-Report-Dec17.pdf.

18   Ibid.

19   Simonetta Longhi, "The Disability Pay Gap," Equality and Human Rights Commission, https://www.equalityhumanrights.com/sites/default/files/research-report-107 -the-disability-pay-gap.pdf.

20   Ibid.

21   Heather McCulloch, "Closing the Women's Wealth Gap," https://womenswealthgap. org/wp-content/uploads/2017/06/Closing-the-Womens-Wealth-Gap-Report-Jan2017 .pdf.

22   The use of "spoons" in this sense was coined by Christine Miserandino in 2003 in her essay "The Spoon Theory," https://cdn.totalcomputersusa.com/butyoudontlooksick .com/uploads/2010/02/BYDLS-TheSpoonTheory.pdf.

23   Audre Lorde, *Sister Outsider: Essays and Speeches* (Berkeley, CA: Crossing Press, 2007).

Chapter 10

1   H. Rockliff, A. Karl, K. McEwan, et al., "Effects of Intranasal Oxytocin on 'Compassion Focused Imagery,'" *Emotion* 11, no. 6 (2011): 1388–96, https://doi.org/10.1037 /a0023861.

2   bell hooks, "Theory as Liberatory Practice," *Yale Journal of Law and Feminism* 4, no. 1 (1991), https://digitalcommons.law.yale.edu/yjlf/vol4/iss1/2.

3   Holly Truhlar, "About Grief," https://www.hollytruhlar.com/grief/, accessed January 3, 2020.

4   Jon Kabat-Zinn, *Meditation Is Not What You Think: Mindfulness and Why It Is So Important* (New York: Hatchett Books, 2018).

5   S. Bowen, K. Witkiewitz, T. M. Dillworth, et al., "Mindfulness Meditation and Substance Use in an Incarcerated Population," *Psychology of Addictive Behaviors* 20, no. 3 (Sept. 2006): 343–47.

6   K. A. Garrison, T. A. Zeffiro, D. Scheinost, et al., "Meditation Leads to Reduced Default Mode Network Activity Beyond an Active Task," Cognitive, Affective & Behavioral Neuroscience, 15 no. 3 (2015): 712–720, https://doi.org/10.3758/s13415-015-0358-3.

7   L. Bacon and L. Aphramor, "Weight Science: Evaluating the Evidence for a Paradigm Shift," *Nutrition Journal* 10 (2011). https://doi.org/10.1186/1475-2891-10-9.

8   Personal communication, November 5, 2019. The concept is well detailed in Christy Harrison, *Anti-Diet: Reclaim Your Time, Money, Well-Being, and Happiness Through Intuitive Eating* (Boston: Little, Brown, 2019).

9   M. L. Westwater, P. C. Fletcher, and H. Ziauddeen, "Sugar Addiction: The State of the Science," *European Journal of Nutrition* 55, no. S2 (2016): 55–69.

10 Judith Matz and Ellen Frankel, *The Diet Survivor's Handbook: 60 Lessons on Eating, Acceptance and Self-Care* (Naperville, IL: Sourcebooks, 2006).

11 Linda Bacon, *Health at Every Size: The Surprising Truth about Your Weight*, 2d ed. (Dallas: BenBella, 2010); Linda Bacon and Lucy Aphramor, *Body Respect: What Conventional Health Books Get Wrong, Leave Out, and Just Plain Fail to Understand about Weight* (Dallas, BenBella: 2014); Christy Harrison, *Anti-Diet: Reclaim Your Time, Money, Well-Being, and Happiness Through Intuitive Eating* (Boston: Little, Brown, 2019); Judith Matz and Ellen Frankel, *The Diet Survivor's Handbook: 60 Lessons on Eating, Acceptance and Self-Care* (Naperville, IL: Sourcebooks, 2006); Judith Matz and Ellen Frankel, *Beyond a Shadow of a Diet: The Comprehensive Guide to Treating Binge Eating Disorder, Compulsive Eating, and Emotional Overeating*, 2d ed. (New York: Routledge, 2014); Evelyn Tribole and Elyse Resch, *Intuitive Eating: A Revolutionary Program That Works*, 4th ed. (New York: St. Martin's, 2020); Evelyn Tribole and Elyse Resch, *The Intuitive Eating Workbook: Ten Principles for Nourishing a Healthy Relationship with Food* (Oakland, CA: New Harbinger, 2017).

12 J. A. Coan, H. S. Schaefer, and R. J. Davidson, "Lending a Hand: Social Regulation of the Neural Response to Threat," *Psychological Science* 17, no. 12 (Dec. 2006): 1032–39.

13 Citations can be found on their website: http://pediatrics.med.miami.edu/touch -research/research.

14 Y. Joel Wong, Jesse Owen, Nicole T. Gabana, et al., "Does Gratitude Writing Improve the Mental Health of Psychotherapy Clients? Evidence from a Randomized Controlled Trial," *Psychotherapy Research* 28. no. 2 (2018): 192–202, https://doi.org/10.1080 /10503307.2016.1169332.

15 Jennifer Glass, Robin W. Simon, and Matthew A. Andersson, "Parenthood and Happiness: Effects of Work-Family Reconciliation Policies in 22 OECD Countries," *American Journal of Sociology* 122, no. 3 (November 2016): 886-929. https://doi .org/10.1086/688892.

16 OECD, "Universal Health Coverage and Health Outcomes," July 22, 2016, https:// www.oecd.org/els/health-systems/Universal-Health-Coverage-and-Health-Outcomes -OECD-G7-Health-Ministerial-2016.pdf.

17 N.L.T Tran, R. W. Wassmer, and E. L. Lascher. "The Health Insurance and Life Satisfaction Connection," *Journal of Happiness Studies* 18 (2017): 409–426. https://doi .org/10.1007/s10902-016-9729-x.

18 Joana Silva, Victoria Levin, and Matteo Morgandi, "Inclusion and Resilience: The Way Forward for Social Safety Nets in the Middle East and North Africa," The World Bank, https://openknowledge.worldbank.org/handle/10986/14064.

19 A. E. Ezeamama, J. Elkins, C. Simpson, et al, "Indicators of Resilience and Healthcare Outcomes: Findings from the 2010 Health and Retirement Survey," *Quality of Life Research* 25 (2016): 1007–1015. https://doi.org/10.1007/s11136-015-1144-y.

20 J. K. Montez, M. D. Hayward, and D. A. Wolf, "Do U.S. States' Socioeconomic and Policy Contexts Shape Adult Disability?" *Social Science and Medicine* 178 (April 2017): 115–126. https://doi.org/10.1016/j.socscimed.2017.02.012.

INDEX

ACKNOWLEDGMENTS

Radical belonging. The word *radical* derives from a Latin word that means "root." My deepest gratitude goes to my wife, Anne, for providing the ground in which I'm rooted, for showing me every day what belonging looks like through her presence. It is from Anne that I learned the sense of radical belonging conveyed in this book, the idea of unconditional love—loving someone at their very human root—despite and including their rough edges. Gratitude, too, goes to our son, Isaac. That you've grown into the delightful human being you are gives me faith, not only in my capacity for creating and nourishing a home base for belonging, but also for showing me the awesomeness possible when opportunity is provided.

Thank you to the many people who read the manuscript in its entirety, sometimes several times, for your kindness, critical thinking, expertise, and insight; for your insistence that the book was good and that I was good; and at times for helping me up from despair. In alphabetic order: the Bacons—Craig, Dana, Linda, and Shoshi—and Kimberly Dark, Dawn Delgado, Meghan Eliopulos, Melissa Fabello, Jennifer Gaudiani, Lily-Rhyg Glen, Christy Harrison, Da'Shaun Harrison, Mandy Katz, Stephanie Leguichard, Judith Matz (who also inspired the title), Jon Robison, Hunter Ashleigh Shackelford, Holly Truhlar, the anonymous Your Fat Friend, and Stephanie Zone. You all have supported me and inspired me more than you can ever know. Thanks, too, to those who read and provided feedback on portions:

Layla Cameron, Mimosa Collins, Kelly Diels, Laurie Klipfel, Annette Sloan, Rosemary Sneeringer, and Colleen Stinchcombe. And a grateful shout-out to others who have supported me along the way: Robert Hurst, Joe Kelly, Sonya Renee Taylor, Pam Tyson, and Evgen Yurevich.

Thanks to everyone on the BenBella publishing team: Sarah Avinger, Jennifer Canzoneri, Ashley Collom, Alicia Kania, Adrienne Lang, Vy Tran, Susan Welte, Leah Wilson, Karen Wise, Glenn Yeffeth, and others acting behind the scenes, making this a better book and helping get it to those who need it. It's been a pleasure to work with genuinely nice and talented folks with a conscience.

I want to acknowledge those of you who read the book, too. There was a time that I didn't see, though I felt, an invisible wall separating me from you. We are in the same world but made to believe we are not. The focused reflection required to write this book has helped make the invisible more visible and allowed me to better understand the systems that created that wall, how insidiously they keep us apart, and my responsibility in tearing those systems down. I hope the book has propelled you on a similar journey.

Let's not let this messed-up system separate us, okay? I want us to cross this divide, I want to see you, for you to see me, and for us to create pockets of resistance and refuge. I want us to restore radical belonging to our lives and to the world.

None of us can do this alone. Please show up. I need you. We belong together.

ABOUT THE AUTHOR

Dr. Lindo Bacon is fostering a global transformation to a more just world, where all bodies are valued, respected, and supported in compassionate self-care. Best known for their paradigm-shifting research and advocacy upending the weight discourse, Bacon's inspiring message takes us beyond size, to shaping a culture of empathy, equity, and true belonging. Dr. Bacon has mined their deep academic proficiency, wide-ranging clinical expertise, and own personal experience to write two bestselling books, *Health at Every Size: The Surprising Truth About Your Weight* and the coauthored *Body Respect: What Conventional Health Books Get Wrong, Leave Out, or Just Plain Fail to Understand about Weight*. Both are credited with transforming the weight discourse and inspiring a hopeful new course for the global body positivity movement. Bacon is currently spreading the message of *Radical Belonging* through public speaking.

Bacon earned their PhD in physiology from the University of California, Davis, where they currently serve as an Associate Nutritionist. They also hold graduate degrees in psychology and exercise metabolism. Dr.

Bacon formerly taught at City College of San Francisco, in the health education, psychology, women's studies, and biology departments. A professor and researcher, for almost two decades Dr. Bacon has taught courses in social justice, health, weight, and nutrition; they have also conducted federally funded studies on health and weight and published in top scientific journals. Their research has been supported by grants from the United States Department of Agriculture and the National Institutes of Health. Bacon is industry-independent. Their pledge not to accept money from the weight-loss, pharmaceutical, or food industry, signed when getting a PhD almost two decades ago, supports them in speaking truth to power.

Well-respected for their provocative social and political commentary, Dr. Bacon's advocacy for body respect has generated a large following on social media platforms like Facebook and Twitter, health and nutrition listservs and specialty blogs, and the international lecture circuit. They are committed to centralizing the ways in which power, privilege, and disadvantage complicate our experience of our bodies. With a rare dual perspective combining academic expertise and clinical experience, Bacon is adept at providing a link between scientific research and practical application. This enables them to bring authority and compassion to their writing, speaking, and teaching. Dr. Bacon specializes in translating science into practical, actionable terms.

A compelling speaker, writer, and storyteller, Dr. Bacon delivers a unique blend of academic expertise, clinical experience, and social justice advocacy, all couched in a raw honesty and compassion that touch and inspire.

Visit lindobacon.com for more.

BODY SHAMING IS RAMPANT.
BUT IT DOESN'T HAVE TO BE.

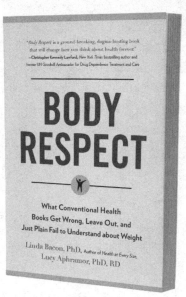

THE MYTHS

1. Fatness leads to decreased longevity.
2. BMI is a valuable and accurate health measure.
3. Fat plays a substantive role in causing disease.
4. Exercise and dietary restriction are effective weight-loss techniques.
5. We have evidence that weight loss improves health.
6. Health is largely determined by health behaviors.
7. Science is value-free.

Much of what we believe to be true about weight is in fact myth. Suspend your preconceptions, re-examine the evidence, and a very different picture emerges, one where it is the machinery of weight stigma that needs dismantling.

Integrating a social justice agenda, *Body Respect* critiques weight science, explains the fallout of a health agenda based on thinness as the goal, and offers an alternative path to compassionate and effective health care.

THE
Radical Belonging
COMMUNITY

"I want us to cross this divide, I want to see you, for you to see me, and for us to create pockets of resistance and refuge. I want us to restore radical belonging to our lives and to the world."
(page 318, *Radical Belonging*)

Join us in the Radical Belonging Community, where we come together in all our magnificent complexity to unlearn the lies and misinformation we've absorbed about ourselves and the people around us and replace them with more truthful, nuanced understandings.

We're a diverse group of people committed to justice, equity, and body liberation, and to valuing all members' identities and experiences. We chat and interact about our lives and the world we live in, connect across our differences, and support and inspire one another in the deep reflection that allows Radical Belonging to emerge.

Whether you are transgender, queer, Black, Indigenous, or a Person of Color, disabled, old, or fat—or you more closely resemble the "mythical norm"—if you are committed to individual and collective healing and liberation and want to better align what you value with what you practice, we invite you to join us.

We belong together.
Visit lindobacon.com to learn more.